Beyond Altruism:
Social Welfare Policy in American Society

Beyond Altruism:
Social Welfare Policy in American Society

Willard C. Richan
Temple University

The Haworth Press
New York • London

Beyond Altruism: Social Welfare Policy in American Society was previously published as a special supplement to *Administration in Social Work*, a quarterly journal devoted to the theory and practice of management and administration in social work and related human service fields.

The Haworth Press, Inc., 12 West 32 Street, New York, NY 10001
EUROSPAN/Haworth, 3 Henrietta Street, London WC2E 8LU England

Library of Congress Cataloging-in-Publication Data

Richan, Willard C.
  Beyond altruism.

  "Monographic supplement #3 to the journal Administration in social work, volume 10, 1986" — T.p. verso.
  Bibliography: p.
  Includes index.
  1. Social service — United States. 2. United States — Social policy. 3. Public welfare — United States. 4. Social work administration — United States. I. Administration in social work, Volume 10 (Supplement #3) II. Title.
HV95.R517   1986   362.5'61'0973   86-29437
ISBN 0-86656-633-3
ISBN 0-86656-756-9 (pbk.)

To Anne, who reads everything before it goes out

Contents

Preface

This is an introduction to social welfare policy, intended particularly for undergraduate and first-year graduate social work students, as well as for a general audience interested in the issues and traditions of social welfare policy. Anyone writing a book such as this is faced with a number of problems from the outset. In the first place, people enroll in a social work school to acquire practice skills — most of them as direct practitioners. Virtually nobody enters in order to learn about social welfare policy. Not only is this content mandatory, but it is usually placed at the beginning of the education sequence. This arrangement has its rationale, but it flies in the face of two time-honored principles. As any educator worth her salt knows, learner motivation is critical, especially for the adult learner. And social workers are advised to "start where the client is."

Secondly, this is a complex subject that knows no boundaries. An occupational hazard of social work generally is the breadth of its domain. Nowhere is this clearer than when one is discussing policy issues. The courses in social welfare policy tend to be charged with supplying any content that is not covered somewhere else in the curriculum. So historical roots going back to the Middle Ages, the latest changes in Medicare rules and issues of social work professionalism all become part of the purview of social welfare policy.

What drove me to undertake this task was the conviction that this *is* essential content for anybody wanting to meddle in other people's lives as a human services professional. That and the belief that it can be made not only comprehensible but also readable. Beatrice Saunders, who has done so much over the years to raise the quality of social work writing, taught us that it does not have to be dull, erudite or incomprehensible to be worthwhile, and that when the reader has trouble understanding the material the writer is more than likely the major culprit.

So I have tried to make this book readable and comprehensible. This does not mean the reader is invited to sit back and relax. If you are not moved to challenge old assumptions—your own and mine—the project will have been a failure. While there has been an effort to maintain reasonable objectivity, the book is not neutral. When one is dealing with matters like the welfare poor and control of threatening behavior and abuse of young children and teenage pregnancy, there are few neutrals. Better to be up front about biases than pretend to be disinterested. More than twenty-five years of teaching this content to social work students has convinced me that they can be trusted to think for themselves.

This brings us to the matter of acknowledgments. I am indebted to the countless students who have taught as they learned. Educators quickly come to realize that they gain at least as much as students in the process. Others have made more specific contributions to the effort. As the dedication page indicates, my wife, Anne Richan, reads everything. Her comments and suggestions go well beyond cleaning up the rhetoric. Scott Wilson and Ronald Vander Weil offered much good advice on early drafts of the material. I thank June Axinn for her suggestions regarding welfare economics and Jane Murray and Barbara Parks for their reactions to the material on teenage pregnancy. Some of the most valuable help came from persons who must be nameless: four manuscript readers whose names were not made known to me. To editor Simon Slavin and Lynne Damien Champoux of The Haworth Press I owe special thanks for their patience, understanding and advice. Finally, I would like to thank Beverly Yeager and Lillian Gibson, who translated all the fine ideas into legible form via the word processor.

Introduction

Welfare. Conservatives say it will be the undoing of capitalism. Radicals say it props up capitalism. The fact that welfare is thus attacked from right and left for diametrically opposite reasons is only one of many paradoxes. Here are others: During the first term of Ronald Reagan, the avowed enemy of the welfare state, spending on social security and Medicare grew faster than the federal budget as a whole. We tend to think of welfare as being for poor people, but the benefits for the nonpoor are greater. And welfare policies designed to force people into the labor market are adopted at a time when the labor market cannot absorb the available workers.

In order to make sense of the strange world of social welfare policy we must get past the rhetoric and see the true nature of this basic American institution. Any society must solve certain problems if it is to survive. In the modern age social welfare programs play an integral part in this—in the United States as well as in other countries, regardless of their political and economic ideology. We can't wish welfare away. In fact if it didn't exist we would have to invent it.

DEFINING TERMS

The language of social welfare policy is confusing. Words and phrases that sound alike mean different things, or their meaning is similar but not synonymous. Different commentators use the same terms differently. The language confusion reflects a subject matter which is by nature hard to define, though the problem is partly the relative newness of social welfare policy as a professional concern.

To the general public, "welfare" means financial aid to poor people: welfare, as in welfare chiseler, welfare fraud, etc. These negative stereotypes are constantly reinforced by the mass media. Not only are they a bum rap, by and large, but financial aid to the poor is only the tip of the iceberg. In its broadest sense, social welfare may refer to the totality of health, education and social service programs, both governmental and private—as when economists talk about a country's social welfare expenditures. This book is about something called *social welfare policy.*

Policy is a way of dealing with problems. We talk of foreign policy as the way the government handles its international relations. More than a single program, it is the set of principles guiding a range of actions in a particular sphere. Policy helps justify action and give it coherence. Sometimes policy is articulated, as when the president makes a major speech on defense spending or farm price supports. But the reality of policy never follows the script exactly and to understand it we have to draw on many kinds of evidence.

Social welfare policy is concerned mainly with the transfer of goods and services to individuals and families, either through government agencies, voluntary nonprofit organizations or profit-making companies. The range of services which are typically included under "social welfare" is awesome indeed: income security, housing, health care and physical rehabilitation, some aspects of education, marital and family counseling, probation and parole services, child care and protection, family planning, mental health, alcohol and drug rehabilitation, nursing home care for the elderly, job placement and training, community dispute settlement, recreation, and many more. If you want an idea of the scope of social welfare in your community, turn to the GUIDE TO HUMAN SERVICES section of the phone book.

In social welfare programs, the usual ground rules between provider and consumer in the market economy do not apply. The market is dominated by exchanges between parties. You give me the automobile or dress or haircut and I give you the money you have determined is the price of the commodity. If I can't come up with the money, I don't get the commodity. I sell my labor to an employer. If I don't work, I don't get paid. In social welfare there is no price, or the charges have no relationship to what is received.

This sounds like a one-sided exchange, but it is one-sided in theory only. The person who receives food stamps has to give up a measure of pride and privacy and personal choice in return for the benefit. A person treated in a mental hospital may pay nothing in dollars for the service but then may pay for the rest of her life in social stigma.

So the real difference between market relationships and social welfare relationships is that in the latter the terms of the exchange cannot be measured. Typically a major part of the financial cost is born by somebody other than the recipient. That is true whether the recipient is a derelict on skid row or a middle class couple getting marital counseling at a family service agency.

Social policy is broader than social welfare policy, since it deals with all courses of action aimed at improving the quality of life. For instance, it includes policies for protecting the environment. *Public policy* is any governmental course of action—social, economic, military, etc. *Public welfare* may refer to all social welfare programs under government auspices but is often used specifically for income assistance and child welfare programs. The *welfare state* is not a physical place but a conception of government's responsibility for the welfare of its citizens. It thus is a philosophical viewpoint as well as a description of government activity. This conception is discussed at length in Chapter 1.

Human services has become popular as a label for these kinds of programs in recent years, as "welfare" has taken on a negative connotation in the public mind. *Social services* is an older term, but its meaning varies widely. In most countries outside of the United States it includes the full range of health, education and welfare provisions, but in this country it usually excludes health care and education and is limited to services that don't involve the transfer of money and other material aids. Some people use *social work services* for this more restricted concept. The problem with that is that social work is not a set of services but a profession. To add to the confusion, the majority of persons in "social work" positions have no professional training. The final section of this book deals with the social work profession.

THE PLAN OF THE BOOK

Part I (Chapters 1-2) presents the basic thesis of the book. We begin with the author's own philosophical perspective on social welfare policy. The reader may agree or disagree with all or parts of it, but it is important to understand it. The final chapter in this part discusses five vital tasks that any society must carry out in order to survive. Parts II-V look at social welfare policies related to each set of tasks.

Part II (Chapters 3-6) addresses two essential tasks: providing the means of survival and seeing that the work of society gets done. Economic security programs are the focus of this exploration. We trace the evolution of income support programs, their impact on recipients and the relationship between work and welfare.

Part III (Chapters 7-9) deals with another societal task, the control of threatening behavior. This time mental health and corrections are our cases in point. At first blush these two fields may seem worlds apart; the former is thought of as humane while the latter smacks of punishment. In reality the two fields have common roots and still have much in common.

Part IV (Chapters 10-12) is concerned with the societal task of preparing people for useful lives. American efforts in this regard have focused on two populations in particular: immigrants and children. We use the field of child welfare as our vehicle for exploration.

Part V (Chapters 13-15) looks at a profession which has been deeply involved with all of these societal tasks: social work. Professionalism, whose roots go back to the middle ages, has been moving into a wide range of occupations in the twentieth century. The tensions within the social work community mirror tensions in the larger society. Therein lie many of social work's problems but also its potential contribution to a viable society.

SOCIAL WELFARE POLICY AS A PROCESS

Social welfare policy is not just a set of decisions about certain issues. It is also a set of activities through which decisions are made and carried out. Certain chapters in this book serve a double purpose by both presenting substantive policy issues *and* illustrating different activities involved in policy making.

Defining social problems. Policy is developed in response to social conditions defined as "problems." Chapter 12 shows how society comes to view a set of conditions as a problem and how interest groups cast the problem in very different terms. The case in point is teenage pregnancy, which suddenly became an "epidemic" in the late seventies.

Debating social policies. Policy is shaped by being argued by contending interests. Some observers are inclined to be cynical about the public debates over policy, believing that the "real" contest takes place in smoke-filled rooms. But even powerful interests have to justify their positions publicly. Chapter 14 is a debate on the question of licensing of social workers.

The politics of policy. While public debates on the issues are important, one should not ignore the role that power, formal and informal, plays in the shaping of policy. Chapters 5 and 15 deal with this dimension of social welfare policy. Chapter 5 uses economic security policies to illustrate the structure and process of policy-making in the political arena. Chapter 15 discusses the activities of social workers in that arena.

The financing of policy. Most social welfare policies involve the spending of money, large sums of money. The economic base of social welfare policy and programs is discussed in Chapter 6. Again, economic security programs, which include the largest government expenditures of all, are the case in point.

Implementing policies. Abstract social welfare policies become reality when they are translated into services delivered to target populations. The organizations through which services are delivered are a critical factor in what happens to the consumers of services. Chapter 8 examines service delivery systems, using correctional and mental health agencies as illustrations.

Public and private social welfare. While most social welfare dollars come from taxes and public programs are the giants in the field, private agencies—profit and nonprofit—play a significant role in welfare work. Chapter 11 focuses on the private sector, as seen in programs for children and youth.

The policy cycle. The picture of a neat sequence in which a problem is recognized and solved through a new social welfare program is misleading. The reality goes more like this: Groups with enough political power to get their way define a condition as a problem and are able to pass a law intended to deal with it, and this leads to a program, which creates *new* problems, whereupon the cycle is re-enacted. Chapter 9 describes this cycle in relation to the use of closed institutions for the care of offenders and the mentally ill.

This book is intended neither as an encyclopedia of social welfare policies and programs nor as a manual for policy analysis. Rather it is meant to give the reader a basic grounding in social welfare policy—its parameters, history and key issues. Specific programs are used to illustrate general points. Anyone wanting to study services to the homebound elderly or alcohol and drug rehabilitation programs in depth can find this information elsewhere. This book is a basic introduction to a complex field in hopes that it will shed light on the subject and lure the reader onward.

THE END PRODUCT IS ACTION

The contents of this book may be reassuring or distressing or both. Some of it may make you angry. One thing I hope it does not evoke is cynicism. The purpose of analysis in this field is action. The idea of becoming a policy advocate or program reformer may be a bit intimidating at first, but those are human beings out there running the show. Washington, that power center of social welfare policy, is in many ways like an overgrown small town. If we are to be frightened, it should be at the thought that so many major decisions are made on the basis of relative ignorance. That is where we come in. By the time you have read this book you will know a great deal more about social welfare policy than most of the people who enact the legislation that shapes it. That remark is based not on arrogance but on an appreciation of how little is known about this field by those who control its fortunes. We have an obligation to teach as well as learn.

The worst enemy of action is not the outright rejection of an idea by avowed opponents but the certainty among supporters that action will do no good. Yet how quickly our assumptions are overturned by subsequent events. Who would have guessed in the afterglow of his 1984 re-election triumph that Ronald Reagan would be struggling to regain the public's trust a few years later, his administration mired in the Iran-Contra debacle?

This book makes a number of predictions about the future. All are made in the full knowledge that history may prove them dead wrong. That element of uncertainty and surprise should be enough to spur the most hardened cynic to keep on working for those things one believes in.

PART 1

Getting One's Bearings

Finding one's way through the complexities of social welfare policy is a lot like the problem facing the explorers of centuries ago. Even if our instruments are state-of-the-art, they are crude in relation to the demands of the search. We are not crossing uncharted lands, others have been there before, but the maps and charts they have drawn may bear only slight resemblance to what we see. We even have our own counterpart of the humbugs and superstitions that bedeviled the mariners of old: habits of mind and shared bits of conventional wisdom that can keep one from asking nosy and provocative questions. Yet it is precisely those kinds of questions that allow us to break out of old thoughtways, an essential step if one is going to understand social welfare policy.

Think of this book as a road map. It does not tell you where you should end up but it can be helpful in getting there. An imperfect road map is generally better than none, so it is possible to disagree with a great deal that one finds in this book and still learn from it. This suggests a particular kind of critical mindset with which to read about social welfare policy: skeptical, yet ready to consider the merits of an argument. There are two tests of any map: Is it accurate? And is it useful? Different questions, and the user should be prepared to ask both.

In order to make sense of a road map, you must know where you are starting from. The analogy for a book about social welfare policy is knowing where the author is coming from. There are two basic premises on which this book is based: that social welfare policy in this country is a creature of American liberalism, and that social welfare can be understood only in relation to certain vital functions of society. Chapter 1 deals with the first of these premises and Chapter 2 with the second.

To understand the welfare state within the United States, one must see its historic relationship to the liberal tradition. Liberalism is a much misunderstood and much abused philosophical orientation. One hesitates to use the term ''doctrine,'' for one of liberalism's strengths as well as weaknesses is the fact that it eludes precise definition.

It is the author's belief that social welfare policy's significance goes far beyond humanitarian concern for others, beyond altruism. Every society—including those which do not seem humane at all—is confronted with a number of tasks it must perform to survive: seeing to it that goods and services are obtained and distributed; averting threats to its stability posed by disruptive behavior; assur-

1

ing that members have the will and ability to perform essential roles; and building and maintaining sufficient internal solidarity to keep from disintegrating (see Gilbert & Specht, 1974, pp. 4-5; Warren, 1963, pp. 51-66). The complexities of modern society have given rise to specialized institutions to assist in carrying out these tasks. Social welfare figures prominently in this process.

Chapter 1

Social Welfare
and the Liberal Tradition

Hardly a day goes by without someone somewhere castigating the welfare state. And what worse insult than to be called a "welfare state liberal"? It is time to meet this twentieth century monster.

More than a set of social programs or a certain percentage of government spending, the welfare state is a principle of government responsibility for the welfare of the citizenry. At its most expansive, it has been defined as "a polity so organized that every member of the community is assured his due maintenance" (*Oxford English Dictionary*, 1955, Addenda) and a state "that provides benefits for virtually all types of hazards that any person might encounter" (Handel, 1982, p. 16). More typical is Schottland's (1967, p. 10) reference to "a modern, democratic Western state in which the power of the state is deliberately used to modify the free play of economic and political forces in order to effect a redistribution of income."

Modify, not eliminate. The general conception is of a system within a market economy. Typically the focus is on health, education and welfare benefits directed to individuals and families, though some definitions also include a measure of control over the means of production. (See Girvetz, 1950.)

But the principle of government responsibility for the welfare of the citizenry is not restricted to democratic, capitalistic societies. The Soviet Union can be said to have a well developed welfare state, as can the Union of South Africa and most Latin American dictatorships and European democracies. In fact, most nations of the world have gone further in assigning responsibility for health, education and welfare to government than has the United States. That may come as a surprise to many Americans, who are constantly told about the "excesses" of government welfare programs. The extent and kinds of benefits and, more so, who gets them on what basis, vary widely from country to country and even within countries. But throughout the civilized world today, the welfare state is the rule rather than the exception.

The American welfare state is a creature of liberalism. To understand it requires us to clear away a lot of current political rhetoric about "liberals." Historically, they were *not* the "bleeding hearts" accused of giving away the store in order to make life easy for the shiftless element at the bottom of the heap. On the contrary, those whom today we call "conservatives"—those opposed to government intervention on behalf of the poor, affirmative action and regulation of industrial working conditions—are much closer in spirit to the original liberals than the people who now bear that label.

LIBERALISM

One of the difficulties in understanding liberalism is the fact that it has been less a precise doctrine than a historical movement. Though one can trace its antecedents to ancient Greece, modern liberalism started in the Renaissance. Its central tenet was freedom, its central character the private individual. In politics, the liberals fought the absolutist state. In religion, they were at the vanguard of opposition to the hegemony of the church. In economics, they were the quintessential capitalists.

Freedom meant more than liberty from externally imposed restraints. In fact, the bourgeoisie who were the backbone of liberalism feared the unbridled passions of the masses. The individual who symbolized the movement was the self-directed man of reason, separate from nature and separate from his fellow human beings (Arblaster, 1984).

Interpreted in this way, freedom was "not a means to a higher political end but was itself the highest political end" (Bullock & Shock, 1956, p. 121). Starting from this core belief, the liberal faith embraced tolerance of difference, privacy (of person and property), the rule of reason, and law as the ultimate protector of freedom.

Above all else was fear of any excessive concentration of power, the ultimate threat to individual freedom. In the beginning that meant church and state absolutism. Liberalism was a secular faith. Insofar as it could be said to have a religious doctrine, it was a belief in progress. Finally, liberalism was and is pragmatic, a quality which has led it to be called at best amorphous and at worst immoral, and, depending on the speaker, a tool of either radicalism or capitalism. But it is its pragmatism that has allowed it to survive over the centuries.

Consent of the governed was a central part of the philosophy, although the early liberals had trouble with the notion of democracy, rule of the majority. Liberalism was the credo of the *un*common man, and mediocrity was the object of derision in the intellectual realm and fear in the political. Democracy posed the threat of mob rule. So liberals were caught between their aversion to centralized authority, on the one hand, and too wide an extension of sovereignty, on the other.

American Liberalism

The liberals who founded this nation said, "We hold these truths to be self-evident," and indeed most Americans accept the liberal credo in the abstract without giving it much thought. The rightness of private property, a free press, religious tolerance, a political opposition and the right to a public trial are taken for granted.

But liberalism does not mean the absence of oppression. Classical liberalism in particular was capable of great cruelty and harshness. In this country this non-doctrine has been forced to come to terms with a number of internal contradictions. Four in particular stand out: political elitism, slavery, economic exploitation of the lower class, and militarism.

Opening Up the Political Process

The founders of the Republic shared the traditional liberal fear of domination by the masses. They hedged the system of governance with barriers to direct expression of the popular will. The president was to be chosen by electors who in turn were named in whatever manner the respective state legislatures chose. Senators were to be chosen by the state legislatures—a principle which stayed in effect until this century. Most states limited the franchise to males who owned property and paid taxes and put stringent qualifications, based on property ownership, on the right to serve in office.

Thus those who had fled tyranny abroad established their own elitist system in the United States, and in its early years the country was ruled by a small circle of aristocrats. Even Thomas Jefferson, the chief spokesman for popular rule, accepted the underlying assumptions of republicanism, with its indirect expression of the popular will (Beard & Beard, 1960, pp. 203-204).

But the liberal principles on which the new nation had been founded bore within them the seeds of a different kind of representation. If the rule of law applied equally to all and the sanctity of the free individual was the beginning and end of society, it was contradictory to exclude from these principles the vast majority of citizens who happened not to have been born into wealth. It was not simply the illogic of this rarified brand of liberalism which was its undoing but even more the changes occurring in society in the early nineteenth century.

Democracy is an infectious idea. For large numbers of people to help fight a war of independence and hear the inflammatory rhetoric of their leaders but be barred from political participation was an ideal recipe for upheaval. The French Revolution added fuel to the fire. The population was growing rapidly, further undermining the carefully crafted system of governance. Between 1790 and 1820, the population more than doubled; ten years later it had more than tripled.

As the frontier was pushed westward, the eastern seaboard states began to lose their dominant position. But agitation was forcing democratization there also. By the 1820s eight of the original thirteen states had removed property ownership as a condition for voting, extending the franchise to most adult white males. The dramatic changes can be seen in the number of ballots cast in presidential elections: from a little over 361,000 in 1824 to more than a million in 1828.

It was the election of 1824 which crystallized the issue of elitism versus populism. In that year Andrew Jackson—self-styled man of the common people—won more electoral votes than any of the other four candidates running, only to see the presidency go to John Quincy Adams, scion of the Boston family which had dominated American politics from the beginning. It was the last time that the old elite would control presidential politics without having to deal with the insurgents. Four years later Jackson came back to claim the prize. In the ensuing decades massive immigrations further opened up the political process; urban bosses and rural populists challenging the eastern "establishment."

The events of the early nineteenth century helped resolve a basic contradiction within liberalism, between its devotion to liberty and its aversion to democracy. Not that large numbers of Americans were not still denied an effective voice in the affairs of the nation, most notably women. Real democratization of the political process would wait another eighty years. But an even more blatant discrepancy remained to haunt the nineteenth century exponents of "liberty and justice for all."

The Anomaly of Slavery

In drafting the Declaration of Independence, Thomas Jefferson inserted language accusing King George III of perpetuating the slave trade. The passage came out before final adoption (Arblaster, 1984, p. 202). This was the price of keeping southern colonies on board. But liberalism itself spoke with two voices on the question of slavery. As against the principles of personal liberty and equality before the law, slave states asserted the right to property and freedom from central government control. In the words of historian Staughton Lynd (1967, pp. 179-180), "almost without exception the [Founding] Fathers felt that slavery was wrong and almost without exception they failed to act decisively to end it."

The issues of property rights and states' rights were basically different. The latter required no approval of slavery in principle. The belief in the right of each state to have a maximum voice in its own affairs was akin to Voltaire's famous dictum, "I disapprove of what you say, but I will defend to the death your right to say it." But the right to dispose of one's property as one saw fit was at the very center of the liberal creed. Here the liberals were trapped by the universality of their principles. It was not only their own freedom they spoke for but the freedom of all humanity, as a natural right. How then could they acquiesce in the enslavement of any human as the property of another?

The answer lay in how one defined the slaves. By viewing them as half-human, or perpetual children in need of supervision, it was possible to reconcile slavery with liberalism. Thomas Jefferson, who hoped for the eventual abolition of slavery though he himself was an owner, believed blacks were "inferior to the whites in the endowments both of body and mind," as did most of his contemporaries (Arblaster, 1984, p. 202). Thus racism was the veil that allowed liberals to ignore the inherent evil in the slave system. It was a system, after all, in which few hands were clean—the ship owners and merchants of New England being implicated fully as much as the plantation owners of the South.

In time liberals came to abandon their uneasy tolerance of slavery. Many were to be found in the vanguard of the abolitionist movement. But the center had also moved. Abraham Lincoln, who at one time had disavowed the desire to tamper with either the institution of slavery or states' rights, ended up repudiating both.

For Lincoln the central issue at the time of the Emancipation Proclamation was not slavery but the preservation of the Union. The war over which he presided settled once and for all the question of the pre-eminence of the national government over the several states. In so doing, it paved the way for an active role of central government far different from that conceived by the early liberals.

Economic Liberalism

Unlike slavery, the exploitation of the industrial work force was totally consistent with the tenets of classical liberalism. Not only did the entrepreneur have a right to the rewards of enterprise, but the relationship of employer and employee was a free and voluntary exchange between equals, in a legal sense. After all, the worker had the option of quitting; no matter that the alternative was likely to be starvation.

Many abolitionists saw no contradictions between fighting to end slavery in the south and ignoring "wage slavery" in the North (Glickstein, 1979). Southern apologists for their system of involuntary servitude claimed that the main difference between slaves on the plantation and workers in New England cotton mills was that the latter lacked protections afforded the former (Fitzhugh, 1960). But in the minds of many abolitionists economic competition was crucial to the development of character—no less in the worker than the entrepreneur. Freedom was the key to salvation of the individual and the attainment of a just and fruitful society. Thus slavery, no matter how benignly administered, was an abomination, if only in the fact that it was a consciously imposed denial of liberty. Poverty of the free citizen, no matter how wretched, was a result of personal failing and no occasion for social guilt. In fact, poverty was a blessing, for it served as a necessary prod to the idle and improvident (Glickstein, 1979).

Social Darwinism, with its belief in the survival of the fittest, provided the intellectual justification for laissez-faire capitalism and its byproduct, oppression of the weak by the strong. Not only the capitalist held this view. The following statement by a charity worker in 1893 stemmed from the same assumption that misery of those at the bottom was their own fault:

> The moment it is understood by the idle and shiftless in a community . . . that they can, on the ground of destitution, claim a certain amount of support while still remaining at large and enjoying the sweets of liberty, the door is opened to a perfect flood of pauperism and consequent vice. (Huntington, 1893, p. 102)

But economic liberalism had one ironic twist: Individuals might go it alone in matters of thought and conscience, even as voters if they so chose, but it was impossible to engage in productive enterprise in isolation. The more one's appetite for profit, the more dependent one was on other humans, as laborers and consumers. Adam Smith, the architect of laissez-faire economics, saw the division of labor—the natural foundation of interdependence—as central to industrial enterprise.

> The greatest improvement in the productive powers of labour, and the greater part of the skill, dexterity, and judgment with which it is anywhere directed, or applied, seem to have been the effects of the division of labour. (1776, p. 5)

It was interdependence that would eventually erode the paternalism with which liberal entrepreneurs directed their operations. Even more than the earlier threat of secession, it was economic liberalism that forced Americans to take a new view of central authority. The relations between trading partners and between employer and employee would require the intervention of the only force powerful enough to interpose its will, the national government. Periodic breakdowns of the economic machine created human misery unknown to earlier generations. Aside from compassion, it was necessary for the sake of social stability to minister to the needs of the destitute. The industrial expansion of the nineteenth century brought with it unprecedented immigration to the United States and this, too, would require an active role of government.

A New Meaning of "Liberal"

By the end of the nineteenth century the fears of church and state power were overshadowed by a new monolith: economic concentration. Having cheered the growth of a massive industrial machine as the ultimate expression of individual enterprise, liberals now shrank from the monster they had created. They were not alone in their opposition to the monopolies and trusts. A burgeoning labor movement and a variety of radical factions were even more outspoken in their condemnation of corporate greed. The common enemy would in time help to forge an alliance between liberals and trade unions and lead some liberals to drift toward socialism.

But at the turn of the century, the dominant element in the trade union movement took a dim view of government as the instrument of social reform and eschewed the political arena, preferring collective bargaining tactics instead. For their part, socialists tied specific reforms to a general aim of fundamental change in the social order. This alienated the rank and file of workers as well as their union leaders. (See Foner, 1980; Dick, 1972, pp. 111-135; Austin, 1949.) Thus the early labor leaders were too parochial and the socialists too doctrinaire to lead the fight against entrenched economic power.

Instead it was liberal reformers who became the center of the struggle. Characteristically, the forces of reform were loosely organized, coming together around specific problems rather than following a coherent plan. Corruption in big city political machines based in immigrant populations was as much a target as corruption in the corporations that oppressed the same immigrant groups. The crusade was thus actually a series of crusades and the reform movement was constantly in danger of falling apart over the diverse agenda of the several factions (Lustig, 1982; Filler, 1962).

But there was a central theme to the struggle: that government was the instrument best suited to protect the common good. If one wished to clean up political corruption, the answer lay in passing new legislation. If one wished to challenge the power of the trusts, one needed the countervailing power of the U.S. government. The man who symbolized this new liberal orientation to government as a positive force was President Theodore Roosevelt.

Roosevelt was an authentic liberal. Born into upper class gentility, he was a firm believer in hard work, individual initiative and, most of all, results (Hofstadter, 1957, pp. 206-237). These same values that had justified laissez-faire economics were now turned against it. Roosevelt's main mission in domestic policy became the breaking up of the trusts. The actual achievements in that sphere were less significant than the expansion of government's role in social welfare—in particular the enactment of state workers' compensation laws and various pension programs, and the establishment of the U.S. Children's Bureau. Limited though these steps were, they pointed the way toward the welfare state.

The birth of the American welfare state is usually placed in the early 1930s, when the federal government was propelled into action by the worst depression in the nation's history. Strictly speaking, the federal government had been in the business of "welfare" long before that. In the early nineteenth century, U.S. funds aided a few institutions for the deaf (Trattner, 1976); and in the post-Civil War era, the Freedmen's Bureau gave assistance to blacks (Axinn & Levin, pp. 83-86). But it was not until the Depression that protection was extended to the general population.

While twentieth century liberalism in American politics has tended to be viewed as anti-business by its critics, largely because of its alliance with organized labor, the record of policy initiatives belies the reputation. Franklin D. Roosevelt's first actions upon entering office in the depths of the Depression were directed to business recovery. John F. Kennedy pushed through tax cuts designed to stimulate business. And many actions of these and other liberal presidents have more indirectly worked to the benefit of private industry.

If there is a consistent thread in twentieth century liberalism, it is the promotion of social welfare aims through the use of government, a striking departure from the kind of liberalism which preceded it. How did this metamorphosis occur? It is important to understand that there was from the beginning a strong thread of social responsibility in the liberal fabric. It can be seen in the statesmanship of a Franklin or an Adams, the active role of liberals in nineteenth century philanthropy, the universality of the doctrine itself (liberty and justice for *all*). It was what kept liberalism from degenerating into hedonism. Just as their forebears had had to come to terms with the illiberalism of slavery, twentieth century liberals saw that freedom meant little to the worker mashed under the heel of industry. And government was the only institution capable of redressing the imbalance. Thus the historic principle of equality under the law was broadened to encompass a more general meaning of equality—redistribution of resources and opportunities. This posed a new quandary for liberalism: the dilemma between liberty and equality. To this we shall return shortly.

Liberals and the Military

Today we face a new concentration of power, one that combines centralized authority, largely unaccountable to the citizenry, and unprecedented destructive potential. It is the defense establishment. Liberals have yet to find common ground in dealing with it.

To many, World War II was as clear a contest between good and evil as any war before or since. Liberals perceived the true nature of nazism before conservatives did and were readier to intervene in the struggle. The liberal Franklin D. Roosevelt drew a reluctant country along with him into rearming. On the heels of the defeat of Germany and Japan, Americans became alarmed about a new threat: the Soviet Union. There followed a schism among liberals which is still with us, the schism between "hawks" and "doves."

The order to drop atomic bombs on two Japanese cities was a natural sequel to the wholesale slaughter of civilians throughout the war. The order to develop the hydrogen bomb was part of the Cold War against the Soviets. Both orders came from a liberal president, Harry Truman. Liberal and conservative administrations alike have contributed to the arms build-up since then. Lyndon Johnson is best remembered for two wars: the war on poverty and the war in Vietnam. The American labor movement has been fiercely anti-communist, with many elements avowedly pro-military.

Other liberal voices have counseled restraint and pointed to the danger of excessive military power. One concern has been the use of American military might on behalf of oppressive regimes abroad. Both factions have used the same basic argument in this dialogue: the right of the individual to life, liberty and the pursuit of happiness, whether the individual be a Soviet Jew or a Vietnamese or Salvadorean peasant. Liberals have also seen a huge defense apparatus as threatening basic liberties and taking resources away from social welfare programs.

THE DILEMMA BETWEEN LIBERTY AND EQUALITY

It is not that the welfare state actually equalizes the life chances of all Americans. In fact, in some respects the people who reap the greatest benefits are the well off (Abramovitz, 1983; Titmuss, 1969, pp. 34-55). But it is clearly the intent of the welfare state to mitigate the effects of inequality, especially as they fall on the least fortunate. The largest social welfare program in the country—social security—is redistributive; that is, it shifts resources downward. If we expand the notion of welfare state to include not only direct benefit programs but affirmative action and other opportunity measures, the explicit purpose is the redress of inequality.

How does one reconcile this aim with the central liberal tenet of personal liberty? As the machinery for implementing social welfare policies has grown larger, more complex and intrusive, the question has become more difficult. Is this a zero-sum problem, that is, one in which equality can be served only at the price of liberty?

We must first ask what is meant by liberty. For the original liberals it was liberty for people like themselves. In time liberalism came to terms with the fact that "liberty for all" had no meaning unless it extended to the least among humans. In the real world, this could not come about without some interference with the autonomy of others, especially those with the power to oppress. Gunnar Myrdal (1960) has envisioned a "welfare society" in which the voluntary good will of all would supplant much of the present welfare state machinery. Such a society seems a long way off, if indeed it is ever attainable. In fact, as Myrdal sketches out his notion he includes a far more extensive role of government than is presently true of the American welfare state.

Rawls: Justice as Fairness

Philosopher John Rawls (1971) has sought to reconcile liberty and equality by means of the concept of justice as fairness. He asks us to start by supposing that we do not know who we are nor anything about our circumstances. That is appropriate if we are designing a justice system which will apply to all persons of all circumstances. What kind of a system will we choose? One that best protects *our* interests.

As a liberal, Rawls assumes our own personal liberty will be paramount to us. Since we don't know who we are, we will want to make sure that one person's liberty is gained at the least risk to another's. Furthermore, for all we know, we may be at the bottom of the heap, so we need to take special account of the position of the underdog. It is this last point that brings equality into the discussion and separates Rawls from the liberals of old. Two guiding principles stand at the center of Rawls's theory of justice:

1. Each person is to have an equal right to the most extensive total system of equal basic liberties compatible with a similar system of liberty for all.
2. Social and economic inequalities are to be arranged so that they both (a) work to the greater benefit of the least advantaged, and (b) are attached to offices and positions open to all under conditions of fair equality of opportunity.

Rawls assigns highest priority to liberty, an ordering which may differ from those of many present-day liberals. It might be argued, for example, that liberty is a rather remote issue for the homeless person struggling for sheer survival. But the significant thing about this conception is that it incorporates both concerns of the welfare state: liberty and equality. An active role of government in providing for the needs of the destitute is consistent with Rawls's principle, as are a wide range of other social welfare functions. Depending on how one defines "fair equality of opportunity," affirmative action and school desegregation policies may also be consistent with it.

The important word is *may*. Liberals disagree sharply over such issues. Many persons who were totally identified with the civil rights movement of the early sixties recoiled at the more militant side of welfare rights and black power in the late sixties. Liberals also differ over specific program priorities. Should priority be given to the need for income supports or better housing or legal assistance or counseling or institutional care? This question becomes more urgent as welfare resources shrink. Meanwhile, the welfare state per se faces a more fundamental kind of questioning, from the left and the right.

WELFARE AS A TOOL OF CAPITALISM

From a Marxist perspective, the welfare state is primarily a means of supporting capitalist exploitation of the masses. It uses benefits to discipline the work force. It teaches clients to be submissive and love the system, instead of mobilizing them to demand their rights. Furthermore, such seductive counsel is substituted for material resources that are the real need. The welfare state is an apologist for capitalism, in that it perpetuates the myth that problems lie, not in the economic and political order, but in the pathology of the victims. Ostensibly dedicated to equality, it actually serves the rich and powerful through everything from subsidies to tax write-offs.

A similar indictment—though not primarily from a Marxist perspective—is that the welfare state is the tool of white racism. It is said to perpetuate the myth of black inferiority—couched in the benign language of the therapist—give preferential treatment to whites and keep minority populations in a state of servitude through public assistance policies, child welfare practices, mental health and corrections.

The critics differ as to the degree of knowing complicity in the crime. Galper (1975), for instance, sees social workers and other welfare state functionaries as well-intended. It is not that they are deliberately evil but that they lack both the power to make necessary changes and the insight to recognize the true nature of the problem. But he sees them as potential allies in the struggle against capitalist oppression (pp. 188-227).

The criticism on the left should be taken seriously. Many of the specific complaints are true. For the writer the question is not so much the particulars as it is the sweeping nature of the analysis and the implications for what should be done. Interestingly enough, few critics on the left propose scrapping the welfare system as a bankrupt idea. In fact, they want more, not fewer services, an improvement on what exists. Their real target is capitalism itself; for short of abolishing or fundamentally changing that, they see no hope of significant change in social welfare. Some critics whose main concern is racism share the goal of abolishing capitalism, while others call for a separate welfare system under minority control but with resources provided by the larger society.

That the American welfare state is an integral part of the larger social order is clear. As is spelled out in detail in the next and subsequent chapters of this book, it serves important functions for maintaining existing political and economic structures. It is inherently American, although it has borrowed concepts from other societies. This being so, what is to be done about its negative aspects? Abolish the present political-economic system? To be replaced by what? Some may be sufficiently optimistic to hope that the new order would be an improvement over the old. My own perception is that it would be a revolution of the right, not the left, more fascistic than socialistic, given our experience to date. It was Stalin, not Kerensky, who came to power after the Russian Revolution. In France, it was not the moderate Danton who prevailed but Robespierre and ultimately Napoleon.

But the question of radical change is academic. American capitalism has never been seriously threatened from the left. It has managed to absorb all such efforts—with the help of the welfare state, to be sure. The liberals who dominate welfare state policy and its critics on the left share many of the same values and aspirations. As Galper says, we are potential allies. The real issue may be, who will define the terms of the alliance? To date the respective parties are too far apart to contemplate marriage or any of its present-day equivalents.

The critics on the left perform an important function in forcing the center of gravity over a few notches. In effect, they make it easier for the liberals to be truly liberal in the twentieth century sense, harder to be reactionary. They are thus reformists, however much they deride that role.

WELFARE AS A BAD IDEA

Unlike the critics on the left, those on the right believe the welfare state *is* a bad idea, one which should be scrapped. Their arguments touch a responsive chord in a society which has never felt comfortable with the notion of getting something without paying for it and which still harbors great fear of big government. Until the last decade and a half, they seemed to be a vocal minority that appealed to passion more than reason, thus were not taken seriously by many liberals. This is no longer true. In fact, they present a more logically consistent case than the defenders of the welfare state, partly because they hold a distinct ideology.

Robert Nozik represents this point of view in perhaps its purest form. The advocates of the welfare state, according to Nozik (1974), have abandoned the principles of true liberalism, which he defines in terms reminiscent of the Social Darwinists. He calls for a "minimal state," whose functions would be limited to protecting people and their property and enforcing contracts. Private citizens would be free to band together to provide education, health and other services, but government would not be involved. Nor would anybody have a claim on benefits. There is nothing inherently wrong with charity, as long as it is a voluntary act and carries with it no sense of obligation nor entitlement.

Not only has Nozik frozen liberalism in an earlier time, in repudiation of its evolutionary character, but he has distorted it in the process. His theory omits any thought of social responsibility, an essential component of liberalism. He thus resolves the liberty-equality dilemma by ignoring it.

Others who share Nozik's opposition to the welfare state use more substantive arguments. By taking from the rich and giving to the poor, it simultaneously undermines economic growth and pauperizes its supposed beneficiaries (Gilder, 1981). It interferes with the operation of the market (Freidman, 1962). By displacing the family and local community as the sources of nurturance for the individual, it weakens these vital social institutions (Glazer, 1971). And always there is the persistent question of unfairness; the bleeding of hard-working citizens for the sake of those who will not help themselves.

This last charge is the easiest to answer. As Abramovitz (1983) points out, we are all "on welfare" in a sense. Almost 50% of American households receive some direct government benefit (*This Week in Washington*, 1985). The universal programs that cushion the retirement years of the middle class—social security and Medicare—take the lion's share of federal welfare expenditures; more than ten times the outlay for food stamps and Aid to Families With Dependent Children (AFDC). It is medical professionals, not their patients, who receive health care dollars. Similarly, farmers benefit from food stamps, and construction workers and landlords profit from housing programs.

These are the direct welfare expenditures. The indirect, in the form of tax deductions, work mainly to the benefit of the best off, as do subsidized fringe benefits in industry (Titmuss, 1969). If we look beyond the welfare state per se, we find the biggest "hand-outs" going to defense contractors, a kind of welfare that conservatives are least willing to reduce. Even welfare for the poor benefits the nonpoor, because one thing the welfare recipient cannot do is hold onto assistance, it must be spent. So welfare dollars find their way into the general economy and ultimately the pockets of the hard-working taxpayer.

Does the welfare state sap the initiative of the poor by fostering dependency? The impact of welfare on the work incentive is a major issue, one that we consider in Chapter 4. Suffice it to say at this point that the evidence is mixed, and the most likely answer is that benefits both increase and decrease participation in the work force. But for the vast majority of those receiving welfare benefits, the question is moot: they are the elderly, the physically and mentally disabled and young children.

Does the welfare state undermine the role of the family and the local community? Indeed, haven't things gotten worse every time social programs expanded? (See Murray, 1984.) One is reminded of the tongue-in-cheek observation that the quality of medical care causes cancer, since both have risen in the same period. The reasons for family breakdown and neighborhood dissolution are complex. The same forces in industrial society which have contributed to these problems have also prompted enactment of welfare state provisions. However, some welfare measures *have* clearly harmed family and neighborhood integrity. AFDC rules requiring that the breadwinner be out of the home in order for an impoverished family to qualify for aid may have a destabilizing effect on families. Urban renewal programs have destroyed neighborhoods in the name of community progress. The answer is not to eliminate the benefits but to change the rules so that they do in fact support families and communities. Welfare state proponents have been among the strongest advocates of such steps.

Yet there remain serious questions about the impact of welfare on the sense of personal responsibility and family integrity. After avoiding them for many years—because even raising them seemed to carry racist overtones—liberals have had to face these issues squarely. Eleanor Holmes Norton, a black woman who formerly chaired the U.S. Equal Employment Opportunity Commission, has expressed concern about the future of the black family. Widespread dependence on public assistance, children who give birth to children, and young men who shun responsibility for their offspring are facts of life. But unlike the welfare state critics who would simply take away financial support, Norton sees these patterns as adaptations to a catch-22 situation; one in which society denies blacks and other minorities access to meaningful work, uses the monthly welfare check as a way of keeping them quiet, and in other ways undermines the values it preaches. The issue of social welfare policy and black family life is discussed in Chapter 10.

One of the more ingenious arguments for dismantling the welfare state runs this way: Either it has succeeded, in which case it is no longer needed, or it is a failure that should never have happened. More typically, it is the former side of the proposition which is advanced: Welfare served a useful purpose during the Depression, and even some of the non-financial forms of service in the War on Poverty had their place, but the welfare state has outlived its usefulness (Anderson, 1978). Why then does it continue? Because social workers (by implication all welfare bureaucrats) want to keep their jobs.

There is a kernal of truth in this last assertion. Notwithstanding the real dedication of many workers in the human services, the expansion of welfare programs over the last fifty years has created an "industry" to which many careers are tied. Professionalization and unionization of staffs have helped to solidify vested interests in the welfare establishment. For example, some attempts to

close down half-empty hospitals and transfer patients to other facilities as an efficiency move have been met by fierce resistance. A reformer who tried to bring
about a more enlightened juvenile justice program in Massachusetts by closing
down warehouse-like training schools found a similar reaction (Richan, 1980).

In this way, social welfare personnel are no different from other workers. The
overall effects of such rearguard actions on the total welfare system may be
small. Certainly their economic impact is limited, since personnel costs of the
welfare state are dwarfed by direct transfers of money, as in social security payments. But the vested interests of welfare workers are not a reason for doing
away with welfare.

Has the welfare state been so successful as to work itself out of a job? One
problem with this sort of question is in finding clear evidence regarding the effects of welfare programs. Research on the issue presents special problems.
Ethically we cannot give benefits to one set of destitute families and withhold
them from another in order to arrive at a scientifically valid test of the proposition. Another problem is the intrusion of a multitude of external factors to mess
up the data. Does the success or failure of an employment program reflect the
qualities of the program, the fact that it is directed to those least competitive in
the labor market or the availability of jobs?

One obstacle to good research on this and other welfare issues is that social
welfare itself is in a goldfish bowl, with various constituencies ready to pounce
on any shreds of evidence which support their case. That has led to premature
expansion of certain programs and premature abolition of others. Often the
evidence is simply ignored. Countless reports showing conclusively that the
average AFDC family leaves the rolls in a few years and that work is out of the
question for a majority of welfare recipients make little difference to a society
convinced that most people on welfare are there because they choose to spend
their lives on the dole rather than face the prospect of honest work.

Is there still a need for the welfare state? One way to answer that is to consider
the consequences of dismantling it. Let us start with the big ticket items, social
security and Medicare. These will have most meaning to those with aged parents
or who are themselves approaching retirement. Next in terms of size are other
income security programs, which include not only aid to the poor but also unemployment benefits for the worker who gets laid off because of a plant closing.
Just what that hard working taxpayer and his family will do to make ends meet is
no longer the federal government's concern.

Next to go will be support of health care and all education, training and employment services. After that will come veterans' benefits, housing and community development and farm income supports. There are welfare state expenses
hidden within other items, but the foregoing would suffice to produce a different
kind of government—and a different kind of society. It is a society nobody under
the age of fifty has ever known, a fact that may make it easier for critics to talk
so freely about dismantling the welfare state.

No doubt states would pick up some of these programs, but they are not capable of mounting social security and Medicare. Typically the federal government has taken on a responsibility only because states and the private sector failed to deal with it. The states are notoriously uneven in the human service area, those in the region with the greatest poverty—the South—being most reluctant to support welfare. We must also keep in mind that many state and local services are heavily subsidized by the federal government.

To be consistent, the dismantling of the welfare state must also include indirect welfare, in the form of tax exemptions. That will hit both state and local public services and private charity. People with enough surplus income will invest in individual retirement accounts (IRAs), but investment income of this sort will now be taxed.

The vast majority of the working class will be pushed into the ranks of the poor when they reach the age when they are no longer of use to the post-industrial economy. Private health insurers will exclude the people at high risk from most coverage, as they are now doing with potential AIDS victims.

The dismantling of the welfare state would have two other indirect consequences. One is that nearly 80 cents of every federal tax dollar, except for the interest on the national debt, would go for defense, foreign military aid and the space program, which is predominantly military. The warfare state would supplant the welfare state instead of coexisting with it. The other consequence is that, being deprived of necessities and amenities formerly provided with federal government aid, the American people would be even less disposed to be generous to either their own poor or the wretched millions in the two-thirds of the world which has not shared in the benefits of industrial progress. That in turn would lead to more reliance on police power at home and military means abroad.

THE END OF THE WELFARE STATE?

The merits of the welfare state aside, is it due to go the way of the nickel cigar and the horse-drawn buggy? Not that we have ever achieved in practice anything approaching the conception of government responsibility for the welfare of all. Nonetheless, for half a century this country has subscribed to the belief that the federal government does have an obligation to protect the citizenry from the worst ravages of poverty and other social ills. It came about dramatically in the Great Depression of the 1930s, when the traditional view that poverty was self-inflicted became manifestly absurd in the face of world-wide economic collapse.

In recent years, the terms of the debate over welfare have shifted. In the United States and several European countries, governments favoring less welfare have come into office. In a sense the center of gravity has shifted to the right, with conservative critics of the welfare state being more vocal and liberal defenders sounding more defensive and less liberal. Aside from the efforts to trim welfare costs, there has been a shift in this country toward less federal and more state responsibility for social programs. In 1981, Congress consolidated more than 50 separate programs into nine broad categories, with more of the decision-making about specifics left to the states; at the same time the funding was cut by 25%, with states, localities and the private sector left to make up the difference or reduce programs. This general thrust continued into the mid-eighties.

On the surface, then, the trend seems indeed to be away from the welfare state concept of (national) government responsibility for social welfare. But before we get too far with the funeral preparations, we should step back and get a little more perspective on events. Has this country abandoned the welfare state? There are several reasons to think not, nor that it will in the future.

Mixed political messages. Ronald Reagan's resounding electoral victory in 1980 was widely interpreted as carrying with it a mandate to cut back on the federal government's role in domestic affairs. Deregulate industry, slash federal taxes and, in particular, reduce federal spending and control in social programs. Henceforth, went the script, federal activity would be limited to provision of a social safety net for the most needy. Such welfare-state initiatives as housing subsidies, school lunches, mass transit support and urban redevelopment would be the responsibility of others. In Reagan's first one hundred days in office—reminiscent of Franklin D. Roosevelt's first hundred days of dramatic action to stem the effects of the Depression—Congress responded by pushing through major tax cuts, a massive defense build up and reductions in many social programs.

But the Reagan Administration soon discovered that one facet of the welfare state was sacred territory: the retirement insurance system under social security. An attempt to restrict benefits in that program brought open revolt from the President's own party in the Senate, and the plan was scrapped. A deep recession which hounded the early years of Reagan's presidency fueled a resurgence of the Democratic opposition, and the Republicans suffered significant losses in the off-year 1982 congressional election. This slowed but did not stop the administration's efforts to reshape the country's political agenda. A brisk economic recovery and Reagan's personal appeal led to a landslide victory in the 1984 election campaign. But even here the messages were mixed: Was it Ronald Reagan's policies or his charisma that gave him such a resounding vote? The fact that he ran against a lackluster and fumbling opponent further muddied the water.

Reagan's second term was marked by reversals and strategic retreats by the administration on a number of critical issues. Ironically, setbacks in the policy arena seemed not to make a dent in the President's popularity. But there were clear signs that the dramatic changes that had occurred in his first year in office were unlikely to be repeated. In fact, public opinion polls found that the percentage of Americans who favored welfare state programs for the poor was higher at the end of 1985 than at the beginning of 1981 when Ronald Reagan took office (*New York Times,* 1986). It is fair to ask, then, how much of a setback the welfare state had suffered.

The nature of the damage. The most striking thing about the revolution of the early eighties was what it did *not* achieve. While there were significant cutbacks in certain programs, the basic benefits like social security, Medicare, food stamps and AFDC were left intact, though eligibility for the latter two programs was tightened. Not that there weren't significant inroads on welfare provisions, but the worst scenario didn't happen, and the Congress elected in 1982 restored a number of cuts that had been made in 1981. In government the bottom line is money. Despite all of the rhetoric about rolling back social programs, total federal expenditures for social welfare[1] rose by more than 20% during Ronald Reagan's first term in office.

These are all short-term developments, and events could quickly move in a different direction in response to new pressures. The retrenchment of social welfare programs predated the election of Reagan. It went on under Democrat Jimmy Carter as well as his Republican predecessors. Undoubtedly many of the cutbacks that occurred under President Reagan would have happened without him.

In the early and mid-eighties colossal federal budget deficits were leading all factions to look for ways to rein in costs of government programs, including social welfare. All this could change abruptly—say, if the economy went into a tailspin as it did in the thirties. More significant for the longterm prospects of the welfare state than any of these events, however, are underlying forces in American society.

The arithmetic of age. An overriding factor in the degree to which a society allocates its resources to social welfare is the age of the population. This is true regardless of the ideological, political and economic order (Miller, 1976). And this society is getting old. As is spelled out in detail in Chapter 7, the frail elderly, those over 80, are increasing faster than any other group. These are the people who will need more income support, health services and nursing home care in the coming decades. Even if we were disposed to turn our backs on this segment of the population, their political clout will assure that they will be listened to. Thus, if we decided to scrap every other social welfare benefit and concentrate all our resources on the elderly, expenditures would continue to increase.

The vital functions of social welfare. We won't scrap every other social welfare benefit, because we need them to function as a society. Put aside all notions of charity, all humane impulses. A modern society needs income security and health care benefits for persons of all ages. It needs programs to curb antisocial behavior and redirect energies in constructive directions. It needs help in keeping the social fabric intact. Conceivably, we could manage many of these functions by imposing a police state. But interestingly enough, no police state in modern times has felt free to dispense with all welfare provisions. Hitler didn't. Stalin didn't. We recoil at the way they used social welfare programs, but these extreme cases make it clear that we will not dispense with them either.

---

[1]Community and regional development; education, training, employment and social services; health; social security and Medicare; income security; and veterans' benefits and services. Data are for fiscal years 1981 through 1984 (U.S. OMB, 1985).

To wish to get the federal government out of the business of social welfare is to wish for a time when life was untroubled and bosses knew all their workers by their first name and folks got along together without anybody feeling downtrodden and parents didn't abuse their children and drinking and drugs weren't a problem and women and blacks "knew their place" and were contented. It's a time that never existed.

Chapter 2

Beyond Altruism:
The Vital Tasks
of Social Welfare Policy

There seems little question that altruism is a powerful engine in human affairs. Titmuss (1971) found, for example, that this was the most important reason why people were willing to part with that most precious of possessions, their life blood. But altruism does not explain why societies expend huge resources on social welfare. To understand that we must look elsewhere.

Suppose you had to start things all over again. Not just you but you and a group of other people. Cut off from the rest of humanity and destined to spend the rest of your lives on your own.

In his chilling classic, *Lord of the Flies,* William Golding (1962) puts a group of English choir boys on a deserted island. In learning to survive, these cherubs show that they are capable of every form of baseness including murder. Golding is trying to make a point about human nature. He is saying, in effect, we are all little beasties underneath the choir robes. Let us use the same situation to make a different point: how societies large or small survive.

You are on an airliner that develops engine trouble in mid-Pacific and has to ditch on a deserted island. Miraculously you and the other 99 occupants live through the ordeal, but you have no way of communicating with the outside world. Now all you have to do is figure out how to survive.

Your first job is locating water, food and shelter, managing the supplies of these resources and working out a system for distributing them. Notions of rugged individualism will be scrapped in a hurry. Democratic decision-making may also have a tough time. Such niceties will not be uppermost in the minds of the group. If any of you are going to make it for very long, you will have to work together.

Your next worry is maintaining order in the group. A few members are on the verge of panic and must be kept under close watch. They cannot be allowed to endanger the rest of you, even if it takes harsh measures to control them. Fights between group members must also be dealt with firmly. These are desperate times, when the best and worst in us comes to the surface.

Those elementary steps may suffice for the time being, but over the long haul the group must be assured that the work of survival goes on. If anybody has a special skill, such as medical treatment, others have to be trained so you are not

21

dependent on that one person. People will also have to be taught to kill game or grow food, repair shelters, and so forth. Along with the knowledge will have to come the willingness to carry out these tasks. If the group is to continue into future generations, children will have to be taught these same survival skills and motivated to use them for the good of the group.

If this community is like most, it will reach low points when nothing seems to go right and factions turn on each other. It would be fatal to let this kind of disarray continue, so steps have to be taken to build a sense of identity with the community as a whole.

This small society of castaways has had to accomplish five basic tasks: providing the means of physical survival, assuring that work gets done, controlling threatening behavior, preparing people for useful roles and keeping the community as a whole from falling apart. But you don't have to go to a deserted island to see the same thing. You could start with the family in which you grew up.

Food, clothing, shelter and health care were basic necessities. Let any of these be cut off, even temporarily, and the family had a major crisis on its hands. If the breadwinner became ill or died or was laid off or left home, somebody had to step in to take over. Domestic violence or even the threat of it would have posed a different kind of crisis. Nor could dangerous behavior on the part of a child be tolerated. Not just physical threats but anything that might undermine existing relations and norms of good behavior. You became acutely aware of this when you reached adolescence and began testing limits you had previously accepted.

You may have been less aware of the process of learning your proper place in the family and taking over attitudes and skills from your parents and older brothers and sisters, but that was one of the primary functions of your family. The lessons ranged from subtle signals that certain age-mates were undesirable to the teaching of language skills, career goals and sex-role behavior.

Family solidarity is more complicated. Very often certain ties are close and others weak within the same household. But if there is not a basic bond among members the viability of the family itself is threatened. Separation from a parent through death, divorce or desertion is always a crisis. Most families adopt symbols of solidarity such as special holidays, inside jokes or stories about a favorite relative. You can supply the rest of the illustrations of family solidarity from your own childhood.

SOCIETAL TASKS

Just as with face-to-face groups, nations must accomplish these five tasks. The reason for the production and distribution of basic life-supports is self-evident, as is making sure work gets done. Social control of behavior considered threatening and preparation of children and newcomers for their proper roles are also understandable requirements. Social solidarity, though less obvious, is needed if society is to continue into the future. But while these tasks may be obvious, the way in which they relate to societal values and practices is not.

Q. Who should work for a living?
A. Everybody should work for a living.
Q. Why?
A. Because it's right (fair) (good for one's character).
Q. Should children below the age of fifteen work for a living?
A. That's different. They're only kids. Their parents should support them.
Q. Why should they?
A. It's their obligation as parents.
Q. Should people over seventy work for a living?
A. No, they deserve to be taken care of.
Q. Why?
A. It's just right, that's all.

Until fairly recently most Americans believed a mother's place was in the home, bringing up her children. Many Americans still hold that value. During World War II, when a large percentage of the men in the labor force were in the military, women were needed to work in factories. Somehow we found it acceptable at that time for women to place their children in the care of somebody else and go to work. In rural areas many husbands commute to industrial jobs while their wives do the heavy farm chores that tend to be thought of as "men's work."

Q. Why should children treat parents and teachers with respect?
A. Because without respect discipline would break down.
Q. Why is discipline important?
A. It's for the children's own protection. Also, if they don't respect teachers and parents they won't learn anything and they'll never get anywhere.
Q. Do we know for a fact that respectful children do better in life than disrespectful ones?
A. It stands to reason that they will.
Q. Why should Americans stand when "The Star Spangled Banner" is being played?
A. To show their loyalty to their country.
Q. Suppose they are loyal but don't want to show it in that way.
A. People should stand up for their country.
Q. Suppose they are not loyal.
A. That's something all Americans owe their country. If they don't like it they should get out.
Q. Why is it bad to have Americans who feel no loyalty to the United States remain here as long as they don't cause trouble?
A. What are you, a Communist?

My point is not to question those beliefs but to show that, while they are usually stated in terms of the person's welfare or just what is right, their significance goes much deeper. They are means by which society gets its members to carry out the survival tasks. No matter that the beliefs may lead to behavior that is inefficient or self-defeating, their underlying meaning is societal.

The way in which basic necessities are produced and distributed is central to everything else. Somehow society has to make sure that people with the right skills will carry out the work of providing goods and services. Totalitarian states often rely on direct coercion to make that happen. A democratic country with a mixed economy like ours uses more indirect means. People have to be recruited to do needed work and motivated to be productive. They also have to be able and willing to buy what is produced.

Disruptive behavior has to be kept under control. Again, it is not as easy to use direct coercion in a democracy as in an avowed police state, so more indirect means come into play. In either kind of society, the formal machinery of control depends on a high degree of self-restraint and the support of the majority of the population.

Newcomers to the society may lack the skills and motivation and ways of behaving to take their place in the order of things. Depending on where they come from, they may have to get rid of some old cultural baggage.

In all societies, families or something approximating families play a critical role in all this. It is no accident that modern societies prize the nuclear family, in which children are prepared to move away from home and pursue careers different from their parents' and challenge the ideas of the older generation. That kind of flexibility fits the needs of a high-tech post-industrial system. Traditional extended families that stay in one place and where the elders rule the roost work better in agrarian societies.

Likewise, a modern economy relies on a universal education system where children are taught basic literacy, technical work skills, rules of punctuality and work organization. Even competition in school sports prepares young people to compete in the world of work, thus fostering ever-higher standards of excellence. And permeating all of these institutions are values of loyalty to one's group and one's country. Thus the individual members carry around their own personal gyroscopes to keep them on course without the need for the heavy hand of an oppressive regime.

At least that is the way it is supposed to work.

THE FLAWED REALITY

It is a real question whether life should revolve around the maintenance of a well-oiled production-consumption machine. In a material sense it has yielded many benefits for the majority of Americans, but has material well-being of the majority been purchased at too high a price in fundamental humanistic values?

The question makes us uneasy, but the basic assumptions underpinning the existing order have never been seriously challenged by most Americans.

So let us take the American post-industrial society on its own terms. *Post-industrial* because the production of goods has yielded center stage to the production of services, and information processing has become more important than materials processing. The dynamics have changed, but the basic tasks remain the same. Has this society yielded the benefits that are claimed for it? Clearly in many ways it has not.

The most dramatic instances of failure have been the periodic recessions which have tipped some families into poverty (some of these permanently) and shaken the economic security for many more. We know that unemployment has a devastating impact on a person's life, going way beyond the loss of income. Recessions pass, but the grinding poverty that entraps a significant part of the population does not pass. A fifth of all American children live in poverty; among black children it's more than two fifths (Children's Defense Fund, 1984). Female-headed households—29% of all households—average less than half the income of those headed by males.[1]

We are so familiar with the dismal statistics on blacks and other minorities that we may tune them out. It is important that we do not. Black babies are twice as likely as white babies to die in the first year of life. Fifty-four percent of black men are employed, as compared with 78% of white men. Black men are six times as likely as white men to be murdered and 75% more likely to suffer from hypertension.

In 1982, there were 13 million crimes known to have been committed in the United States. That amounts to one for every 18 Americans. Our murder rate, as of 1978, was three times the rate in Finland, six times the rate in Israel, eight and a half times the rate in Japan, and ranged from six to 19 times the rates in Western European countries. Even bloody Northern Ireland has only three-fifths the rate of this country.

Almost one out of five Americans is estimated to have a mental disorder, according to studies by the National Institute of Mental Health (NIMH). Many of these, especially among men, are masked by alcohol and drug abuse (*New York Times*, 1984f). About one out of a hundred Americans is schizophrenic.

The nuclear family structure which fits so smoothly with the needs of an industrial economy creates a number of problems. It is marked by a close and intensive relationship between parents and children while the latter are growing up, then a sharp break when the children leave home. Parent-child relationships in the extended family are neither so close during childhood nor so detached afterward. Adolescence is the period when children make the transition between these two stages of family life, so not surprisingly it is a time of major stress. Conflicting messages about rights and responsibilities and the commercialization of the teen culture compound other problems.

---

[1]Unless otherwise indicated, figures are from U.S., Bureau of Census (1983).

Nearly one in five arrests for serious crimes in 1982 involved persons between the ages of 15 and 17, though they were only one-sixteenth of the population over the age of 14. As of the end of the 1970s, over a million teenagers became pregnant each year, and over 600,000 became mothers before reaching adulthood. The highest unemployment rate is among young people aged 16 to 24. More than one out of ten high school students drops out before graduation. Among blacks the rate is more than one in seven.

Cases of child abuse and neglect which are reported are believed to be only the tip of the iceberg. In 1981 there were 846,000 reported cases, an increase of almost 40% in three years. With women entering the workforce in unprecedented numbers, family life has been in the midst of a revolution. We are fast approaching the point when a majority of children under the age of six will have working mothers; and of these, half will be cared for outside their own homes (Waldman, 1983; Kamerman, 1983a). Changing roles have been attended by increased family violence and breakdown.

At the other end of the age scale, the post-industrial society tends to discard old people and treat them as second-class citizens, in contrast with many traditional societies in which the elders maintain their position at the head of clan and community. The marketing of physical beauty and vigor further demeans the status of the elderly. As a result, they suffer income and role loss and social isolation at the same time as their health is declining rapidly. In 1982 the poverty rate among Americans in the 45 to 64 year age bracket was 10%; among those 65 and older it was 15%. Rates of suicide and mental hospitalization are highest among the elderly.

So even if one accepts the values of materialism and me-firstism, the system has basic flaws.

SOCIAL WELFARE: REPAIR SHOP OR FRONT-LINE INSTITUTION?

As discussed in the previous chapter, major expansions in social welfare policy have had to overcome resistance, some of it fierce and protracted. Even when catastrophes such as the Great Depression forced the country to move in a different direction, the measures were modest, guided by precedents from the past.

This conception of social welfare policy is called *residual* (Wilensky & Lebeaux, 1958, pp. 138-140). It assumes that the social order will normally keep things on track. From time to time there are breakdowns requiring interference with the "natural" order of things. It is at these times, according to this conception, when social welfare programs should come into play. When things are set a-right, the program should be cut back or dismantled. How come social welfare policy seems to be cumulative, that is, does not go away? It is because those who run the programs have a vested interest in keeping them going, and the beneficiaries become dependent on them, i.e., less self-reliant. This is the "repair shop" approach to social welfare policy.

A different view of social welfare is that it is part of the basic fabric of life. Policies are enacted, not just in response to breakdowns, but to meet society's obligation to all its citizens. This is the *institutional* view of social welfare policy. Programs continue, not because people become addicted to them, but because they are an intrinsic part of an enlightened society. Our policies are a mixture of residual and institutional, but the general outlook in this country is still basically residual. It has sometimes been said that Americans learned their lesson during the Great Depression and never again would we allow people to go without basic necessities because of opposition to an active role by government. Expansion of programs in the sixties seemed to confirm that idea, but in recent years the principle of government responsibility for human welfare has been challenged.

The most obviously "institutional" program is the social security retirement system. It was enacted in the 1930s in response to a crisis, but it was seen from the beginning as part of the national economic fabric. Retirement was not an anomaly to "solve" but a normal and legitimate sequel to a productive life. The belief that social security undermines thrift is still heard occasionally, but most Americans seem thoroughly committed to this program. Virtually every other social welfare policy in this country is viewed as "residual," regardless of how large and loyal its constituency of supporters. People should be able to keep a job, take care of their medical bills, handle their family relations, avoid mental disorders and stay out of trouble with the law. If they can't, there is something wrong with them. It is a way of saying all's right with the system; the exceptions are caused by the failings of individuals.

We cling to this outlook despite massive evidence to the contrary. The post-industrial system depends on income security programs to manage the supply of labor and child welfare programs to prepare children for entering the work force. Society needs programs to curb violent impulses, turned inward and outward, that result from societal stresses. The family needs supportive programs, not because of occasional aberrations, but because of inherently conflicting demands on it. And all of these institutions need measures to help maintain the solidarity of the whole, a solidarity undermined by forces growing out of the system itself. These are the vital tasks of social welfare policy.

PART 2

Survival and Workforce Tasks

When two persons meet for the first time, one of the first questions asked is about occupations. Knowing what somebody does for a living is shorthand for inferring a great deal else about the person: general income level, social class characteristics, educational background, maybe even place of residence. If a woman says, "Just a housewife," it doesn't take the conversation long to get around to her husband's occupation. If a person says "student," the next question will be about the field of study, with the same object in mind of placing the person in the socioeconomic spectrum. The next time you are among strangers, say at a party, you might see how long you can avoid bringing occupations into the conversation.

Work is indeed closely associated with income in this as in most societies. We presume *that income is based on work—either current or before the person retired. Similarly, in social welfare policy there has always been a close tie between work and income provision, but of a somewhat different sort. Wedded to the belief that income gained through work is good and income acquired any other way is bad, we have hedged financial benefit programs around with work requirements, treated benefits based on past work as more respectable than those which are not, and used employability as a basis for denying benefits to people.*

So the societal tasks of providing the means of survival and getting the work done are closely intertwined. These are the bedrock functions, the most elemental of all. The earliest social welfare programs were concerned with these two functions, and they continue to represent the largest part of social welfare expenditures. Part II traces the history of these programs and issues which dominate them today.

Chapters 3 and 4 describe the evolution of economic security policy. In Chapter 3 we meet the two worlds of welfare—that reserved for people considered adequate, normal, hard-working but in need of protection against misfortune; and the other, inhabited by those considered weak, shiftless, unreliable and the cause of their own misery. Chapter 4 explores the relationship between work and welfare. Policies ostensibly intended to move the nonworking into the active labor force don't always work that way. Attitudes about work and welfare are mixed up with other attitudes, particularly those involving race and sex.

Chapters 5 and 6 deal with topics that cut across societal tasks. Chapter 5 looks at the political processes through which social welfare policies are enacted, while Chapter 6 is concerned with the economic base of policy. The illustrations are from economic security policy, but they could just as well have been from some other aspect of social welfare.

Chapter 3

Economic Security

The best way to begin is to tell about two imaginary boys, Paul and Mark, and their families.

Paul, aged 7, lives on the second floor of a two-family house in a small city with his mother and his sister, aged 3. His friend Mark, also aged 7, lives on the first floor with his mother and his brother, aged 9, and his sister, aged 11.

Each month Mark's mother receives money from the government, to support her and her children. The money kept coming when the family moved here from Michigan last year and it increases a little every six months to keep up with the cost of living.

Each month Paul's mother receives money from the government, to support her and her children. When Paul and his family moved here from California two years ago, his mother had to make a new application for support. That meant bringing in a lot of records to prove to the worker that she was too poor to support her family. The worker suggested to Paul's mother various ways of supporting her family such as having his sister stay with a neighbor while she worked. Paul's mother told the worker about her health problems that make it hard to hold a regular job, but he seemed skeptical and implied that she could manage on her own if she really wanted to. But the biggest blow was the discovery that the government checks in this state would be about half of what they were in California. Luckily she would continue to get the same allotment of food stamps, vouchers she could cash in at the supermarket.

In addition to the checks from the government, Mark's mother receives quarterly dividends from some investments her husband left her. They go right into an education fund for Mark, his brother and his sister. They are a net bonus on top of the government checks. When Paul's grandmother died last year she left a few thousand dollars to Paul's mother. This had to be reported to the welfare department, resulting in the loss of government checks for a few months until the inheritance was used up.

The other kids in Paul's school pick on him sometimes and call him a welfare cheat. Nobody says that to Mark. Paul has learned to hide the fact that his mother gets a government check when the teacher asks what people's parents do for a living. The teacher doesn't call him a welfare cheat, but she lets him know she doesn't think much of people who get a government hand-out.

You may be wondering what Paul did to deserve all this. It's not what he did but the fact that his father walked out on the family and hasn't been heard from since. His family would be in the same situation regarding welfare benefits if

Paul's mother and father had never married or the father had never been able to hold a steady job for a long enough period of time. Mark's father, on the other hand, died after holding a good job for several years. So Paul and Mark, good friends living a few feet from each other, inhabit different worlds: the two worlds of welfare.

THE TWO WORLDS OF WELFARE

Paul's family is receiving Aid to Families with Dependent Children (AFDC), while Mark and his family get survivors' benefits under social security. AFDC, a public assistance category, is a *selective* benefit program. People become eligible for these benefits selectively, on the basis of a careful review of their individual circumstances. The survivors' provisions under social security are part of a *universal* benefit scheme. Not literally universal, in the sense that everybody qualifies. Rather, persons falling into a clearly defined category—in this case the surviving spouse and minor children of a deceased person—are automatically eligible, regardless of how needy they are.

The basic difference between selective and universal welfare programs is one of *presumption*. Under a universal scheme, persons are presumed to need the benefits. That places the burden of proof on anybody wanting to deny them the benefits. With selective programs, you are presumed *not* to need the benefits, so the burden of proof is on you. That is why Mark's mother had so little trouble showing that she was eligible for government support, while Paul's mother had to prove to the caseworker that she was poor enough to need help and must continually demonstrate need.

The Means Test

The mechanism through which Paul's mother establishes her right to benefits is called a *means test*, a test to show that she lacks the means to support herself and her family. Given the public attitudes toward poor people in general and those on welfare in particular, means tests in public assistance are generally very humiliating.

When Paul's mother got a windfall, this placed her above the level of need established in that state for AFDC eligibility, so she "failed" the means test for a number of months. But there is no means test for survivor's benefits under social security, so Mark's mother can simply salt away any amount of money she gets in dividends without its affecting her benefits. There are limits on how much she can earn in a job, however, without affecting her eligibility.

The same distinction between the two worlds of welfare is also found in other benefit programs. You may qualify for health care under *Medicare*, in which case there is no means test and you are presumed to be eligible if you fall into the right general category, or for medical assistance or *Medicaid*, which is means-tested. If you are old or disabled, you may qualify for retirement benefits under social security, without a means test, or Supplemental Security Income (SSI), which is means tested. Some people qualify for SSI in addition to their social security benefits.

There is another difference between AFDC and survivors' benefits: variations from state to state. Recall that Paul's family's benefits dropped sharply when they moved to their present location, while it made no difference where Mark's family lived. While means-tested programs are also more likely to be state-based programs, this is not always true. Food stamps, a means-tested benefit, are uniform across the country. The income under unemployment insurance, which has no means test, varies among states.

So it is an oversimplification to talk of the two worlds of welfare as if the line of demarcation were very clear between them and there were no differences within the respective worlds. But the selective or universal character of a program is of overriding importance. Where did these concepts come from? For that we turn back fifty years to the most important piece of social welfare legislation ever enacted in this country.

THE SOCIAL SECURITY ACT OF 1935

You have heard or read about the Great Depression of the 1930s, but unless you experienced it directly you probably have a hard time getting a feel of what it was like. The typical movie or TV treatment is to flash a montage of newspaper headlines of the stock market crash, followed by glimpses of men standing in soup lines and maybe a picture of a farm surrounded by a dust storm and then a convoy of jalopies on their way to California. Music up and out and on to World War II.

The first thing to understand about the Depression is that poverty did not suddenly occur on October 29, 1929, the day the floor gave way under the stock market. Despite the illusion of prosperity during the 1920s, buoyed by lavish spending by the affluent few and dreams of riches among the less affluent, the ship of state was developing serious leaks below the water line. In the "peak" year of 1929, more than a fifth of the families in the United States were making less than $1,000 a year and having to spend an average of $350 more than they were taking in just to stay afloat. Three out of five families were living on less than $2,000 a year, considered a bare subsistence income at the time (Axinn & Levin, 1982, pp. 175-176). The farm economy had been depressed since 1922. These factors helped to push the country deeper and deeper into a full-scale depression.

In the immediate aftermath of the stock market crash in 1929 it was the financiers and small investors who felt the impact. For the nation as a whole, President Hoover's assurances that this was "just another panic" from which the country would soon recover were convincing. But as things continued to get worse and the situation dragged out into months and then years, the seriousness of the collapse hit home to the general population.

The visible signs of disaster were everywhere. Everybody had a relative or friend or neighbor who was out of work. The hopelessness was written on the faces of young people—no longer just "those" young people who you knew were never going to amount to anything, but the children of respectable families. Blacks were ground down worse than most, though in those days blacks were the invisible poor, assumed to be satisfied with their lot in life, happy-go-lucky and unperturbed. But you couldn't ignore the once-proud men standing and begging on the street corners.

Or picking through your trash cans. That is my vivid recollection as a young boy in Maine. I grew up on the edge of poverty, respectable poverty to be sure. We were never well off, though we weren't pushed to the point of utter desperation, either. Tuesday was trash collection day, and we waited until the last possible minute to put the cans out by the street so the men would have less chance to pick through them. We didn't say to each other, "Isn't it a pity that the economic situation has driven proud people to this." Instead we cursed the bums for poking around our trash and creating a scene on our nice, quiet, well-mannered street. And we knew that the poorest families in town were that way because of their own inadequacies.

The attitudes were a little schizophrenic. If a family got burned out, everybody came running to help. Children trooped to school with canned goods for the Thanksgiving and Christmas baskets, and businessmen dropped coins in the cups of beggars. But all the while they knew they were better than "those people" and that anybody with a little gumption could make it. If relief had to be provided, it should come from private charity. If government had to be involved, let it be local government.

> The first responsibility of taking care of people out of work who are lacking housing, clothing or food . . . is upon the locality; then, if the locality has done everything that it possibly can do, it is the duty of the State to step in and do all the State can possibly do; and, when the State can do no more, then it becomes the obligation of the Federal Government.

Those are the words, not of some throw-back to the dark ages, but of Franklin D. Roosevelt,[1] the activist liberal president, spoken in the depths of the Depression. Somehow that outlook had to come to terms with the reality that private charities and local governments were going bankrupt as resources plummeted and the need for help skyrocketed.

---

[1]Remarks to relief administrators, June 14, 1933, as quoted in Rosenman (1938), p. 238.

The Two Worlds Established in Law

It was one thing to see poverty engulf "those people." It was another to face the risk of being there yourself. Losing your life savings in a failed stock scheme might not send you directly to the poor house, but it shook your confidence in the future. The golden years were beginning to look a little tarnished. The Roosevelt administration and Congress responded to the national mood by putting together an economic security program intended to deal with both the destitution of the poor and the insecurity of the majority. For those already in poverty, limited financial aid geared to discouraging dependency. For those still able to provide for themselves, protection against the threat of future unemployment and the unavoidable dependency of old age. This was the Social Security Act of 1935.

The greatest virtue of this two-stage system, other than its political acceptability, was the fact that it established the responsibility of the federal government for the general welfare in terms that had never before been conceived. It wasn't enough to protect the country against foreign invaders, we owed our citizens protection against want as well. Its greatest weakness was that it established just as firmly the conception of two worlds of welfare.

The United States government typically avoids making quantum leaps but instead relies heavily on past precedent in writing new policies. That is one reason it took an economic catastrophe to bring about enactment of the Social Security Act. It also led the policy-makers to shape the act along lines already well established. We now turn to the historical roots of the two sides of the policy.

THE POOR RELIEF TRADITION

When the authors of the Social Security Act created plans for assistance to the poor, they looked to existing welfare laws in the states. These had come into being piece-meal, as political pressure from various groups overrode the general resistance to the states' involvement in poor relief. By 1935 a majority of states had some combination of old age pensions, aid to the blind, and "mothers aid," for dependent children in families where the breadwinner was dead, disabled or missing.

For persons who did not qualify for any of these—for example, a retarded adult—there was a patchwork of local poor houses and charities. These "able bodied" poor were assumed to be less deserving than the elderly, blind and widows and orphans, and in many places were expected to fend for themselves, go to jail or get out of town.

These state programs had several features in common, including:

— The means test. A requirement that you demonstrate a lack of means to support yourself in order to qualify for aid.
— Separate programs for the different categories of poor, such as aged and blind, with different standards of eligibility and size of grants.

— Residence requirements. Eligibility limited to persons having resided in a particular place for a specified number of years.

— Less eligibility. Benefits pegged low enough so that any recipient made less on welfare than the lowest paid worker made through honest toil. (The worker would thus be "less eligible" for help than the recipient.)

— Relative responsibility. Adult children responsible for care of their parents, parents for their adult as well as minor children, siblings for siblings, etc. This responsibility frequently extended to grandparents and grandchildren.

Rather than set up a wholly new assistance system, the planners of the Social Security Act left the states to fashion their own programs. By meeting certain federal rules, a state could get matching funds for its own expenditures up to a designated cut-off point. This led to great unevenness in eligibility rules and grant levels from state to state as well as between categories of assistance within the same state. The roots of this kind of public assistance system go all the way back to before the dawn of western industrial society.

The Elizabethan Poor Law

Feudalism in the middle ages provided a built-in work-welfare system. Bound together by a set of mutual obligations, the lord could count on a captive labor supply and the serf could count on his family's being cared for if he died or became too old or sick to work. The demise of this system was hastened by the Black Plague around the middle of the fourteenth century, which wiped out two-thirds of the English population. The labor shortage forced wages up sharply, leading the government to impose harsh measures to require workers without means to accept employment from anybody willing to hire them and to stay within their home parish. Beggars were subjected to punishments ranging up to mutilation and death.

Meanwhile, the church was taking over a major part of the work of caring for the aged and infirm. In the towns, guilds provided aid for their members in need. But by the sixteenth century these private efforts were not equal to the need, so government began to regulate the welfare function as well as the supply of labor. Henry VIII is usually remembered as the bloated tyrant who disposed of a number of wives and broke with the Catholic Church, but he is also the ruler under whom the English government first took responsibility for the welfare of its subjects in an organized way.

Under Henry and later under his daughter, Elizabeth I, a series of laws was enacted which spelled out in ever more specific detail the responsibility of local officials for the poor. These humanitarian steps went hand in hand with statutes designed to deal harshly with vagrants, unauthorized beggars and other able-bodied persons who would not work. These various laws were replaced by a single act, known as the Poor Law of 1601, or as we say today the Elizabethan Poor Law (de Schweinitz, 1943).

What is striking is the similarity between the major features of this legislation and what the designers of the Social Security Act used three and a third centuries later as a model for their public assistance policies.

There were three categories of poor: (1) The impotent poor—the aged and the mentally or physically disabled. They were either housed in almshouses or given "outdoor" relief in their own homes. (2) Dependent children—who were abandoned or whose parents could not care for them. They were bound out to the care of a local citizen, and at an early age they were expected to work for their upkeep. (3) The able-bodied or "sturdy beggars." They were assigned to the workhouse; and if they refused, they were flailed or put on public display in the stocks. No one was allowed to give them alms.

The parish was responsible for its own, but a person who had lived in the parish for less than three years was denied help.

Relative responsibility extended to grandparents and grandchildren as well as parents and children.

The American Response

The American colonies looked to England's poor-law tradition as the model for their own relief activity. But the New World was not England. The struggle for survival, together with a religious doctrine that material wealth was a sign of God's favor, conspired to undermine the sense of local government's responsibility for the poor. Instead of an urban environment, America was predominantly open country and small hamlets, so what relief activities there were tended to be informal—neighbor-to-neighbor help in times of crisis. There were food, clothing, firewood and utensils to be doled out to the most impoverished, but the emphasis was on deterring dependency. Newcomers had to establish residency for as much as five years before being eligible for help. Public shame and the whipping post were used liberally to discourage begging.

As industries and cities began to dot the countryside in the early nineteenth century, more organized means of dealing with poverty were needed. Increasingly, towns turned to the almshouse as the solution to poverty. This might be a single dwelling, a farm or a cluster of buildings where everybody from the insane and criminal to widows and dependent children was housed. Almshouses were seen as less costly than "outdoor" relief; they allowed better control over the lives of the recipients and they could also provide useful work. Saving money was the first priority, so almshouses varied greatly in quality. Some were well run. Many were drafty and dilapidated dumping grounds where ages and sexes were thrown together in common quarters, beds consisted of piles of straw and food was abominable. Overseeing the enterprise might be an unemployed couple unable to find other work. This was not the universal pattern, but it was common enough so that almshouses became an object of scandal. They were eventually abandoned, not only because of the miserable living conditions, but also because of concern for the younger residents' morals. But a major factor, especially in the larger urban centers, was the sheer magnitude of the problem of poverty.

Dealing With the Waves of Immigration

During the nineteenth and twentieth centuries American society was transformed by successive waves of immigrants from Europe. Between the end of the Civil War and 1900, roughly 13.5 million persons entered the United States. That was a million more than the entire population of the country in 1830. In contrast to earlier immigrants from northern and western Europe, the newcomers from the southern and eastern countries stayed in the large cities. Most were poor and unused to urban life.

The growing industrial machine welcomed this source of cheap labor—made special efforts to recruit it, in fact—but when hard times hit, the new arrivals were expected to fend for themselves. When they came in enough numbers to become a political force, the public dole—one in which aid was often traded for votes—was the standard response. Meanwhile, private charities tried to fill the gap.

The charitable impulse doesn't always operate in orderly ways. As charities sprouted up in American cities in the mid- to late nineteenth century, different groups worked at cross-purposes, some needy families were overlooked and the more enterprising made the rounds from organization to organization. To bring order out of chaos, philanthropic leaders began to form *charity organization societies* (COS). Originated in London in the 1860s, the COS found fertile soil in this country. The pattern of coordination of relief efforts throughout a city, systematic investigation of requests for aid, and record-keeping was taken over by state welfare programs that appeared in the early twentieth century. The COS, one of the most influential institutions in American social welfare, pioneered many present programs and was largely responsible for the origins of the social work profession. These facets of its work are dealt with in other parts of the book.

The Role of the States

Although Franklin D. Roosevelt and others still stressed local responsibility for relief in the early thirties, the wall against state participation had begun to crack by the turn of the nineteenth century. It was in the Progressive Era—from the 1890s to World War I—that the states became particularly active. Women and children were a special concern: the denial of the vote to women, the exploitation of child labor and the economic plight of widows and orphans. The White House Conference on the Care of Dependent Children, called in 1909 by President Theodore Roosevelt, declared that no child should be removed from its own home for reason of poverty (Friedlander & Apte, 1980, p. 91). This set the stage for a drive for state financial aid to dependent children; and by the time of the Social Security Act in 1935, most states had such laws.

Initially state "mothers' aid" was bitterly opposed by leaders of the charity organization movement. They asserted that public aid, as opposed to what they called "scientific philanthropy," would undermine professional standards of service. They also worried that public aid would weaken the support for private charity.

Similar campaigns were launched for assistance to those with special disabilities. By 1935, 24 states had aid to the blind (Axinn & Levin, 1982, p. 200). Old age pensions were on the books in 34 states, but in many states the laws were little more than lipservice, not backed by appropriation of funds. By 1935, only ten states were actually operating such programs (Kurtz, 1943, p. 358). Why the belated and half-hearted efforts for the elderly? We should remember that before the Social Security Act, there was no conception of *a* retirement age in this country. You worked until you were too old or feeble, then your children or other relatives took you in, or you went to the local poorhouse to live. Besides, people didn't live all that long, especially poor people.

Progress by Degrees

The people who designed the Social Security Act improved upon this accumulation from the past. They stipulated that assistance must be in the form of cash, thus protecting the right of self-determination. They made client information confidential, to assure the right to privacy. They required uniformity throughout a state, thus assuring the right to equal treatment. The client would have the right to a fair hearing of grievances. Residence requirements were not abolished but limits were placed on the length of time a person had to live in a state before becoming eligible for aid. To assure honest and efficient administration, welfare personnel had to come under civil service. There were flaws in these measures and in later years there were retreats in the face of political pressure, but the program launched in 1935 represented a major advance in social welfare.

Excluded from this system was general assistance, the catch-all aid for persons who did not qualify as old enough or young enough or blind. The traditional ways of dealing with the "sturdy beggar" would continue. In the depths of the Depression there were emergency relief programs of various kinds, but once the economic crisis was past, many states would deal with this population simply by not dealing with it.

INSURING THE MAJORITY AGAINST POVERTY

In the private sector, insurance is intended to protect you against something that you hope won't happen, or else a known risk far in the future. That is basically how certain programs under the Social Security Act work. Our young friend Mark's parents didn't assume that Mark's father would die until the children were grown up and able to support themselves. The same is true of employed workers who are insured against being laid off from work.

These *social insurances* may seem like welfare for the well-off. Mark's mother can receive her government check whether or not she collects stock dividends. Shouldn't social insurance benefits be limited to only those who are poor, or at least kept from those who are rich? The first thing to understand about this kind of benefit is that instead of being a matter of charity for the down-trodden, it is sought by the nonpoor for their own protection. The fact that it is redistributive—that is, it does shift resources downward in the economic scale—is more a matter of accident than design. One indication that social insurance is more related to self-interest than altruism is the fact that the largest share of federal expenditures for income security go into retirement benefits under social security, not to food stamps and AFDC and other means-tested programs.

This does not mean that self-interest plays no part in the growth of public means-tested aid. During the Depression the construction industry was a main beneficiary of low-cost public housing. Farm-state senators and representatives in Congress are major supporters of food stamps. The threat of disorder from the poor has sometimes prompted the majority to accept expanded public assistance, though the longterm reaction is more likely to be punitive than charitable. For a period in the late sixties and early seventies, welfare recipients were able to wield considerable political influence in their own behalf, but they have always had to rely heavily on allies. So, unlike social insurance, advances in means-tested programs have tended to be a result of somebody's worrying about somebody else's economic conditions.

Not surprisingly, social insurance did not happen until those in need of it had sufficient political power to make demands. It occurred first in Germany in the 1880s, a time of political ferment among workers. Otto von Bismarck, "the Iron Chancellor," sought to quell a political threat by the socialists by placating the workers with a system of sickness and accident benefits and old age pensions (Holt & Chilton, 1918, pp. 265-270). Instead of being based on need, these were insurances which covered all workers against future threats to their economic welfare.

Workers' Compensation

In contrast with industrial countries in Europe, the United States resisted the notion of social insurance. The liberal ideology of individualism was firmly established among workers and their unions as well as employers. Just as workers entered into free "contracts" with their employers, they were also "free agents" when it came to compensation for work-related injuries and ill-nesses. First of all, you should not be so careless as to have accidents—no matter that you might be a 12-year old on a 12-hour shift. And if you felt it was the employer's fault, you were free to sue the company: Joe Newcomer who was in chronic debt and barely knew English versus the United States Steel Corporation or a New England textile manufacturer.

Enter organized labor, and with it a shift in the balance of power. Joe Newcomer could not hire a good lawyer but his union could. The unions began suing and winning some cases—enough of them to worry the corporations. But it was not only management that wanted a change. Most of the money which was being paid out in insurance premiums and court settlements was ending up, not in the workers' pocket, but in the hands of the insurance companies and lawyers.

We might expect manufacturers to oppose the intrusion of government into this arena and labor unions to support it, but there was a time when this situation was reversed. The corporations were anxious to clamp a lid on the escalating cost of injury case settlements, while labor leaders opposed government protection of workers as undermining their own role as protectors. So the National Association of Manufacturers became a champion of workmen's compensation and Samuel Gompers, the union leader, fought it.

Workmen's compensation (later changed to workers' compensation) was enacted in most states in the early twentieth century, the first social insurance program in this country. Depending on the particular state, employers either contributed to an insurance pool or covered their workers with private insurance. A worker who suffered from a work-connected disability would receive benefits according to a set of formulas. Each state had its own law, some very restrictive. The architects of the Social Security Act left workers' compensation intact. Thus a patchwork and inadequate system still covers work-related illness and injury today.

Unemployment Insurance

As the Depression deepened in the early thirties, a problem far more formidable than accidents in the workplace confronted workers: job loss due to cutbacks in production or plant closings. Here again, traditional American attitudes about individual self-reliance began to shift because of the economic crisis. In 1932, the point of highest unemployment, Wisconsin enacted an unemployment insurance law aimed at protecting workers against lay-offs. By the time of the passage of the Social Security Act in 1935, four more states had passed such measures.

Today the idea of insuring workers against lay-offs and providing retirement benefits for the elderly is not controversial. In fact, it is attempts to cut back on these systems which create political furor. Conversely, the newspaper headlines scream about fraud and indolence on AFDC and general assistance, and these programs are continually under assault in the legislative arena. Fifty years ago it was the other way around. In the depths of the Depression the need for federal funds to bail out state and local relief efforts was obvious, but the idea of getting the federal government into the insurance business on such a large scale was un-American in the eyes of many conservatives.

The National Association of Manufacturers labeled the concept "socialist" and the head of the American Bar Association said it would usher in "the inevitable abandonment of private capital" (Schlesinger, 1959, p. 311). Such alarums did not reflect the mood of the country, wracked by the fear of unemployment, but authors of the Social Security Act were concerned that a conservative Supreme Court might find the whole package unconstitutional. So instead of a single national scheme, they opted for separate state programs under federal regulations.

Unemployment insurance would have no means test. The level of benefits would be determined not by need but by the level of previous wages up to a maximum. A worker was required to have worked in a designated number of quarters (three-month periods) to qualify. All of this meant that those in the lowest-paying, irregular jobs—the worst off—would benefit least. There was no means test but a kind of work test: the recipient had to sign up for available employment in order to receive the compensation. The cost of the program would be born entirely by the employer, an incentive to keep lay-offs to a minimum. This is the system of unemployment insurance in effect today. There are several problems with it. One is the existence of separate state programs. In states dominated by a few industries and those with weak labor unions, the programs reflect employer interests over workers'. Under these circumstances, the intended inducements to keep down lay-offs can work against the employees. Instead of reducing unemployment, employers can keep costs down by pushing for state legislation which provides for an extended waiting period before workers can start collecting benefits or limits the length of time over which benefits are to be paid. The benefit levels themselves can also be set so as to limit the cost of the program. The question of what constitutes "suitable" work frequently comes up. For instance, should an unemployed musician be required to accept a job as a ditch-digger?

Some social policy analysts have questioned the use of an employer-only tax. Presumably this simply gets passed on to the workers in reduced wages. And politically, labor representatives might be in a stronger position if the workers were also paying into the system. It has also been suggested that the government contribute from its general tax funds as a way of spreading the cost of unemployment to the total society. (See Burns, 1951, pp. 154-155.)

Income Security for the Elderly

The Depression hit older Americans especially hard. In the intensified competition for jobs, they were no match for younger and more vigorous workers. By the 1930s people were living longer, and this growing segment of the population was beginning to find its political voice. Also concerned about the plight of the elderly were their children, often saddled with their parents' care when they themselves were under economic stress.

Not surprisingly the Depression was a time of great political ferment and radicalism of the right and left. Many names which have since become synonymous with demagoguery came to prominence at that time: Huey Long, the "Kingfisher" from Louisiana; Upton Sinclair, the End Poverty in California

(EPIC) crusader; Father Charles Coughlin, the radio priest whose radicalism eventually degenerated into anti-semitism; and many others. But the man who became the folk hero of the elderly was anything but a ranting demagogue or even an eloquent orator.

Dr. Francis E. Townsend, a 66-year-old unemployed physician (yes, there were many) from Long Beach, California, looked out of his window one day in 1933 and beheld three old women pawing through his garbage cans looking for food. Instead of becoming angry at *them*, the way my family might have, he became incensed that this sort of thing should happen in America and decided to do something about it.

He wrote a letter to the *Long Beach Press-Telegram* in which he proposed a scheme for solving the problem of unemployment and caring for the elderly: Everyone over sixty years of age would receive a monthly pension on condition that he or she would not work and would spend all the money received. The plan was to be supported by a national sales tax. It was an idea whose time had suddenly arrived. The Townsend plan spread like wildfire. Townsend clubs sprang up across the country. It mattered little that economists, on analyzing the financing scheme for the plan, said it would cost about half the national income (twice as much as existing federal, state and local taxes combined). Townsend had unleashed a political hurricane, and political leaders found themselves forced to run with the tide or at least not appear to oppose it (Schlesinger, 1960, pp. 29-41).

The Townsend movement didn't create the Social Security Act, any more than other radical schemes did, but it helped silence the opposition to the idea of social insurance for the elderly. Unlike unemployment insurance, old age insurance had no precedent in this country. This fact, together with the enormous costs projected, gave impetus to a single national scheme instead of separate state plans. Old Age Insurance (OAI) would be a *contributory* plan—the worker and the employer each paying half of the cost. There was to be no means test but a retirement test: you were limited as to what you could earn and still collect OAI benefits.

The initial social security system represented a major leap forward in American social welfare policy. For the first time, the federal government had major responsibility for the economic security of its citizens. The majority of industrial workers and their families were protected against destitution due to economic dislocation and old age. For elderly and blind adults and dependent children living in poverty, there was a system of subsistence income. From the perspective of today it was a grossly inadequate system, but it set the framework.

CHANGES SINCE 1935

The Social Security Act has gone through several major expansions since its adoption in 1935. In 1939, insurance coverage was extended to surviving spouses and children, and in 1956 the disabled were included. In 1965, health insurance for the elderly (Medicare) was added. In other ways, the insurance programs have been liberalized. These, after all, are protections for the "deserving" majority; and once the traditional shibboleths against "socialism" were stilled, political pressure tended to push for broadening the insurance provisions. This expansionary philosophy together with population and economic changes have combined to pose threats to the fiscal soundness of the system, as is discussed in Chapter 6.

Health Insurance

The architects of the Social Security Act wanted to include health coverage but were overruled by President Roosevelt, who feared that opposition from the medical profession and others might jeopardize the entire bill (Witte, 1962). By 1950 the United States was the only major industrial country without national health care protection. After an abortive attempt by President Harry Truman to revive the idea in 1949, health insurance lay dormant until the 1960s. By that time the increasing lifespan, greater political awareness of the elderly and the manifest failure of private insurance to provide adequate coverage combined to bring the issue to the front burner.

In 1965 a three-layer system was enacted: hospital care; physicans' and related services (optional); and, for the poor, means-tested medical assistance (Medicaid). Once again, the two worlds of welfare had been established. In the ensuing years, the fact that people's income was less of a factor in the ability to demand medical care, without an effective system of cost control, would help to escalate health care costs rapidly. How a later effort to solve the problem became mired in politics is discussed in Chapter 5.

Consolidating Public Assistance Categories

The original Social Security Act designed public assistance on the basis of state pensions for the aged, blind and widows and orphans. In 1950 a new category was adopted, aid to the permanently and totally disabled (APTD). In 1972 the three "adult" categories—aged, blind and disabled—were lumped into a single program of Supplemental Security Income (SSI).

Instead of subsidizing state programs under federal guidelines, SSI would be a single national scheme administered jointly by federal and state governments. There are still state-to-state variations in benefits in this program because states have the option of supplementing the federal grant. But for the first time, a floor was placed under cash assistance for these adult recipients; not so, Aid to Families with Dependent Children (AFDC), which continues as a state-administered program with the minimum grant level dependent on what a state is willing to make it.

Meeting Special Needs

The Social Security Act introduced the principle of unrestricted cash grants, on the belief that people's dignity and ultimately their ability to help themselves is aided by having control over their own lives. But some assistance programs involve earmarked funds or subsidies to consumers, because of the large sums and unpredictable need (medical assistance), because of a mistrust of the recipients' judgment or ability to manage, or because of the vested interest of an industry in promoting business (farmers' support of food stamps and the construction and housing industries' support of housing programs).

These programs don't all come under the Social Security Act, but they are part of the nation's economic security system. Of all these special programs the one that has had the biggest impact on poverty is food stamps. The stamps are traded at the grocery store like money. Adopted in 1964 with the blessing of the food industry as well as reformers who judged the existing dole of surplus commodities to be demeaning to the poor, food stamps were an instant success. By 1969, 2.9 million persons were using them, and by 1976 the number had climbed to 18.6 million.

Food stamps have been widely criticized for many of the same reasons that other programs for the poor are. But there is convincing evidence that food stamps have succeeded in raising the standard of health among low-income Americans. In the late sixties, medical researchers funded by the Field Foundation found widespread hunger and malnutrition in rural Mississippi. Ten years later they retraced their steps and found that, while poverty was still a major problem, hunger and malnutrition of the sort they had witnessed were no longer in evidence. They attributed the difference to food stamps and other federal nutrition benefits (U.S., Congress, Senate, 1979). The program's flexibility allows it to respond to special crises, such as recessions, and more than 95 cents of every dollar spent goes directly into food benefits.

Veterans' Benefits

Special pensions, health care and other assistance to veterans have traditionally enjoyed wide acceptance as well as active political support from veterans' organizations. Up until World War II, the typical response was the one-shot bonus, delivered no doubt with an eye to the next election day, and care of those who had been injured or disabled in action, in veterans' hospitals. After World War II, the concept was broadened to include a broad array of health, educational, insurance and housing benefits for all veterans (Friedlander & Apte, 1980, p. 89).

Chapter 4

The Work-Welfare Link

To understand the relationship between work and economic security you first have to understand the place of work in the post-industrial order. In a market economy such as ours, it is the task of managers of industry to maximize the output of labor at the least cost. During this century, and particularly since the 1930s in this country, this task has been complicated by the organization of workers in unions. So labor and management are natural antagonists, but each needs the other. It is only as they are able to organize that workers have any significant leverage in their dealings with employers.

The period from the 1930s through World War II was marked by major gains by unions, some by direct confrontation with management, others through legislative victories. After World War II there was a stable if uneasy balance of power. In recent decades that balance has been upset by several factors. Since it reached a peak in the midfifties, union membership as a percentage of the workforce has been declining—from a third of all nonagricultural jobs in 1955 to less than a fourth by the end of the seventies (U.S., Bureau of Census, 1983, p. 439). Changing technology and the resultant decline in blue collar jobs has been a major factor in this. The organizing of white collar and service workers in the public sector has slowed but not reversed the trend.

Two new developments are further upsetting the balance of power: competition from overseas and the ability of capital to move rapidly from one place to another. The overseas competition is related to an overvalued dollar, which in turn is related to our mammoth federal deficit, discussed in Chapter 6. As for the mobility of capital, a large company can close a plant in one part of the country and open up in another virtually overnight. Or it may move its operations to another country with low wage scales. Or it may simply threaten these actions if labor makes too many demands (Bluestone, 1982). Attempts to enact legislation requiring firms to give advance notice of plant closings and otherwise protect the community have met with little success.

The early eighties have witnessed a new phase in labor-management negotiations: major concessions by unions, including the powerhouses of the labor movement. The unions further demonstrated their diminishing strength by an unprecedented early endorsement of Walter Mondale for president and his subsequent trouncing by Ronald Reagan in the 1984 election. Decisions by the National Labor Relations Board (NLRB) have also indicated a less friendly environment for labor. Two rulings in 1984 allowed companies to scrap in effect their contracts with unions by moving their operations to new locations (*New York Times*, 1984a).

The economic security system plays an integral part in the relations between industry and its workforce. In this chapter we explore the linkages between work and welfare.

THE EVOLVING RELATIONSHIP

The earliest relief provisions had the dual purpose of meeting survival needs and regulating the supply of labor. That is also true of many economic security programs today. Organized relief came into being at a time when the nature of work was changing—from peasant labor, tied to the manor, to "free" labor able to move from one employer to another. Policies geared to keeping a supply of workers in an area or, when there was a lack of work, keeping beggars out predated the industrial era.

Post-industrial capitalism faces two major challenges: making sure the workforce has the capacity and willingness to perform, and dealing with the cycle of boom and bust. In Part IV of this book we explore one facet of the first challenge: preparing children for future work roles. In this country there has been an added challenge: dealing with populations which have been systematically excluded from full participation in the world of work, notably racial minorities and women.

CREATING A WORKFORCE

When production becomes industrial, people have to learn a new meaning of the word "work." In traditional agrarian societies, the weather and the length of sunlight were controlling factors in how long or often one worked. You might do enough to fill the larder for the winter, then turn your attention to more pleasant pursuits. Not that there would be much time for the latter. But the idea of going daily to a central place for a designated number of hours, come rain or shine, to carry out assigned tasks was foreign to the people recruited to the industrial workforce.

The flood of immigrants to this country in the nineteenth and early twentieth centuries was an essential ingredient in building the American industrial machine. The primary need was for masses of cheap, unskilled labor, and the main task was to convert peasants into a dependable and compliant workforce, able to work long hours for little pay. The exploitation of children in this regard is discussed in Chapter 10.

In the previous chapter we saw how the charity organization societies developed a coordinated system of private philanthropy in American cities. These were a major source of relief for the immigrants. Aside from managing the giving of life-supports, the COS's primary function was instilling the work ethic in the newcomers. The early settlement houses and character building organizations such as the YMCA were likewise involved in this transformation process, offering cheap, clean lodgings, as well as lessons in the world of work, to immigrants and rural American youth.

The task of converting a peasant population to an industrial workforce has not been peculiar to this country nor to capitalism. When the Soviet Union, under Stalin, embarked on a course of rapid industrialization in the 1920s, it was faced with a labor force made up largely of peasants with no conception of factory life. According to Rimlinger (1971), economic security programs played a crucial role in regimenting the workers. Benefits were tied not only to continuous employment but also to willingness to accept work of types and in locations deemed necessary by the state.

A DIVISION OF LABOR: WELFARE AND EMPLOYMENT POLICIES

Government's role in managing the workforce was historically a divided responsibility in the United States. Not only do public welfare and employment services exist in relative autonomy from each other, but there has been considerable tension between them over the years. A factor in this dichotomy is the respective origins of the two. It was only in times of great economic stress that the society considered financial aid to employable persons, then only with reluctance. Such measures were mainly for those clearly unable to enter the workforce, such as the old, the disabled and young children.

Meanwhile, the industrial system required outside help in channeling good workers into vacant jobs, and government was brought in to fill this role. Employers' interests were paramount in setting up state employment services. The practices in these agencies reflected this set of priorities; experienced and productive workers were placed in jobs while others were shunted aside in a practice known as "creaming" (taking the cream and leaving the milk). In more recent times labor unions have also been active in relation to employment policies. Unemployment insurance—a protection for the mainstream of the work force against lay-offs—became the domain of state employment services.

In the sixties the country was producing a growing population of persons who could not be readily absorbed into the workforce, particularly young blacks. Traditional employment services had little understanding of this population, and the public welfare system and special poverty programs became the main repository for services targeted to them. So those with the best access to private industry job opportunities continued to concentrate on the highly employable, while those who worked with the hard-to-place lacked the right connections.

MANAGING THE UPS AND DOWNS IN THE ECONOMY

It is well known that market economies are subject to periods of boom and bust that throw the balance between labor supply and demand out of kilter. Less well known is the part economic security policies play in dealing with the cycle.

Not only does the economy as a whole go through such ups and downs, but changes in technology, resources and markets cause more limited crises. The production-distribution system relies on a labor force which is flexible enough to adapt to these changes—to be available when needed. The welfare system is able to maintain a pool of labor at a high enough level of subsistence to be useful, but at a low enough level to prefer working to not working. This has been its classic function for centuries.

But what happens when the labor market is overloaded? You can maintain a surplus of workers at the ready—quiescent yet eager to work—for only so long. These are not robots but human beings who have been taught to be dissatisfied with idleness and the inability to buy what is produced. Piven and Cloward (1971) have given us the best explanation of how the system deals with this problem. In times of recession, they say, the welfare system expands to absorb the excess of unemployed workers. This keeps the lid on potential civil disorder. It doesn't solve the problem of idleness but it does get money into consumers' hands. When the economy gets back in stride and the demand for labor goes up, the welfare system contracts, forcing workers into the labor market. According to this theory, then, the economic security system plays a counterpoint to the main melody, expanding when the economy is down and cutting back when the economy is up. Piven and Cloward offer a large amount of evidence from recent decades to support their thesis. But there are certain patterns in economic security policy that appear not to follow the script.

The Paradoxes of Welfare Policy

If the function of welfare contractions is to force people off the rolls and into the labor market to meet the demands of industry, one would expect employers to grab them up eagerly. The opposite is true. Job applicants must often learn to hide their former welfare status if they hope to be hired. Employers—susceptible to the same stereotypes about welfare recipients as the rest of us—will even turn down tax incentives to hire the welfare poor rather than have to deal with them.

The theory holds that the welfare system will become expansive when the job market is tightest and restiveness of the unemployed threatens public order; that it will contract, forcing potential workers into the labor pool, when the job market is expanding. But the late sixties, when the economy was booming, saw a liberalization of welfare eligibility rules, and the seventies, when stagflation was restricting employment opportunities, were a time of new welfare restrictions.

Pennsylvania enacted a welfare reform law which limited employables to three months of assistance per year, at a time when the state had high rates of unemployment. At the time this bill was being argued in the state legislature, it was estimated there were forty persons seeking work for every available job in the two major metropolitan areas of Pennsylvania (Berglund et al., 1980). Of course welfare recipients would be the least qualified for those jobs. In the sluggish seventies, similar restrictive actions took place in other states.

Not only do drastic cuts in the welfare rolls compound the problems of a saturated labor market, they also pull money out of circulation, putting an added drag on the economy. A 1972 study for the U.S. Department of Commerce found that every dollar in AFDC benefits generated $2.05 in industrial activity (Stein, 1975, p. 17). That is, each dollar received by the AFDC recipient is spent on goods and services, and this money then creates additional value as it moves through the hands of landlords and retailers, wholesalers, and so on. This is what economists call a "multiplier" effect. The net worth of the money is multiplied through economic activity. Sharp cuts in welfare thus create an *inverted* multiplier effect, with money being pulled out of the economy at a faster rate than the reduced grants alone would suggest.

When Ronald Reagan took office in 1981, one plank in his welfare reform platform was *workfare*, a policy requiring able-bodied recipients to work off their grants in public service jobs. It sounded reasonable enough: Let recipients pay for what they get through honest toil, give them experience in the world of work, and get confirmed freeloaders off the rolls. Congress agreed, allowing states the option of adding a workfare requirement to their AFDC laws. A year later, only three states had put workfare into effect statewide. Nineteen other states had adopted part of the package—ranging from a few pilot projects to allowing counties to decide whether they wanted workfare (Jobs Watch, 1982). For some reason, workfare in reality was a pale shadow of workfare in the political rhetoric.

There were practical reasons for the footdragging by states. Workfare is costly to run and is an administrative nightmare. People working off their grants on jobs they didn't choose are hard to supervise, as are the employers who are looking for cheap labor. Because the "pay scale" for workfare was at minimum wage, recipients were working only part-time, making work sites harder for the welfare department to monitor than would be the case with full-time assignments. Then there were the problems of finding jobs that didn't displace union workers and handling workers' compensation payments and fringe benefits. In fact, after Pennsylvania enacted workfare, its welfare officials charged with implementing the program acknowledged publicly that they would not monitor its operation closely, nor would they make special efforts to prevent or punish violations (*Philadelphia Inquirer*, 1983).

Reagan's own experience with workfare as governor of California in the early seventies gave little support to the belief that it would do what was claimed. The policy was enacted in 1971. By the end of 1972, only six counties had put it into operation and only 184 out of 2,707 recipients referred had actually been placed on work assignments (Evans, 1972, p. 354). It was discovered that welfare clients in nonparticipating counties had found employment more readily than those in the participating counties (California, State Legislature, 1974, pp. 7-11; see also Goodwin, 1981, p. 20; Joe, 1975; Sklar, 1968; U.S., General Accounting Office, 1985). Of a different nature are work programs which invest in development of work skills and job readiness as well as placement in the private sector. As is discussed at the end of this chapter these latter programs have had more success in moving people into the workforce. But this was not the predominant thrust in the seventies; rather it was compulsory workfare that supposedly was to push recipients off the rolls but did not do so in fact.

What is one to make of a private labor market that rejects the welfare poor it should be eagerly seeking; welfare reforms that push people into an over-saturated job pool and draw money out of a sluggish economy; and compulsory workfare that doesn't move people into the workforce? Is the system haywire, or is something wrong with the theory that welfare contractions have the function of creating a cheap labor pool?

It is sometimes said that the demand for cheap labor is a thing of the past, but the figures tell a different story. Between 1950 and 1982 the percentage of all workers employed in blue collar industrial jobs declined, but common laborers and service workers rose from 17% to 28% of the total labor force (U.S., Bureau of Census, 1983). It is these latter categories of jobs that make up the cheap labor market. So one must look elsewhere to explain the apparent contradiction.

One possible explanation is that only one side of the Piven-Cloward thesis is valid—that is the part that says welfare will expand to absorb more people in times of unrest. It may simply be that the prevailing American opposition to welfare for employables is temporarily suspended when disorder threatens. The "contractions," in other words, are the normal state of affairs, with the periodic expansions an anomaly. According to this reasoning, whether or not people are pushed into taking menial jobs is coincidental. There is an alternative explanation, one that involves people other than the welfare poor themselves.

Beaming Political Messages

The cheap labor thesis is right as far as it goes. At one point Piven and Cloward say the main target of the degradation of welfare recipients is not the recipients at all but the working poor (Piven & Cloward, 1971, pp. 173-174). Highly publicized scandals about the misdeeds of welfare cheats deter people who might be tempted to leave their dead-end, demeaning, unpleasant, under-paid jobs and accept public aid. It was found, for instance, that a public exposé of the Washington, D.C. welfare system by Senator Byrd of West Virginia sharply reduced the numbers of persons in the District applying for public assistance (Piven & Cloward, 1971, p. 174). So one "message" from the welfare system is aimed at the people who are already supplying the cheap labor.

But the fear of having to become a welfare recipient reaches beyond those on the bottom rung of the ladder. The lurches of the economy during the seventies and early eighties were throwing into the ranks of the unemployed, people who never imagined they would be there. More fundamental is the disenchantment with work that has been growing in recent years. Increasingly industrial workers are viewing the job as a necessity but not a source of satisfaction, and this raises questions about America's continued adherence to the work ethic, the belief that work is intrinsically good (Macarov, 1978, p. 224). The issue was posed sharply during the late sixties and early seventies by a generation of youth, many of whose members dropped out, did drugs or just lost interest in "getting ahead."

For the majority, the ones who haven't dropped out, the message has a different meaning: assurance that *we* still believe in the work ethic, we are not like *them*. Degrading the welfare poor helps reaffirm the commitment of the majority of the population to the work ethic when it is in danger of being undermined.

Finally, there is the message to the poor: a warning, not against laziness, but against assertiveness. In 1969 membership in the National Welfare Rights Organization (NWRO) reached its peak and then fell off rapidly and with it the momentum behind the drive for welfare rights (Piven & Cloward, 1979, pp. 295-296). Two attempts to pass a broad welfare reform act which would have placed a national floor under AFDC and other welfare categories ended in frustration as conservatives weighed the measure down with work incentive clauses and finally killed the bills. Some observers blamed the death of the bills on NWRO's having asked too much (see Moynihan, 1973). That was part of the message. The national floor under welfare was salvaged—for categories of public assistance *other* than AFDC—in the form of Supplemental Security Income (SSI). Meanwhile a form of income guarantee known as Earned Income Tax Credit (EITC), under which employed workers who fell below a certain income level would be subsidized, was enacted. These, too, were part of the message to the welfare rights activists: Don't make waves, don't ask too much or you may get left out while others benefit.

The political message to the welfare poor was more than simply a warning to the activists. In demeaning those on welfare it inverted the revolution of rising expectations. It is when the poor both believe there is hope and define themselves as worthy that they begin to make demands on the system. By not simply denying the welfare poor benefits but by systematically degrading them, the system undermines that self-perception and with it the revolution. But the degradation has a larger function.

THE "UNDESERVING" AMERICANS

Between 1972 and 1982, the percentage of managerial positions in the United States held by women rose by more than half. The increase in the percentage of black managers was 30%. In fact, during that period the ranks of professional, technical, sales, clerical and craft workers all became more female and black. The percentage of blacks completing four years of college increased 184% between 1960 and 1982; the increase for women was 140%. But somehow the revolution missed the people at the bottom.

Just as the folklore of the soldier-hero affirms Americans' faith in the rightness of their country and themselves, evidence that all is not well in the republic poses a threat. If indeed this is the land of unlimited opportunity, how come a lot of people never make it out of the depths? The answer is clear: they didn't have the intelligence or the backbone to seize the opportunity when it was offered. It is the same phenomenon that once allowed liberals to rationalize slavery, as discussed in Chapter 1. Similarly, native Americans were nonhuman demons; it was they who invented scalping (not so); they who deprived the settlers of life, liberty and the pursuit of happiness instead of the other way around (also not so).

One obstacle to creating an enlightened and humane welfare system has been the mythology of welfare: All welfare recipients are assumed to cheat, though investigations have consistently turned up less fraud than occurs in income tax returns. But as recounted in Chapter 1, this and other welfare myths defy all evidence to the contrary. No matter that the facts have been presented in countless documentaries and news articles. The myths serve to reassure the majority that the welfare poor are that way because of their own failings.

The dismal statistics cited in Chapter 2 underscore the failure of American society to live up to its rhetoric about equality. The two worlds of welfare reflect two societies, and technological advances appear to be driving them further and further apart. As generations of middle class Americans—mostly white but with a sprinkling of blacks and other minorities—join the computer age, the economy and an aging society will still need people to perform menial services. Scientific progress has not reduced the number of low level service jobs but rather increased them, relative to the total work force.

The people filling the ranks of this secondary labor force are recruited primarily from third-world Americans locked in blighted central city areas. The faces are new but the patterns are familiar: Asian and Hispanic immigrants fighting with blacks for a place in this nether world of American economy, just as generations of immigrants fought among themselves for a toehold. In a simpler time this was the first rung on the ladder of success, and indeed a few with more than ordinary grit and brilliance still make it to the top. But the computer age is unfriendly to a population with limited education. As of 1982, a majority of adult Americans of Hispanic background and 45% of black adults had less than a high school education (U.S., Bureau of Census, 1983). Among black males the percentage employed fell from 75 to 54 between 1960 and 1984 (Joe & Yu, 1984).

These trends have led some to speak of a permanent underclass and acceptance of welfare as an unavoidable condition for a segment of the American population, an abandonment of the historic assumptions about work and welfare.

UNHOOKING WORK FROM WELFARE

The early church accepted poverty as a fact of life and the obligation to succor to the needs of the poor in similar terms. You didn't punish the poor because you had no expectation that they could respond. This air of pessimistic tolerance could not survive in an age of industrial capitalism, when all were expected to strive for something better. But in eighteenth century England occurred a remarkable experiment in separating work from welfare. This was the Speenhamland Law of 1795 (Polanyi, 1944).

At a time of great economic distress it was decided to guarantee to each family the cost of bread, regardless of employment status and earnings. If a breadwinner earned less than this minimum, he received enough to make up the difference. Not only did this remove an economic incentive to work, but employers could cut wages knowing that the family would still get its minimum income. As a result of this policy, says Polanyi, productivity sank steadily, and it was only after "Speenhamland" was abandoned that England began to develop industrially.

Far more sophisticated versions of a guaranteed income have been proposed in recent decades. The plan based on a so-called "negative income tax" is the best known. Your income tax is figured on the basis of your income; generally the more you earn the higher the tax you pay. The *negative* income tax turns this principle on its head, so to speak. The further a poor family sinks below the poverty line the more assistance it receives. Some schemes actually call for administration by the Internal Revenue Services along with the regular income tax.

In 1969 the Republican President Richard Nixon, identified with conservative views generally, surprised the country by unveiling the Family Assistance Plan, which incorporated elements of the guaranteed income. Aid would be based purely on need, so that those below a certain level would be brought up to it. However, work incentives were an important part of the plan. In time this bill foundered, as did a second version of the Family Assistance Plan, but out of that struggle came the merging of the adult assistance categories into Supplemental Security Income (SSI) and agreement to test the guaranteed income concept in a few locations.

THE NEGATIVE INCOME TAX EXPERIMENTS

Different versions of a guaranteed minimum income using a negative income tax were tested in several parts of the country in the 1970s. The results were mixed, but fears of wholesale desertion of the workforce were not confirmed. The scientific validity of the experiments was weakened by the fact that they were all for a limited number of years—thus a participant knew that the program would come to an end—and in one case the study was still in progress when the program was extended to the entire welfare population, making valid comparisons impossible (Cogan, 1978).

However, the fact that similar results occurred in several different locations gives some credence to the findings. Brown (1983) has done the most comprehensive analysis of the full set of experiments. The *New Jersey-Pennsylvania* program used only families with an able-bodied male present; they found that labor force participation was not significantly affected by the availability of the income guarantee. For blacks the rate actually improved. Cogan (1978) challenged these findings; his own reanalysis of the data showed a decline in labor force participation. But Cogan limited his work to those who accepted the option of the income payments. A true test of the impact of an available benefit on the work incentive should include everybody who has the opportunity to receive assistance, not only those who are willing to take it.

Experiments in *North Carolina and Iowa* found virtually no loss of labor force participation among men, but a substantial decline among women. Similarly, in *Gary, Indiana*, there was an average 7% decline in hours of work for men and a 17% decline for women. In *Seattle and Denver*, the figures were 5% for men and 22% for women, with female heads of households reducing their participation 11%.

Are women less committed to the work ethic than men? The more reasonable explanation for the differences in the respective rates of work force participation is that women have two major roles in the family: breadwinner and child rearer. That would explain why in Seattle and Denver female heads of households fell in between the men and women as a whole.

The results of these experiments have of course been seized upon by various factions to prove a point. Liberal supporters of a negative income tax latched onto the early data from New Jersey, before the full findings were available. Conservative critics have been just as eager to show instances where people dropped out of the world of work.

A fair reading of the full range of experiments suggests to this writer that there is limited, but by no means wholesale, withdrawal from the workforce when people are guaranteed an income, but the decision to work or not work, and the ability to do so, are extremely complex. Confidence in one's ability to get and hold a job enters in. So do home responsibilities, health, and distance from the work sites. But these factors are no doubt overshadowed by the fit between skill level and the demands of available jobs. At one time, the President suggested that the newspapers are full of job ads, implying that anybody could work who really wanted to. You might carry out your own experiment, by going through the help wanted ads in your newspaper and seeing how many jobs are for people without advanced degrees or several years of special experience. Of course one needs to be able to read English to make much sense out of help wanted ads. Most jobs, however, are not obtained through reading the paper but through personal contacts. Those with parents and relatives and friends already in good jobs are the most likely to hear about openings and to be hired.

Clearly, America of the 1980s is not Speenhamland of the 1790s. The work ethic is so deeply ingrained in most of us that we will keep on working even if we can do better financially by accepting public aid. The psychological and social costs of becoming unemployed are enormous. On a practical level, work is the only realistic way that people in poverty escape from it.

The notion of unhooking welfare from work, through a negative income tax or any other plan, appears to be an idea whose time has come and gone. The last attempt to promote a version—a watered-down version— of the scheme was by President Jimmy Carter in 1977. It never made it past the committee stage of deliberation in Congress.

CAPITALIZING ON THE WORK ETHIC

The defeatism implicit in writing off the productive potential of large numbers of Americans has struck many observers as an unconscionable waste of human resources. Rather than a means of exploiting the masses for the capitalistic machine, work can be a way of enhancing the life of the worker while producing benefits for the society. We know that employment has important meaning to a person beyond providing income. This may be a result of inculcation of the work ethic and not an inherent tendency in humankind, but it is a fact of life, nonetheless. The problem, of course, is that technological changes generate labor surpluses, at least for the short run. What to do with the excess capacity is one of the major challenges facing our society. Relying on supply and demand to make people eager to take demeaning jobs, that or starve, is both inhuman and inefficient. As some have pointed out, there is much work to be done—cities to be cleaned up and housing to be built, elderly persons in need of personal care and children in need of day care, and an environment in need of being rescued from the ravages of pollution. Our society spouts the rhetoric of the work ethic, but the ethical problem is our failure to provide meaningful work for all who are capable of doing it.

During the early eighties, several states experimented with more creative ways of bringing able-bodied welfare recipients into the workforce. Instead of simply requiring that clients take dead-end public service jobs to work off their grants—the original workfare concept—they built in education and training options, provided transportation and day care and counseling services and in one case offered the state employment service a $1,000 "bounty" for each recipient placed in a private sector job. By then a majority of states had some sort of work requirement.

The most highly touted program, Massachusetts's employment and training (ET) plan, claimed that 20,000 welfare clients were moved into employment in the first two years and that 86% of them were still working twelve months after placement; average pay was said to be more than twice the average welfare grant. The original investment in state and federal funds was said to be more than offset by the reduction in welfare rolls (Atkins, 1986). A major factor behind the success was the fact that Massachusetts had the lowest unemployment rate of any large industrial state at the time. But more generally, early surveys of states with similar programs indicated they could have a positive impact (Gueron, 1986).

In what is perhaps the crowning irony, just as investment in work and training

programs appeared to be showing promising results, the Reagan administration's 1987 budget called for the elimination of federal spending for such
initiatives. This would leave compulsory workfare—which had been notably unsuccessful in moving welfare recipients into stable employment—as the main
federal policy in this area.

More generally, the administration's budget proposals would be most
devastating to programs which could help to move poor people into productive
work—summer youth employment, work incentive benefits and job training—
while basic income transfers such as AFDC and food stamps would continue intact. Somehow the actions did not fit the rhetoric that excoriated welfare
dependency and celebrated the work ethic. To understand the apparent contradiction one must look beyond the avowed goals of policy to its political context. It is this context to which we now turn.

Chapter 5

The Politics of Social Welfare Policy

The most powerful person in the world is the president of the United States. He presides over the biggest economy and the most awesome military machine. Almost invariably, he puts his stamp on the national life during his tenure in office. This is different from saying that the president always gets his way. Take, for instance, economic security.

Harry Truman tried to get a national health insurance program and failed. John F. Kennedy tried to rein in the costs of public assistance by providing rehabilitation services; instead the costs of public assistance went up. Richard Nixon tried to get a guaranteed income program and failed. He tried again and failed again. Jimmy Carter tried to get a watered-down guaranteed income program and failed. He also sought a law to control hospital costs and failed.

Ronald Reagan promised to cut back on the cost of Aid to Families with Dependent Children and succeeded. He also tried to make modest cuts in social security and backed off in the face of a revolt among the members of his own party in Congress. Such are the ups and downs in the life of a president. Aside from the content of the policies he is promoting, there are limitations on a president's power within the decision-making machinery itself. In this chapter we look at these and more generally the politics of social welfare policy.

There are some built-in advantages for a president. He has a raft of experts and the best sources of information available to anybody. Though he must often contend with dissension within the executive branch and more than a little subversion of the official game plan down in the ranks, he has the power to enforce discipline among his subordinates. Contrast this with the relative anarchy in Congress, where any initiative is met by resistance from some quarter and can be stultified by a combination of rules and the heavy hand of tradition.

The president is the nation's number one newsmaker and can beam his message directly to the voters via television when he wishes. Reagan has used this asset to maximum advantage. The Senate has the power to block presidential appointments to key offices but rarely does. Presidents vary greatly in their ability to capitalize on their power, and a presumably strong president can quickly fall from grace. The fact that only two persons have served out at least two full terms in the last fifty years (Roosevelt and Eisenhower), though all the others except Kennedy lived to become ex-presidents, says something about the hazards of office.

Many of the limits on presidential power were intended that way—part of the division of responsibility with which the liberal founders of the Republic sought to restrain centralized authority. Others are unofficial, a result of powerful interests that seek to impose their own agenda on policy-making. A president may also have to contend with subversion of his game plan by people within the administration itself.

LIMITATION #1: THE OFFICIAL FAMILY

Every president in recent decades has entered office promising to give the cabinet a major role in policy-making, and each has ended up relying mainly on the White House staff and relegating the cabinet to a secondary role. One reason for this is that the department secretaries who make up the majority of the cabinet are often selected as much for their political value as for their knowledge of policy. They also may be powers in their own right, with loyal constituencies outside of the administration, and a president may feel the need to counter their influence with a hand-picked cadre closer to him.

When President Jimmy Carter wanted a guaranteed income proposal to send to Congress, he turned the job over to the Departments of Labor and Health, Education and Welfare. Conflicting views between Labor Secretary Marshall and Welfare Secretary Califano and their respective aides had to be resolved before a plan could be produced. Eventually it was, but Califano's less than enthusiastic support of the final product made it hard to convince a skeptical Congress (Lynn & Whitman, 1981).

The differences within the Carter cabinet were miniscule compared with those in some earlier administrations. The issue has nothing to do with how strong or decisive a president is. In the administration of Franklin D. Roosevelt in the 1930s, two top aides—Harold Ickes and Harry Hopkins—carried on a public feud over relief policies punctuated by threats to resign (Schlesinger, 1960, pp. 341-351).

When David Stockman became Ronald Reagan's director of the Office of Management and Budget, he created resentment on the part of some department heads with his insistence on cutting back their budgets. Stockman made public statements which were potentially embarrassing to the administration. Reagan valued Stockman's work sufficiently to keep him on despite this. On the other hand, Health and Human Services Secretary Margaret Heckler was forced out when she was judged not to be implementing administration policies to the satisfaction of the president and his top advisers.

Cabinet members and other senior officials are expected to support the president's views, so they generally toe the line or leave. Not so the rank below them.

The Bureaucracy

The growth of the federal bureaucracy in recent decades is a well-established part of American folklore. The fact is that in 1950 there were 2.1 million civilian employees of the federal government and from then through 1982 the number never went above 2.9 million, despite a greatly expanded federal role and a 53% population rise. The greatest increase in government has been at the state and local levels (4.3 million in 1950 to 13.1 million in 1982). The 2.9 million federal employees include everyone from agency heads in Washington to mail carriers in the boondocks.

The federal bureaucracy has sometimes been called the fourth branch of government, and in fact its ability to shape policy is impressive. This is where most national policy is formulated; and when Congress enacts a piece of legislation, it is the bureaucracy that then translates it into programs and regulations. Neither presidents nor cabinet secretaries nor members of Congress can attend to the myriad of details that go to make up the reality of policy, so out of necessity much of the responsibility for policy-making is delegated to the bureaucracy.

It is more accurate to refer to bureaucrac*ies*. That has its good and bad sides. It is frustrating to see internecine warfare within the federal establishment slow progress on an urgent piece of business or create an unbreakable impasse. But democracy would quickly die if all the bureaucrats suddenly started working in concert. The federal employees below the top echelon are protected by civil service, so they outlast the elected and appointed officials to whom they are supposedly beholden. This allows hold-overs from a previous administration to frustrate the plans of the incoming executive to "clean up the mess in Washington."

In 1973, the Nixon administration sought to cut back sharply the use of federal funds for social services. The task fell to the head of the Social and Rehabilitation Service (SRS). He put out new regulations encompassing the changes and invited comments; since the power to write regulations is an administration prerogative, there is no need to respond to the comments. The proposed rules set off an uproar in the social welfare community, which feared that services and professional careers would both be eliminated. Knowing that many subordinates, especially those who had served under the previous administration, shared the sentiments of the protesters, the SRS commissioner gave strict orders that they were to have no contact with "the enemy." Eventually some of the more frustrated members of the SRS violated this order, paving the way for a compromise with the critics (Richan, 1981, pp. 164-176).

One secretary of Health, Education and Welfare under Nixon, Elliott Richardson, developed a proposal for consolidating human services and with the president's blessing sent it to Congress. Meanwhile, staff members within the Department were quietly undermining it, openly sharing with congressional staff members their skepticism about the bill. It died in committee, as did subsequent legislation with the same objective (Richan, 1981, pp. 121-150). A very powerful body in the executive branch is the Federal Reserve Board. It is discussed in Chapter 6.

LIMITATION #2: CONGRESS

While the saying that the president proposes and Congress disposes is an oversimplification, it is true that most major legislative proposals come from the administration, and nothing comes out of Congress the way it went in. There are basic differences in the operation of the respective houses.

The Senate

The rules and customs of the Senate reflect the fact that its 100 members include many recognized national leaders. Debate is allowed to proceed at a leisurely pace, in fact until recently it was practically impossible to cut it off, and generally there is an air of deference to individual senators. Several measures may be dealt with at the same time, so it is possible to drag out consideration of any one measure almost endlessly. One senator may hold several key committee or subcommittee posts simultaneously, since there is a limited number of members to conduct business. Individual senators have strong power bases, thus are less beholden to committee chairs and party leadership than is true in the House of Representatives.

The House

It is more than four times as large as the Senate, and its members are constantly running for re-election and heavily burdened with "case work" (constituents' problems). Yet the House usually operates more efficiently than the Senate. It has to, because of its size, but also its leaders tend to wield more power than their senate counterparts due to the relative anonymity of most of its members. You will be hard put to name more than a handful of U.S. representatives; you may even have trouble remembering the name of your own. Efficiency is also aided by the rules of operation: one item of business is disposed of on the floor before another is taken up, and the rule of germaneness (that an amendment to a bill be relevant to the content of the original motion) is stricter than in the Senate. It is also easier to cut off debate.

Committees

Much of the actual business of both chambers is conducted through their standing committees. The *Senate Finance Committee* and the *House Ways and Means Committee* deal with social security and other income maintenance legislation. They are also the tax-writing committees, which gives their chairpersons a great deal of power in their respective bodies, since taxes are such an important political issue. Chapter 6 discusses the roles of congressional committees in the budget-making process.

Wilbur Mills was one of four U.S. representatives from Arkansas, a state with nine-tenths of one percent of the nation's population. Yet while he chaired the House Ways and Means Committee no welfare legislation got enacted that he personally opposed. His power was derived not only from the importance of his position but also the fact that over the years he had become an expert on the ins and outs of both public welfare policy and the way to make the House rules work for him. The committee operated under a closed rule, under which any legislation coming from his committee had to be voted up or down on the floor, without amendments. Mills ran the committee with an iron hand, and all deliberations took place in the total committee.

When alcoholism and a personal scandal forced Mills to give up the chair in the 1970s, he was succeeded by Al Ullman of Oregon. Ullman was more democratic and less assertive in the way he ran the committee, with the result that he was less of a force in determining the fate of welfare measures. However, he still was very influential by dint of his position as Ways and Means Committee chairman.

Senate Finance Committee Chairman Russell Long of Louisiana had a major role in derailing Richard Nixon's Family Assistance Plan and forcing major changes in another version of the same proposal. Later, when Jimmy Carter tried to get his own welfare reform plan passed, Long was still the major person to deal with on Capitol Hill.

Reconciling the Differences

By the time each house has completed action on a bill, the two versions are different. These have to be ironed out so the president can receive a single bill for his signature. This is accomplished by means of a *conference committee*, composed of members of both houses who are chosen on the basis of their leadership positions or relationship to the matter under discussion. Sometimes conference committees virtually write a new piece of legislation, so their power can be considerable. Once the conference committee has completed its work, the revised measure is sent back to the two houses for final ratification. By then it is too late to make major changes, though one or the other house may refuse to pass the bill in its final form.

LIMITATION #3: THE JUDICIARY

Just as the founding fathers had intended, the judicial branch of government is a restraint on the power of the president and Congress. Federal judges, including justices of the U.S. Supreme Court, are appointed for indefinite terms, so once in office they are free of the usual political pressures on public officials. Thus it is not always easy to predict how a particular justice will approach policy issues. Earl Warren, a Republican nominated to be Chief Justice by the moderately conservative Dwight Eisenhower, led the Court through its most liberal reform period in the 1950s and 1960s. Byron White, nominated by Democratic liberal John F. Kennedy, was a "swing" member of the Court who tended to line up with the conservative bloc.

The terms "liberal" and "conservative" have more than one meaning when applied to courts. In addition to the usual political meaning, of left and right, they may refer to consideration of social and economic factors in judical decisions (liberal) versus reliance on legal precedent and strict construction of constitutional language (conservative), or judicial activism (liberal) versus avoidance of broad decisions (conservative). Typically the three kinds of conservatism go together, but not always. The Burger court, generally to the right on the political spectrum, has sometimes played an activist role on behalf of conservative principles and placed consideration of national security ahead of a strict reading of traditional legal protections of individual rights (see *New York Times*, 1984e).

Whatever their political coloration, nominations to the bench are among a president's most important actions, for the appointee stays on to influence decisions long after the president has left office. Of the Supreme Court's nine justices in 1984, four were named by Richard Nixon, who resigned from office in disgrace a decade before and three others were nominated by presidents who had since died.

During the sixties, the federal courts made a number of decisions which liberalized public assistance policies. Notable among them was the Supreme Court's action striking down state residence requirements in the federal public aid programs (349 U.S. 618, 1969). But the most important decision on economic security policy came in 1937, when the Supreme Court decided whether the Social Security Act itself was constitutional.

When the Social Security bill was in the works, both administration officials and leaders of Congress were apprehensive about having the measure struck down by the Supreme Court, which was then dominated by conservatives. As a result they avoided radical departures from the past. Their fears were understandable, because the Court had rejected the major part of Roosevelt's New Deal legislation by the time it heard arguments on the Social Security Act in 1937. If this, too, were struck down, it might be extremely hard to resurrect it, so this decision was critical for the future of the American welfare state.

On the first of three cases, the justices upheld the Act by only a five to four vote. The others were upheld by larger margins. One explanation for the decisions, which contrasted with the previous anti-New Deal actions, is political. President Roosevelt had been trying to get legislation which would change the Court, undermining the power of the conservative majority. Shifting to a more liberal stance on the Social Security Act was a way for the justices to blunt the support for Roosevelt's scheme. As one columnist put it, it was "the switch in time that saved nine" (Altmeyer, 1966, p. 56; Burns, 1956, pp. 291-315; *New York Times*, 1937).

Because of the importance of the judiciary and the fact that appointments to the bench usually outlast the administrations that select them, they are frequent subjects of controversy. In the 1970s, Richard Nixon named Clement Haynsworth to the Supreme Court. In most cases the Senate confirms such appointments with little trouble. However, in Haynsworth's case enough questions were raised so that the nomination failed to receive the requisite two-thirds vote. Nixon then came back with a second nomination, that of G. Harrold Carswell. When civil rights groups mounted a major campaign against Carswell because of his alleged racism, he was also rejected by the Senate (Harris, 1971). The man finally nominated to fill the seat was Harry Blackmun, who often lined up against Nixon's other appointees on judicial questions.

In the mid-eighties, some liberals noted that President Reagan was likely to have named a majority of the federal court judges by the end of his second term, and charged that the selection process was too political, in contrast with previous administration (Goldman, 1985). In earlier years, some conservatives sought to impeach the liberal activist Chief Justice Earl Warren. The country has consistently rejected attempts to interfere with the courts, the nomination process, and the prerogatives of presidents doing the nominating.

LIMITATION #4: THE FEDERAL SYSTEM

Chapter 3 describes the traditional reluctance of Americans to entrust responsibility for welfare to the federal government. The importance of states in the federal system and their ability to limit the power of a president involve more than simply the structural division of responsibilites laid out in the Constitution.

The pattern of representation in Congress and the allocation of Electoral College votes are both based on states, increasing the importance of that level of government. Our national political parties are weak, mobilizing themselves for a few hectic months of presidential campaigning every four years, then lapsing into relative inactivity. It is not unusual for one or both houses in Congress to be in control of the party other than the president's. Thus it is the state organizations which are dominant in party politics.

Ronald Reagan's efforts to shift many activities of government from the federal to the state level have met with mixed reactions from the states. While state and local officials like the freedom to chart their own course, they are wary of being burdened with a greater share of the cost. Changes in the financing of services that have taken place under Reagan are discussed in the next chapter.

The old rivalries over state versus federal control still go on, but the fact that states and localities now depend heavily on federal funds has changed the nature of the debate. The federal bureaucracy is the component that has the direct dealings with state and local agencies. The latter are more concerned about the nuts and bolts of funding and the endless forms to fill out than they are about ideological issues of centralism versus freedom.

Counties and municipalities are creatures of the state, and everything from their taxing power to the way they run their business is subject to the will of the legislature. In the 1960s in the heat of the urban unrest, the federal government bypassed the states in funding a number of anti-poverty programs in the cities. The states insisted on being dealt in on the action and eventually state clearance became a regular feature of local programs. The local level of government becomes most important in the delivery of services. We look at this in Chapter 9, which deals with the translation of policies into services to the consumer.

The Growing Importance of State Government

The "new federalism"—the shift of decision-making from the national to the state level—has received its strongest support from conservatives, and it has been conservative Republican presidents, Nixon and Reagan, who most actively pushed the concept. But the trend toward greater power in the state capitals, relative to Washington, is a more basic development in American government. The next chapter discusses the economic side of the new federalism, revenue sharing, which was first proposed in the administration of liberal Democrat John F. Kennedy.

Although state government resembles the federal government in structure, each state has its own peculiarities. The most important political differences among states are based on regional identity, rural-urban composition, economic base, size and demographics. Typically large urban centers are in competition with suburban and rural districts. The domination of a state by a few large in-dustries or a single political party can limit its ability to respond to citizen needs. On the other hand, contending interest groups—for example big industry and powerful labor unions, or ethnic and religious groups which are closely matched in size—can create impasses in decision making.

Two factors which will influence the ability of states to meet the challenge of increased responsibility in the coming years will be technical sophistication and visibility. Historically, government operations in many states tended to be highly politicized, relying on party faithful with little technical expertise. In recent years most state bureaucracies have become more professional, though the level of performance varies greatly from state to state.

Visibility continues to be a major problem. Question: Who are your state representative and state senator? If you cannot answer that question, you have a lot of company. State government is a well-kept secret. Newspapers which carefully report happenings in Washington will virtually ignore the doings in their own state capital. One reason is that Washington makes better copy. The key figures are more glamorous and the arguments about billions for star wars and Medicare grab the public's attention. Television, reputed to be people's main source of news, goes for visual excitement. Will the local station cover a visit by Ronald Reagan or Jesse Jackson? Yes. A warehouse fire or a raid on a local gambling den? Yes. State government? Unlikely, unless somebody is marching on the state capitol or a fist fight breaks out between two legislators. Television's defense is that it covers what the viewer wants to see. So state government is insulated from that most crucial factor in consent of the governed: the opportunity for the governed to know what is going on.

The power of states should not be overemphasized. The ability of the federal government to shape events and set the agenda for the states is still enormous. That comes out clearly in the next chapter on the economics of social welfare policy. But organizations which hope to influence policy decisions have been paying increasing attention to state politics. With the help of computers, national lobbying operations are able to adapt their tactics to local conditions.

In the years following World War II, it was assumed the welfare rolls would go down. Instead they climbed, as thousands of Southern blacks and whites lured to Northern cities by war jobs became casualties of a series of postwar recessions. By 1950 states and localities were beginning to revolt against federal welfare policies. In 1951, Indiana enacted a law requiring the publication of recipients' names, in violation of federal regulations. The action, intended to expose "welfare fraud," threatened to jeopardize Indiana's reimbursement for Aid to Dependent Children. In order to avoid this, Congress threw out the federal confidentiality rule (Indianapolis Chapter, 1952). It was a classic case of the tail wagging the dog, and it demonstrated a state's power to defy the federal government.

In 1960, Louisiana dropped 23,000 children, mostly black, from AFDC because they were said to be living in "unsuitable" homes. According to state policy, presence of an illegitimate child or promiscuous sexual activity or an unrelated adult male was sufficient ground for disqualifying a family. This was in violation of federal regulations. Under pressure from civil rights groups the federal government threatened to stop Louisiana's AFDC reimbursement, and the state backed down (Bell, 1965, pp. 137-151).

In 1961, the city manager of Newburgh, New York, issued a thirteen-point decree designed to make welfare hard to obtain and humiliating to receive. State officials became alarmed: Not only was Newburgh defying state policy but by also breaking the federal rules it threatened New York's federal welfare funding. The state forced the city to withdraw all but one of its new requirements, the most innocuous of the thirteen (Greenfield, 1961; May, 1964). Once again, state and local officials had yielded to federal authority. Regardless of the level of government, an overriding factor in policy making lies beyond the formal structure.

LIMITATION #5: PRIVATE INTERESTS

The ability of special interest groups to influence elections and policy decisions is well known. Too well known, perhaps, because it is possible to conjure up an image of a few faceless individuals running the whole show from outside the government, while elected and appointed officials are jerked this way and that on the end of numerous strings. In 1984, Ronald Reagan was able to cast

Walter Mondale, his opponent, as a captive of such interests. But the intrusion of private interests pervades all of politics. In this day of multi-million dollar campaigns for state as well as national office, it is inevitable that those with money will use it. The fact that elected officials, most of whom receive substantial campaign funding from special interests, are also the ones who must vote on legislation to control such practices makes reform difficult.

Special interests groups don't hide their influence. By allowing the impression to get abroad that they are unstoppable, they can immobilize the rest of us. In Chapter 15 another view of political influence is presented.

When President Jimmy Carter took office in 1977, one of his top priorities was getting hospital costs under control. He had the Department of Health, Education and Welfare (HEW, later Health and Human Services) draft a bill which would impose federal limits on costs if the hospitals could not bring them down on their own in the next three years. A modest effort, but not modest enough for health care interests. In a rare show of unity, the American Medical Association and two national hospital associations set out to defeat the proposal (Demkovitch, 1979a, 1979b).

Over the years all three organizations had established strong ties with members of Congress, but a major strategy was to mobilize their members around the country through a mail saturation campaign. Most members of most organizations pay as little attention to policy issues as the rest of us. It is only as their politically attuned leaders and lobbyists call on them that they get involved, and then only if they can see a connection with their own vital interests. Since an attempt by the government to clamp a lid on health costs was a bread and butter issue for them, they responded. Key members of Congress began to hear from constituents on the subject.

Meanwhile, the Carter administration was not idle. Its main ball carrier was HEW Secretary Joseph Califano. Midway through the process Califano resigned, leaving it to his successor to carry on. Like the opposition, the administration tried to drum up support out in the hustings. Fifty organizations representing labor, consumers, senior citizens and state and local government spearheaded a massive public education campaign on behalf of hospital cost containment.

The opponents countered with a highly publicized program of voluntary cost cutting by hospitals to head off the mandatory federal plan. They were aided by a strong upsurge in inflation, in which hospital costs no longer outran general price levels. In the fall of 1979 administration lobbyists decided it was time to push for a final congressional vote on the bill. The word came back from Capitol Hill: Not now. Head counts showed that the bill would lose, but administration leaders decided it was now or never. The final bill was emasculated with an amendment calling for a purely voluntary effort, something hospitals were already doing. The essence of the proposal was lost (Cohen, 1979; CQ Almanac, 1979, pp. 512-518).

In the wake of the defeat, proponents looked for a scapegoat—poor timing by the administration, Califano's abrasive lobbying techniques, the failure of the president to lobby personally for the measure. But political reality is more complex than that. A key factor was the organizations which led the opposition. They were experienced, had ample resources with which to pay for staff research and mass mailings, and their members included powerful local leaders to whom members of Congress would be inclined to listen. As against this pressure, there was little to be feared from a president whose public standing was suffering.

For the hospitals this was *the* legislative issue. For President Carter it competed with the most harrowing problem of his presidency: the hostage crisis in Iran. And to the constituency supporting the measure, contrary to its foes, cost containment was not the kind of issue likely to evoke a lot of excitement. When a constituency does get excited and sees its own stake in an issue, it can be a powerful force—even when its apparent power is minimal.

The passivity of the poor is a truism of American politics. Like many truisms, it is misleading. Public assistance recipients were assumed for years to lack both the resources and motivation to get involved in politics. In the late sixties, however, the welfare rights movement became a significant force that had to be reckoned with.

THE AURA OF INVINCIBILITY

Carter's inability to enact hospital cost containment legislation seemed further proof of the reputed power of the medical community to get its way on any issue it cared about. The reputation dated back to the thirties, when drafters of the Social Security bill deleted the health insurance section that many urgently wanted, in order not to have the whole package go down the drain. President Harry Truman fought hard for national health insurance and lost. Lyndon Johnson was able to get Medicare enacted in 1965, but the price of victory was allowing the providers of health care to control the operation. The subsequent escalation of medical expenditures was what moved the Carter administration to try to contain health costs. Each time it was the medical profession that loomed as the villain or hero, depending on where one stood.

But the Reagan administration succeeded in pushing through a tough cost-containment measure. This served as one more piece of evidence that Ronald Reagan was invincible. In truth, on most issues Reagan was able to prevail where many of his predecessors had failed. With the exception of the sharp rebuke from senators of his own party over his attempt to cut back social security in 1981, he was able again and again to snatch victory from what appeared to be almost certain defeat. The aura of success itself aided the president by making opposition seem futile. One talent of Reagan has been to sense the tide of events and join the winning side rather than go down to defeat. For example, when his attempt to cut social security backfired, he put together a bipartisan commission to revise the fiscally troubled program, embraced their recommendations warmly and became a staunch defender of social security against any further tampering.

In his second term, the president ran up against a more truculent Congress. However, by shifting his ground even as he took a hard line in his rhetoric, he was able to avoid the aura of vincibility that hovered around Jimmy Carter throughout most of his tenure in office. The one domestic issue that seriously challenged Reagan's control of events in his second term was the economy. Despite a record period without a recession, the nation faced unprecedented federal budget deficits and severe troubles in agriculture and heavy industry. The role of social welfare policy in the national economy is discussed in the next chapter.

THE ART OF THE POSSIBLE

Ronald Reagan says, "Never say never," and that seems like good advice when it comes to the politics of social welfare policy. A piece of legislation which has been defeated more than once is brought back to life and enacted. A human services program that looks secure is overthrown.

The machinery of American government conspires to slow drastic change in any direction, but on the substantive issues it is neutral. Recognizing this, political activists adapt their strategies to the structure. Welfare rights advocates used the federal courts in the late sixties to reform the system. They shifted to other tactics when the courts became less friendly. A member of Congress will try to steer her bill to a committee that will give it a sympathetic hearing and away from one where it will be buried. The same tactics that serve a progressive cause this year will be borrowed by conservatives next year. Knowing this, experienced politicians keep their options open, make gains where they can and accept defeats as part of the game. Unlike the amateurs, they also stay around for the next inning. There is usually a next inning. Chapter 15 discusses the role of social workers in the political arena.

Chapter 6

Paying the Bills

My friend Charlie has a way of cutting through the frosting to get to the cake. "The bottom line," he says in a burst of insight, "is the bottom line." Meaning, in social welfare policy the ultimate issue is the fiscal balance sheet. Do you want to know where a country's priorities are? See where it spends its money. A way to see how much this country invests in social welfare, for instance, is to compare it with the gross national product (GNP), the total of all goods and services produced in the United States economy in a year. By 1986 the GNP was estimated to pass the four trillion dollar mark (four followed by twelve zeroes). In 1982 close to one out of every five dollars of GNP was government funds (federal, state or local) earmarked for human resources programs. Of that amount, 70% was federal money. Total philanthropic contributions for purposes other than religion were only one percent of GNP—about the same as they had been for twenty years.[1]

So when we talk about social welfare spending, we are talking about government spending, primarily federal government spending. In this chapter we'll look at federal expenditures and their relationship to the total economy. The economics of the voluntary sector are discussed in Chapter 11.

The federal budget gives a picture of the nation's spending priorities. The table on page 72 shows the budget breakdown for several areas, including social welfare, for Fiscal Year 1981, the year Ronald Reagan took office, and the administration proposal for Fiscal Year 1986.

In terms of the total budget, defense and net interest have gone up, while social security and Medicare have risen slightly and other items have gotten a smaller piece of the pie. Until the late sixties, social security and Medicare were excluded from the general budget, since they have separate trust funds. Some analysts believe they should not be included now. They say this distorts the amount of spending of our tax money on "welfare." But the social security money that is deducted from your pay check is a tax, which provides funds for current retirees, so it seems appropriate to leave it in. In the future these social insurances will be moved off into a separate budget again. This is supposed to help insulate them from being raided for other purposes.

---

[1]Figure from U.S., Bureau of Census (1983).

	FY1981	FY1986
Total (in billions of dollars)	657.2	973.7

Percentage for:		
National defense	24.3	29.3
Community & regional development	1.4	0.7
Education, employment & social services	4.8	3.0
Health[a]	4.1	3.6
Social security & Medicare	27.2	27.7
Percentage for:		
Income security[b]	13.0	11.9
Veterans benefits & services	3.5	2.8
Net interest[c]	10.5	14.6
Other outlays (net)	11.2	6.4

Source: U.S., OMB, 1985.

[a]Does not include medical assistance. [b]Means tested assistance, unemployment insurance, and federal employee and other retirement programs. [c]Interest on the national debt minus interest income from trust funds.

A way of demonstrating graphically how much money goes for different purposes is to use the human body. Suppose, for instance, a friend complains that the "deadbeats" on AFDC are breaking the backs of honest taxpayers. Have the friend go through the following steps.

1. Stand up in your stocking feet. We will pretend that you are the federal budget for Fiscal Year 1986—$973. 7 billion in all.[2]
2. From the middle of your thigh to the floor is all economic security programs lumped together ($400 billion).
3. Take out social security, Medicare and veterans' income security ($285 billion), and we drop down to a point about eight and a half inches off the floor.
4. Take off unemployment compensation and special retirement and disabili-

[2]This was the administration's proposal, not necessarily the final budget but reasonably close to it. Figures from U.S., OMB, 1985.

ty benefits ($63 billion), mainly for federal employees, and that puts us down to between three and a half and four inches from the floor.

5. Now we are down to those means-tested benefits most people think of as "welfare." Subtract everything but AFDC and you will be about three quarters of an inch from the floor. Eight billion is a lot of money, but very small compared to the rest of the budget. (The taxpayer also supports AFDC with state taxes, though the amount is less than the federal funds.)

My friend Charlie is a born skeptic. He says the federal budget doesn't tell you how much the federal government spends, and he's right. Several major expenditures have been removed from the federal budget—for example, spending by quasi-government corporations like the postal service. Everybody expresses concern about the practice but it still goes on. In the 1985 budget report it was estimated that $14.8 billion in off-budget funds would be spent during the fiscal year (U.S., OMB, 1984, p. 6/11). Sometimes Congress makes supplemental appropriations of funds, for instance if a steep recession requires extra emergency aid.

PUTTING THE BUDGET TOGETHER

The fiscal year begins on October 1 of the preceding calendar year, so FY 1986 began on October 1, 1985. The preparation of the budget began nearly two years before that. The *Office of Management and Budget* (OMB), in the Executive Office of the President, is especially powerful, because secretaries of federal departments, including defense, must present their budget requests to the director of the OMB, who actually puts together the budget that is presented to Congress. Realistically, the Secretary of Defense can and does appeal directly to the president, who may overrule his OMB director. Ronald Reagan came into office on a platform of sharply cutting federal expenditures, and the person he relied on to do the hatchet work was David Stockman, a former conservative member of Congress. In Reagan's first term, Stockman developed a reputation for being a dedicated hatchetman; this was a plus or a minus depending on whose ox was being gored. The OMB monitors actual expenditures and may tell agency heads they are out of line with what their budgets call for.

Federal agencies began developing their spending estimates for FY 1986 by the beginning of 1984. Starting this far in advance means the original estimates must be based on many unknowns—for example, public assistance costs will be affected by future unemployment levels. Agencies charged with specific functions will tend to lean on the generous side in projecting their needs, and the OMB's task is to whittle them down.

By the fall of 1984, the OMB had sketched out the basic dimensions of the FY 1986 budget for consideration by the president, the final arbiter. In February, 1985, the president sent the budget to Congress.

Congress Works Over the Budget

The federal budget has two parts: revenue and expenditures. The taxes to provide the revenue are the concern of two powerful committees described in Chapter 5: the *Senate Finance Committee* and the *House Ways and Means Committee*. Because the Social Security Act of 1935 involved new taxes, these committees have been the major ones regarding that act and subsequent changes in it. There are four other committees with primary responsibility for the budget: the House and Senate Appropriation Committees, and the House and Senate Budget Committees.

The *House and Senate Appropriations Committees* are responsible for coming up with specific spending proposals on which Congress votes. Until that happens, the budget is only a set of proposals. The Appropriations Committees have traditionally operated through subcommittees concerned with different areas of government. For example, the *House Appropriations Subcommittee on Health and Welfare* deals with funding of the agencies under the Department of Health and Human Services. One side-effect of this arrangement is that the subcommittees have an interest in promoting the fortunes of particular departments and are the natural targets of lobbying by the departments themselves and outside organizations.

The Difference Between Authorizing and Appropriating

Deciding that a certain policy should be adopted and agreeing to spend the money to make it happen are two different steps. The first is *authorization* and the second is *appropriation*. My friend Charlie got disgusted when his U.S. representative told a civic group she had voted for a wonderful new program to help the poor, then was quoted in the local paper as telling the chamber of commerce that she would never vote to spend one more dime on the poor. Charlie's resentment is justified, but the representative may have told the truth in both cases. She may have voted to *authorize* the new program but then voted against the *appropriation* which would have funded it.

In 1956 Congress passed amendments to the Social Security Act authorizing states to provide social services and staff training in public assistance. It was six years later that money was appropriated to implement the plan.

Getting Control of the Budget Process

In the early seventies, President Richard Nixon and congressional Democrats were at loggerheads over control of federal spending. Nixon claimed the right to impound funds, that is, refuse to spend what Congress had appropriated. This led to passage of the Congressional Budget and Impoundment Control Act of 1974. Not only was this intended to give Congress more leverage with the White House but also to put its own house in order. The state of relative anarchy of appropriations subcommittees was to be brought to an end by establishment of *House and Senate Budget Committees* and the *Congressional Budget Office* (CBO), a technical arm of Congress.

The CBO provides economic forecasts and projects the effects of different revenue and spending decisions. It helps to offset the advantage of enormous technical resources available to a president. The budget committees develop overall spending targets; once these are agreed to by Congress, other committees are expected to stay within these limits. This gives these committees a lot of power.

HOW THE FEDERAL GOVERNMENT SPENDS MONEY

Programs Run by the Federal Government

Social security, Medicare, and Supplemental Security Income (SSI) are administered by the federal government. In the case of food stamps states have some administrative responsibility. The standards and rules under which these services function are uniform, but in the case of SSI states may add their own funds to raise the level of grants. The use of a single national scheme has the advantage of better fiscal control by the level of government spending the money and assuring uniform standards regardless of the recipient's state of residence.

Aid to States and Localities

Aside from the few income support categories cited above, the typical way for the federal government to fund social programs is through grants to the states. Some special allocations go directly to localities. There are three patterns of aid: categorical grants-in-aid, general revenue sharing, and special revenue sharing. These latter allocations are called block grants.

Categorical funds. These are earmarked for *categories* of need. The federal government passes a law calling for distribution of money to states meeting certain federal requirements. A state then passes a law meeting the federal rules in order to implement the program. States usually must put up a percentage of the money. AFDC and medical assistance are examples of such federal aid, for each state sets up its own assistance program.

The levels of support of such services may vary widely from state to state. Recall the two young friends described in Chapter 3. Mark's family, on survivors' benefits under social security, kept receiving the same amount of money when they moved from another state; Paul's mother had to reapply, and her grant was half of what it had been in the previous state.

General revenue sharing. This means turning money over to the states without any strings attached. In effect, the federal government raises tax revenue for the state. This idea first surfaced during the presidency of Democrat John F.

Kennedy but did not become law until 1972, under Republican Richard Nixon. These block grants are "new" money and don't replace anything already in place. In 1985 and 1986 the administration proposed eliminating these grants.

Special revenue sharing. These block grants replace several categorical grant-in-aid programs with a single general-purpose allocation, for instance in employment and training or community development. States have maximum flexibility in deciding how to use the money, but they are often cautious about special revenue sharing proposals. Each special program has its champions, including state officials, who fear that once the specific service is merged with others it will lose funds. In 1981 Ronald Reagan got Congress to enact a plan for converting over fifty categorical grant-in-aid programs into nine block grants and cutting the funding by 25%.

In 1982, Reagan proposed a new extension of revenue sharing: turning AFDC and food stamps into block grant programs. In exchange, he offered to make medical assistance a totally federal responsibility. The full cost of AFDC and food stamps would eventually fall on the states. The plan was finally withdrawn in 1984, which not coincidentally was an election year. Some states had been pushing to unload AFDC on the federal government instead of the other way around, and they reacted strongly to the idea of having it unloaded on them. Welfare advocates feared that abandonment of a federal role would open the door to some states' scrapping the program or instituting punitive provisions.

Funding the Private Sector

The federal government aids private philanthropic organizations in two ways: through tax exemption and direct expenditures. Most of the direct aid is channeled through state and local governments. Many voluntary agencies were hit by cutbacks in federal support in 1981. Title XX of the Social Security Act, created in 1975, allocated just under $3 billion for social services in FY 1981, much of it going for services in private nonprofit agencies. The next year the funds were cut by 20%. State and local governments made up some of the difference, but the voluntary agencies still felt the impact of the cuts (U.S., Comptroller General, 1984). The funding of voluntary social welfare is discussed in more detail in Chapter 11.

RED INK

My friend Charlie has decided not to vote in any more presidential elections. "It's this way," he told me. "In 1964 Lyndon Johnson said, 'The Republicans are a bunch of warmongers. Vote for me or you'll see the Vietnam War escalate.' So I voted for Johnson," said Charlie, "and look what happened: Soon as he's re-elected, Bay of Tonkin resolution and, whoops, we're in deeper than ever. So then Nixon came along and said, 'The Democrats are a bunch of bleeding hearts who don't believe in law and order. Vote for me, or the criminal element will take over the country.' So I voted for Nixon, and pretty soon the criminal element have not only taken over the country, they're running it—from the White House no less. Then comes Reagan. 'The Democrats are deficit spenders,' he says, 'Vote for me or the federal deficit will go right out of sight.' That sounded convincing, so I voted for Reagan, and what happens? In a few years the federal deficit has jumped from $60 billion to up around $200 billion. This time I'm staying in bed.''

Charlie's solution—dropping out of politics—doesn't make much sense, but it does seem as though speeches on the campaign trail sometimes bear little resemblance to what happens once a person is elected.

Debts and Deficits

The *national debt* is the total of all money the United States government owes to private banks and other lenders. From George Washington's presidency to Ronald Reagan's it gradually mounted up to one trillion dollars. That is a thousand times a thousand times a thousand times a thousand. During Ronald Reagan's presidency it was due to reach two trillion dollars. The reason it rose so fast since 1981 is that the federal government was operating at enormous *budget deficits*. The deficit is the short-fall between tax revenue and expenditures in a given year, and each year's deficit is tacked onto the national debt. For instance, the deficit for Fiscal Year 1986 was estimated at more than $200 billion.

If the national debt is so much larger than the budget deficit, why is it the latter that has caused so much furor? This is why: Regardless of how much money it takes in in taxes, the government is obligated to pay its bills in order to stay in business. Social security checks must go out on schedule, defense contractors must be paid, and the lenders who are holding the national debt must receive their interest payments. So the government must go into the same financial markets as everybody else and borrow the money to pay its bills. A deficit of over $200 billion is so huge, according to this view, that the government tends to crowd out other investors and force up the cost of money: interest rates. That in turn affects the ability of industry to invest in new plants and equipment, which means the economy does not expand as fast as it might and thus fewer jobs are created. It also raises the value of the dollar compared to other currencies, which means foreign imports are cheaper for Americans to buy and American goods are more expensive in foreign countries. The federal deficit thus aggravates the problem of our trade deficit, which has also been at record levels.

This concern about annual budget deficits is not universal among economists. Eisner and Pieper (1984) contend, for example, that the official figures for the gross public debt ignore the accumulation of government assets, which contribute to net worth. They assert that when one adjusts the deficits for inflation the budgets have registered surpluses in several years. Deficits are a problem, they say, but not the crisis that others contend.

No one claims that the national debt—the long-term accumulation—is unimportant. A large chunk of the federal budget is interest on the national debt: almost $200 billion in Fiscal Year 1986. That can be budgeted every year, the way householders budget in their mortgage interest, so it is not like the shortfall between income and expenditures. But it means the government has to spend the same amount as the federal deficit each year just in interest on old debts. Putting it in terms of our human body model, it represents everything from the top of your head to your collar bone. That money could wipe out the federal deficit, or could be invested in economic expansion and other useful purposes.

It would be impossible to pay off the national debt; to do so would take every penny the federal government has to spend—social security, defense, everything—and throw the country into total economic collapse. Even reductions in the annual budget deficits have to be managed carefully to avoid weakening the economy. A sudden withdrawal of money to wipe out a $200 billion shortfall would also have severe economic repercussions. But because of the deficits' impact on everything from interest rates to our trade balance, as well as additions to the national debt accumulation, they have been a major focus of attention.

As of the mid-eighties, there were widely different expectations about budget deficits in the future. Some analyses forecast continuing escalation, while others projected a gradual decline, even without special measures to control deficits. A lot depended on what happened to the economy generally. Continued prosperity would increase tax revenues and cut the costs of maintaining people thrown out of work, thus working toward a lower deficit. A major recession, on the other hand, would increase unemployment, cutting the taxes the displaced workers would have paid, while pushing up welfare costs.

Cutting the Deficit

There are two ways to reduce budget deficits. Raise more revenue through taxes or cut expenditures. As of the mid-eighties, the president was refusing to consider a tax increase, and Congress was not willing to take the initiative with such a politically unpopular move. That left expenditures. President Reagan declared defense spending and social security off-limits, meaning the only budget cuts he would consider would be in other items.

Let us use the Fiscal Year 1986 budget as an example.

If one takes out the interest on the national debt, defense and social security, that leaves only $287 billion (30% of the budget) to work with. Some of that money must go for existing contracts and other legal obligations. Some of it is earmarked for retirement benefits for federal employees, and it would be questionable on both ethical and legal grounds to renege on those. Some of it goes to maintain our overseas embassies and international trade.

We are not even considering the political uproar that would occur if benefits to farmers and veterans, protection of natural resources, and the space program were scotched. Note that no mention has been made so far of health, education and welfare programs, but eliminating those would also be disastrous, for reasons advanced in other chapters of this book.

Controllability

By its own estimate, the Reagan administration's 1985 budget was almost 75% "relatively uncontrollable." That term refers to obligations of the kind discussed above, aside from the politically explosive items. Using this criterion, military expenditures are predominantly controllable; that is, they involve new spending that theoretically could be cut from year to year. If we add together the relatively uncontrollable expenditures and the defense budget which President Reagan has ruled out of bounds, the 1985 budget would have included only $90.5 billion, less than 10% of the total, which could be considered for cutting.

The Open or Closed Faucet

Entitlement programs—those under which persons who meet certain qualifications are *entitled* to receive benefits—are hard to control because by nature they are *open-ended*; that is, the amount to be spent depends on how many people qualify. You cannot tell retired persons on social security, "Sorry, that's all, come back next year." They have a legal claim to the money, once they meet the qualifications. The same is true of AFDC families. States can lower their grant levels, but once the amount has been set, everybody who meets the requirements must receive help. The U.S. Constitution guarantees equal protection before the law, including equal right to federal benefits if one qualifies for them. Other kinds of funding are *close-ended*; a set amount is earmarked for the purpose. When that money is gone, there is no more unless Congress decides to make a special appropriation.

The 1962 amendments to the Social Security Act, which authorized social services for welfare recipients and other low-income persons, were funded on an *open-ended* basis. The federal government would match state funds on a three-to-one ratio, regardless of how much a state appropriated for this purpose. When states began to take advantage of this program to pay for basic state services in addition to the intended activities, Congress clamped down by changing the social services money to a closed-ended appropriation. A total of $2.5 billion was earmarked for this purpose. When states used that up, there was no more to be had.

Seeking a Way Out

As the pressure for action on the federal deficit grew in the mid-eighties, the administration and Congress cast about for a response that would be politically least damaging. The answer they arrived at was the Gramm-Rudman-Hollings amendment, named after its three Senate sponsors, two Republicans and a

Democrat. This called for reduction of the deficit to zero by stages over a period of five years. In the event that Congress and the president did not act on it, automatic cuts would be taken from both defense and other programs. In its final version, the only exempt items would be social security, veterans' pensions, seven poverty programs and interest on the nation debt (*New York Times*, 1985).

The plan was enacted into law in late 1985. However, it was criticized as setting unrealistic targets and restricting the options of policy-makers in responding to national needs; it faced a legal challenge, on grounds that it abrogated the responsibilities of elected officials; and there was skepticism that it would survive.

The Gramm-Rudman-Hollings plan was a political response to a quandary that was both political and economic. In the ensuing years, public officials might be forced to rethink their positions on such issues as tax increases, social security and defense spending. One of the most formidable issues was social security.

THE ECONOMICS OF ECONOMIC SECURITY IN AN AGING SOCIETY

There has been much concern about the fiscal soundness of the social security system. It is sometimes referred to as a crisis. Actually there have been two problems—a short-term one and a long-term one.

The Short-Term Crisis

Originally social security benefits were established by law. Raising them required an act of Congress. This meant that retirees were repeatedly falling behind. In 1972 Congress added a cost-of-living adjustment (COLA) to social security, so that every six months benefits would be raised to keep pace with inflation. It happened just before an oil crisis caused a sharp rise in inflation and at the same time a slowdown in the economy. With people being laid off, less was coming into the social security fund in taxes while the rapid rise in the cost of living was drawing money out faster in benefits.

With the outflow of benefits coming perilously close to outrunning the taxes coming into the social security trust fund, Congress passed legislation in 1977 designed to "rescue" the social security system by raising taxes and reducing the growth of benefits. President Carter announced that the problems of the system had been solved for the next fifty years. Three years later social security was again in danger, thanks to another surge of inflation and a recession (Carlson, 1984).

It was this second crisis that prompted President Reagan in 1981 to call for changes in the system—and walk straight into a political buzz saw in the process. He appointed a bipartisan National Commission on Social Security Reform, which came out with a solution in the eleventh hour, literally saving the system.

Their plan called for reductions in some benefits, higher payroll taxes, a gradual rise in the retirement age, taxes on benefits for those with very high incomes, borrowing from the Medicare trust fund, and inclusion of new federal employees, who had been under their own retirement system (Ozawa, 1984). The reforms solved the short-term problem. Opinions differed on whether they would also deal with the long-term problems of social security. But the more basic issues concern societal changes running into the next century.

The Long-Term Problem

Social security funding cannot be looked at in a vacuum. The Census Bureau estimates that as of July 1, 1985, there were 238.6 million Americans, two-thirds of them in the productive years (15-64), 12% in the retirement years (65 and older) and 2.6% in the "frail" elderly category (80 and older).[3] By the year 2,000 the total population will have increased by about an eighth, the 65-and-over cohort by more than a fifth and the frail elderly by 60%. By 2,050, the nation as a whole will be less than 30% larger, but the 65-and-older group will have doubled, and the 80-and-older population will have doubled and redoubled. This last group is the one that has the greatest need, not only for subsistence but also for a range of health and nursing care and other supports.

At present only two-thirds of the working-age population is gainfully employed, and the percentage keeps falling. Technological changes may further depress this figure, as discussed in Chapter 4. That means fewer workers paying into the system per retiree collecting benefits. Further upward adjustments in the retirement age can lower the ratio of retired to working Americans, but there are limits as to how far that can go. Just as the hopes in the late seventies that social security had been "fixed" for the next half century proved wrong in three years, the optimism of the bipartisan commission of 1983 is probably not well founded (Ozawa, 1984). Discussions of social security financing rarely take into consideration the full costs of health care and other needs of the elderly (see Hudson, 1978).

The "Dependency Ratio" and Government Responsibility

There are two dependent age groups—those too old to support themselves and those too young to do so. While most attention has been focused on the increases in the former, what has been less recognized has been the decline in the latter in recent years.[4] If one considers only the ratio between people in the productive years and people in the older and younger groups, the dependency ratio will not

---

[3]Figures from U.S., Bureau of Census (1982).
[4]The writer is indebted to Dr. June Axinn for her helpful comments on this point.

be that much greater in the future than it was in the past. From a strictly economic standpoint, then, the burden on the middle group could be expected to stay the same.

However, more than age ratios is involved. Historically the nature of welfare activity targeted to the elderly has focused on basic maintenance and, more recently, health care. Except for families in poverty, parents have been presumed to be able to meet the economic needs of their children. The largest outlays have been for education, and the cost of this has been going up, even when the child population declined. The entry of women into the work force in growing numbers is likely to increase the use of alternative child-care arrangements. As government becomes involved in these, the outlays for children will presumably grow. Finally, cross-national studies of social welfare expenditures indicate that as a population ages, a greater proportion of a country's resources go into social welfare (Miller, 1976).

So there is every likelihood that the demand for economic security provisions will continue to rise as American society ages. What this will mean down the line is hard to predict. If care of the aging becomes too disruptive to the needs of the rest of the population, provisons which are now taken for granted can be expected to become more controversial (see Hudson, 1978).

THE ECONOMIC CONTEXT OF POLICY

As my friend Charlie says, "You can't tell if the sailor's standing up straight if you don't know the pitch of the deck." We do indeed have to step back and look at the economic seas on which the American ship of state is riding in order to understand the economics of social welfare policy. So far we have focused mainly on government expenditures. The government has two basic mechanisms for influencing the nation's economy: *fiscal policy* (taxing and spending) and *monetary policy* (managing the money supply and interest rates).

Influencing the nation's economy, not managing it. In contrast to planned economies, the U.S. government's role is largely indirect, but that does not mean an absence of state involvement. Even in the heyday of laissez-faire capitalism in the latter half of the nineteenth century, government played an active role by promoting railroad construction and industrial development. Adventurism in Latin America and elsewhere had a definite tie-in with private capital.

Production, employment and inflation are three critical concerns of the government. We are most familiar with the use of *fiscal* policy to affect them. By lowering taxes or increasing expenditures, we can stimulate production and employment. Depending on several factors, however, this may be inflationary. If the economy is overheated, higher taxes or reduced expenditures can have a cooling effect, but may also increase unemployment. Large federal budget deficits, in which the balance is shifted away from taxes and toward expenditures, has indirect effects on production, employment and inflation. The role of *monetary* policy, regulation of the money supply and interest rates, is less well known.

Monetary Policy

The unit charged with responsibility for monetary policy is the Federal Reserve Board, which directs the nation's central banking system. Through its twelve regional offices it supervises its member banks; since these include all of the major banks in the country the Fed has effective control over the nation's banking system. The Fed is well insulated from politics. The directors who sit on the board are appointed for overlapping fouteen-year terms, so no president can nominate a majority. The chairmen, who has a powerful role, serves for four years. However, Fed chairmen have a reputation for independence from the White House.

The money supply does not refer to the number of bills and coins that have been minted, though it affects the production of these. Rather, it is the amount of money in circulation at a given time: cash plus those things which can be quickly converted into cash, such as checking accounts. An increase in the money supply can stimulate production and employment, but if the money supply outruns the availability of goods and services, inflation may result.

The fed has three ways of regulating the money supply: by buying or selling government securities, raising or lowering the interest rates it charges to its member banks, or requiring that banks hold a larger amount of funds in reserve. These may sound more complicated than they really are.

Trading in Government Securities

There is always a market for these in the financial community and always people willing to sell them. So if the Fed offers treasury notes for sale, this has the effect of pulling money out of circulation, that is, reducing the money supply. If the Fed buys government securities, this increases the amount of money in circulation. This is the "quick fix" in monetary policy.

Raising or Lowering Interest Rates

Interest rates are the price of money. If interest rates are lowered, people are more likely to borrow money and less likely to want to put it into longterm investments. This will tend to expand the money supply. If interest rates are raised, this will tend to make the money supply contract. If the Fed charges more interest for the money it lends to its member banks, they in turn must charge more interest to businesses, home buyers and other borrowers.

The relationship between the money supply and interest rates is complex. It would seem as if an increase in the money supply would automatically depress interest rates, on the old supply and demand theory: a greater supply lowering prices. But a growth in the supply of money may work in just the opposite way. Financial institutions make decisions on the basis of expectations. Knowing that a rapid growth in the money supply is potentially inflationary, banks raise their interest rates in anticipation that the dollars they get back in the future from borrowers will be worth less than the dollars they lent.

Setting Reserve Requirements

The Fed requires member banks to hold a certain amount of their assets in reserve instead of lending them. This provides a cushion against an undue drain on the banks' resources. By raising the required reserve, the Fed can limit the amount of funds available for lending, thus restricting the money supply.

How you view the effect of different fiscal and monetary policies on the nation's economy will vary, depending on which theory you accept. In recent years three have been most prominent: Keynesian, supply-side and monetarist.

Keynes: demand-side economics.[5] Until the 1930s, most economists tended to think of national economies as operating like the private market: Everyone, at whatever level, wanted to maximize his or her interests (e.g., charge what the traffic would bear), and the ruling factors were supply and demand. That government was best which spent least. In the early years of the Depression, for instance, the emphasis was on cutting government spending, with the result that the problems of the economy were made worse.

John Maynard Keynes, the British economist, stood that theory on its head. The idea was to spend more public funds, not less, and lower taxes, to stimulate the economy. In particular, getting money into the hands of consumers through government transfer payments would give business a direct shot in the arm. Lowering taxes and increasing expenditures would cause a deficit, but, Keynes argued, that could be made up when the economy recovered by raising taxes and cutting back on spending. Keynes also favored lowering interest rates in order to encourage investment in industrial expansion. This was demand-side economics: Getting a sluggish economy moving by increasing the demand for goods and services. The apparent success of Keynesian economics during the Depression won this theory many converts.

In the early 1960s, John F. Kennedy used a combination of tax cuts and social welfare expenditures to get the economy out of the doldrums.[6] Again Keynes's theory seemed to work. Under Lyndon Johnson, demand-side economics helped fuel a long period of relative prosperity. But spending for the War on Poverty and war in Vietnam, without commensurate tax increases, heated up the economy to the point where inflation became a major problem.

---

[5]For more in-depth discussions, see Tobin (1982), Chick (1983), and Stein (1982).

[6]The following discussion draws upon Baumol and Blinder (1979), ch. 5, and Dornbusch and Fischer (1984), ch. 1.

By the 1970s the economy appeared to be caught on the horns of an insoluble dilemma: Control of inflation was being purchased at the price of higher unemployment. Stimulate the economy and you brought on more inflation; put a damper on it and the unemployment rolls would go up. Richard Nixon tried wage and price controls for a period; when these were relaxed, inflation shot up.

The wage and price controls came off about the time that this country and others were hit by an energy crisis caused by a shortage of oil and a series of crop failures around the world which forced up food prices. These "supply shocks" were something new. Not only were prices skyrocketing, but the shortages also were driving up unemployment. "Stagflation"—the combination of a stagnant economy and inflation—had arrived. Demand-side economics seemed unable to provide an answer.

Supply-side economics.[7] This theory is Keynesian economics in reverse. It, too, holds that fiscal policies can pull the economy out of a recession. Like Keynes, it calls for lowering of taxes; but rather than stimulating demand by increasing consumers' spending power, tax cuts are tilted toward higher income brackets to stimulate investment in business expansion. According to the theory, this will result in higher profits and employment, which will yield more in tax revenues than is lost by the original tax cuts. Government expenditures, meanwhile, should be cut, though not necessarily enough to avoid deficits. The deficits, like the slow pace of the economy, will be erased by the expanded business activity and resultant higher tax revenue. Also to expand the supply side, government regulation of industry should be reduced, freeing up the country's productive resources.

When the Reagan administration came into office in 1981, it adhered to the supply-side theory. But while it targeted major tax cuts to business investment, military spending rose rapidly and social security and other costs continued to rise. During Reagan's first two years in office, the country entered a severe recession; meanwhile the lower taxes without corresponding cuts in expenditures caused the federal deficit to balloon. Supply-side economics came under heavy criticism. However, in the ensuing years the economy came back vigorously, with a sharp decline in inflation, seeming to vindicate the theory. In economics, nothing succeeds like success. Just as many liberals were convinced that it was Keynesian economics that brought recovery from the Depression of the thirties, supply-side enthusiasts were sure that adherence to their theory brought about the resurgence in the eighties.

The monetarists.[8] Among those who have been skeptical of supply-side theory are the monetarists. Above all, they are concerned about the huge federal budget deficits which have become a regular feature of the Reagan years and the impact of these on interest rates and the value of the dollar in comparison with other currencies.

---

[7]An illuminating and very readable description of this theory can be found in Brooks (1982).
[8]For fuller discussions, see Friedman (1975) and Stein (1982).

For Keynesians, unemployment is the critical issue. For supply-siders, it is lack of business investment. But for monetarists the big problem is inflation. They see this as resulting from too much money chasing too few goods and services. Thus, the key to economic progress in their minds is slow, steady growth in the money supply. If it grows too fast, inflation will result. But if interest rates are pushed up too far, the money supply is restricted and as a result so is economic growth.

Like the supply-siders, monetarists prefer to bring down the deficit by reducing expenditures rather than raising taxes, but they are more open to consideration of a tax hike if that is necessary to cut the deficit. For both supply-siders and monetarists, unlike Keynesians, employment and consumer demand are the result of changes in more critical components of the economy, so should not be manipulated directly by government intervention. Thus, both of these schools are generally opposed to government employment and economic security measures. They believe demand-side stimulation through government social programs is counterproductive in the long run. What does one do in a period of recession, when large numbers of people are thrown out of work and the ranks of the poor grow? The supply-side and monetarist purists counsel against expansion of social welfare under any circumstances.

LIBERALS ON THE DEFENSIVE

Supporters of the welfare state were thrown on the defensive by events of the eighties. Keynesian theory—which had provided an economic rationale for social welfare provisions—was in disrepute among many economists. Concerned about scaling back federal budget deficits, liberals and conservatives alike were seeking to close the gap between taxes and expenditures. There was little talk of expanding social welfare, only which programs to be spared the axe. The Gramm-Rudman-Hollings deficit reduction amendment, which won overwhelming approval in Congress despite serious reservation among economists, expressed a pervasive sense of frustration.

Bedrock economic security programs, such as social security, food stamps and AFDC, were surviving relatively intact. Other social welfare provisions faced more difficult sledding. But the welfare state does not live by bread alone. In particular, social welfare policies concerned with controlling behavior considered dangerous by the majority continue to be an essential part of government. The means of control will vary, depending on who is being controlled and the dominant perspective in society. The next part of the book deals with the control of threatening behavior.

PART 3

Control of Threatening Behavior

Social control runs through all of social welfare policy. Economic security programs have rules and penalties, not just to prevent clients from getting an unfair share of benefits, but also to regulate their workforce activity and sex life. But certain social welfare policies have been targeted specifically on those who threaten the social order or societal values.

As we see in Chapter 7, the threats may have little to do with personal safety and protection of property. Organized deviance poses a special problem to a society more used to dealing with individuals. Mental illness is clearly different from knowing violation of the law, but treatment of the mentally ill has paralleled treatment of criminals throughout most of history. In both instances, society is trying to ward off threats.

The dynamics of the delivery process, through which policy impacts on target populations, is the focus of Chapter 8. We use mental health and corrections systems to look at general issues of service delivery. The gap between policy intent and policy in action is probably widest in these two fields, but they are different from other services only in the degree of the discrepancy.

The final chapter in this section traces the policy cycle: a process in which a social problem leads to the enactment of new policies, which are implemented by programs which in turn give rise to new problems. The case in point is closed institutions. Today's hopeful social invention becomes tomorrow's albatross. In this case the "albatross" is large closed institutions. The solution—deinstitutionalization—appears already to be heading into the "problem" category again. While these turns of the policy cycle may give the reformer pause to reconsider the original optimism, they should not dissuade us from our efforts to solve social problems.

Chapter 7

Crooks, Creeps
and Other Dangerous People

In thinking about social control of threatening behavior, our natural tendency is to focus on the behavior itself—how did it get that way and what can we do to limit or prevent it? There is no question about the need to understand as much as we can about behavior and to help people deal with impulses that get them into trouble, but if we are to understand social control *policies* we must step back and ask a different kind of question. Why do we have such policies? The obvious answer is, in order to protect the public from harm. Like most obvious answers, it is a misleading half-truth. It does not account for voluminous laws against behavior which appears to harm nobody but the perpetrator and often not that person, nor for imprisonments for a crime that is not possible to commit nor likely to be possible in the foreseeable future. It also fails to explain the extreme variations in what different societies at different times have considered to be in need of control.

THE MAN ON THE SUBWAY

The celebrated case of the man who opened fire on four teenagers in the New York subway in December, 1984, is as interesting for the public reaction it touched off as for the details of the event itself. Radio call-in talk shows—those barometers of our extremes of fear and anger—were bombarded with calls, the majority praising the man as a hero, many offering money to support his legal defense. The reaction quickly spread to the entire nation, as far away as Hawaii (*New York Times*, 1985a). In time the concern about armed vigilantes taking the law into their own hands surfaced, turning the issue into a controversy.

Should a man who is asked for money respond by shooting the people who make the request? You get one kind of answer if you ask the question that way. You get another if you say the incident took place on a subway train in New York. Another if you say the man was a 37-year-old Caucasian businessman and the persons he shot were black teenagers. Still another if you say the man shot two of the youths in the back and shot one twice. And again another if you say the four he gunned down had police records and three were carrying sharpened screwdrivers.

In social control, definition is critical—definition of what is considered unacceptable behavior and definition of the persons involved. The more closely a person fits the image of the societal mainstream, the more readily that person's behavior is condoned, both in public perception and in the way the law deals with it. The more marginal a person to society, the harsher the condemnation and the punishment (Black, 1976). If the subway incident had happened sixty or seventy years earlier, at the height of American prejudice against persons with German or German-sounding names, the fact that the man was Bernhard Hugo Goetz might have gotten a different reaction.

The police and news media are powerful determinants of public reactions. By repeatedly referring to the sharpened screwdrivers in the pockets of the teenagers and their criminal records, they cast the incident in one kind of light. By saying the man had carried a gun since being mugged in 1981 and had been active in organizing his neighbors against crime, they further define the situation. And by noting that the man glared at reporters, refused to answer their questions, called them "vultures," and, according to police, was joking one minute and somber the next, they redefine it.

These images are later examined and qualified by attorneys in the courtroom: Sharpened screwdrivers in some sectors of society may be a means of self-defense or a symbol of toughness; any person under arrest might react to questions from TV and newspaper reporters in angry silence. But the court of public opinion seeks certainty at the expense of subtlety.

Public officials often serve as crystallizers of public consensus at such times. The initial view of the New York subway incident presented by both the mayor of New York City and the president of the United States was that private citizens must not be allowed to take the law into their own hands but fear and anger which might lead to such a reaction are understandable and point to a need to curb crime in the streets (*New York Times*, 1985a, 1985b). Such "on the other hand" pronouncements reflect an ambivalence that has surrounded the control of threatening behavior throughout the history of the country.

In matters of social control, then, definition is a critical factor: how an act is defined and particularly how the actor is defined. Let us look at the way Americans have labeled those whom they have seen as threats to social order.

LABELS

It was the liberal reformers of the early nineteenth century who began to draw clear lines between categories of social deviants. If one was to change a person's conduct, it was necessary to describe the conduct in terms which distinguished it from other kinds of behavior. The insane needed not simply food and shelter but refuge from evil surroundings, a place to find order and tranquility (Rothman, 1971). In time elaborate categories of mental disorders would come into use. Though these classifications were the creation of the observer, they would take on the aura of objective reality.

The liberals of the Jacksonian era were as optimistic as their predecessors had been deterministic, and nowhere was their faith in the power of reason and human intervention more evident than in the case of children. It was important to separate the wayward from the merely dependent, for disobedience was a highly infectious disease, but both kinds of children could be expected to respond to a regimen of strict obedience, routine and hard work. The basic distinction between dependent and delinquent youth has continued into present usage, and in recent years a new term, "status offenders," has been used to identify those whose behavior would not be considered illegal if they were adults (Handler & Katz, 1982).

Labeling has had a central place in adult corrections. In the latter part of the nineteenth century, as convict labor became a cornerstone of penal policy, the potential for work became an important distinction (McKelvey, 1936, pp. 93-125). Historically, the seriousness of offenses and the potential for troublemaking have been used to classify prisoners. Probation and parole have required a more individualized approach to offenders, but the old tendency to place people in slots has continued to dominate the corrections field.

The Effects of Labeling

When society sets a group of people apart as "deviant" the label itself changes their status. They are excluded from the mainstream, whether by being housed away from the rest of society or simply denied entry into jobs, housing and other opportunities. This fact affects their own self-concept as well as the attitudes of "normal" people. According to some writers, the act of labeling is a more powerful factor in the person's later adjustment than the original "defect" that led to the labeling in the first place or the prison or hospital experience (Dinitz, Dynes & Clarke, 1969).

A man at work on a factory lathe suddenly stalks over to a co-worker and begins pummeling him. Others nearby rush in and grab the assailant, wrestle him to the ground and call for the foreman. Scenario A: The troublemaker is arrested for assault and battery. He claims that the co-worker has been picking on him. Scenario B: The troublemaker is taken to a mental hospital for observation. He claims that the co-worker has been picking on him. Depending on the opinions of a number of persons labeled as "experts," the man may become (1) a criminal or (2) a patient. He could become both and be housed in a hospital for the "criminally insane," but that is unlikely unless being processed by the official system leads him to more serious behavior.

If he is labeled as an "alleged offender" he will enter a world dominated by law and lawyers. He may be fined, perhaps put on probation. If his behavior is considered serious enough he may proceed into a world dominated by prison guards and later a parole officer who will require him to abide by certain rules of conduct. If the man is labeled "patient" he will acquire more labels—psychotic, unstable personality, emotionally disturbed, or the like. He will enter a world dominated by psychiatrists, psychologists, social workers and other treatment personnel. If he becomes an "inpatient" he will be dealing with psychiatric aides or attendants. His experience may be very similar to what it would be in dealing with prison guards, but he and they will be looked on differently, by each other and by society.

Suppose you had the choice of entering one or the other of these systems; which label would you choose? Being a "patient" would exempt you from fines and imprisonment and rules of probation and parole. But you would also give up certain protections; there would be limits on what a lawyer could do to protect your interests, and there would be no limit on the number of months or years you could be held in custody. Perhaps most important is how society would look on you after you left the official system; it would view an ex-offender differently from an ex-patient: "Seems O.K., but watch it—you know her record." As opposed to, "Did you notice the way she reacted to that other woman? A little strange, I'd say."

It should be clear from what has been said that whether a person is labeled in the first place—in other words, whether the initial entry to either system takes place—has major consequences for that person's life. And that is not just happenstance. According to legal specialist Donald Black (1976), the degree of integration into the mainstream has a direct bearing on the likelihood of a person's being labeled a deviant. One who is marginal to the society—for example a poor person or a member of a racial minority—is most likely to be subject to an official complaint. If the original complaint comes from an "integrated" party (a mainstreamer), it is most likely to be acted upon and result in a conviction. Black says there is a basic pecking order: The most "serious" violation of social standards is one in which a marginal person acts against a mainstreamer. Second in seriousness is action by one mainstreamer against another. Third is an act by one marginal person against another, and at the bottom is an act by a mainstreamer against a marginal person (Black, 1976, p. 54).

It is essential to add "other things being equal." A minor offense by a marginal person against a mainstreamer may be passed off lightly. On the other hand the shooting of four minority teenagers by a white businessman may be treated very seriously. But as a rule complaints from middle class suburbanites get prompter attention than complaints by inner city ghetto residents, and once in the criminal justice system low-income minority group members are the most likely to feel the full impact of the law. (See, for example, U.S., Commission on Civil Rights, 1966, pp. 511-607; Wicker, 1975; Wolfgang, Kelly & Nolde, 1962.) Yet the labeling process is ever changing.

Charles Rumbaugh's criminal career began with a break-in at age six. By twelve he had committed his first armed robbery, and he spent most of his life in jails, reform schools and mental hospitals. In 1985, at the age of 17, he was executed by the state of Texas for a murder committed in connection with an armed robbery. Prison officials were able to prevent two suicide attempts by Mr. Rumbaugh prior to his officially administered death.

The same issue of the *New York Times* that reported on Charles Rumbaugh's execution carried another story about a $25,000 fine levied against Eli Lilly & Company. Lilly pleaded guilty to misdemeanor counts of failing to notify the government about adverse reactions to Oraflex, an arthritis drug which has been implicated in the deaths of at least 26 persons in the United States. The company's former chief executive was fined $15,000 (*New York Times*, 1985d).

A Practice Becomes a Crime: Drug Abuse

We think of the late nineteenth and early twentieth centuries as a straitlaced time compared with today, but before 1915 the use of addictive drugs was widespread and one could buy any one of several opium derivatives at the corner drugstore without a prescription. It was not until the Harrison Act of 1915 that the use of narcotics became a crime nationwide. Even then it was several more years before authorities cracked down on the practice (Chein et al., 1964).

There were two major reasons for the relabeling of drug use: One was the effort by the medical profession to get control of the dispensation of narcotics, a major source of opiates being patent medicines which were peddled widely by the fast-talking salesmen of song and story. The other was Chinese immigration. Early in the nineteenth century the British actively promoted opium use along the China coast in order to create a market for trade. Prior to that the Chinese had need for little that the British could offer in exchange for prized tea and silk. The immigration from China followed a well-rehearsed script: Brought in as cheap labor in the latter half of the nineteenth century, the newcomers became the target of oppression when the job market dried up. Opium was the red flag under which the campaign to bar Asians from America's shores was organized. In similar fashion, Mexicans became associated with marijuana and blacks with cocaine (Helmer, 1975).

A Crime Becomes an Illness: Alcoholism

As the easy tolerance of drink in the early days of the Republic gave way to association of alcohol with pauperism, child neglect and a host of other problems, two attitudes emerged. One was moral outrage embodied in the temperance movement and the Anti-Saloon League of the late 1800s. The other was a quest for miracle cures. By the turn of the century every state had its Keely Institute for the treatment of drunkards. Keely's business acumen was better than his therapy, and the movement petered out soon after his death in 1900, leaving the field to the temperance forces (Lender & Martin, 1982).

The "prohibition" amendment to the Constitution (the eighteenth), was enacted in 1919, as the nation sought to recover from war conditions and reassert the old values. Though the amendment was repealed in 1933, in the eyes of the public the chronic alcoholic continued to be a social leper and the drunk tank in the local jail the proper treatment. By mid-century the popular culture was starting to present the problem drinker as a person with a problem, and the "disease" label became attached to the behavior (Dinitz, Dyne & Clarke, 1969, p. 215). Yet in this enlightened age, drunkenness is still the second most frequent criminal charge in the United States, the first being disorderly conduct. (U.S., Bureau of Census, Statistical Abstract, 1983, p. 183). It appears the public is still catching up with professional opinion.

An Illness Becomes a Life-Style: Homosexuality

Until 1973 homosexuality was officially labeled as a mental illness by the American Psychiatric Association (*New York Times*, 1973). The textbooks prior to that time described methods for curing this "psychosexual disorder." In this case, the life-style revolution of the late sixties, in which former taboos were coming out of the closet, appears to have preceded professional opinion.

With the emergence of AIDS (acquired immune deficiency syndrome) as a major health problem in the mid-eighties, the public definition of homosexuality appeared to be taking another turn, since male homosexuals were a primary risk group and thus a presumed source of contagion. With this as with all deviant behavior, the defining process is integrally related to perceived threats to public order and safety, but also to less obvious concerns.

Drug abuse and alcoholism are seen as greater menaces than that most addictive of all practices, cigarette smoking, though the health hazards of the latter are well known. A major reason for this apparent inconsistency is that cigarette smoking does not threaten two central values of society: order and work. Drug dependence in reality fails to live up to its violent reputation, though its illegal status and resultant high cost force some addicts into crime. But drug abuse interferes with workforce participation, as does drinking. Homosexuality came to be viewed as less of a threat as family forms changed and childbearing became a less central function, and then more of a threat because of AIDS.

THE SPECIAL THREAT: ORGANIZED DEVIANCE

Americans are most comfortable in dealing with wayward individuals. Aside from the greater power that groups can wield, it is harder to define the aberrant behavior of a number of persons together in the same way as we describe the lone deviant. Groups develop a common ideology that is more resistant to reform efforts than is true of the rationalizations of the disruptive individual. On a different level, we may all experience this when we "deviate" from the majority in a work or social situation. The individual student who takes issue with the conventional wisdom among her classmates can be written off as an oddball. But let one other student say, "You know, I see what Mary is saying, she really does make some sense," and the climate suddenly changes. Mary's views are legitimate; the majority may still believe she is wrong, but now they must deal with the substance of her arguments instead of just stigmatizing her.

On a national scale, organized crime has posed major problems for law enforcement authorities, partly because it *is* organized. In certain circles, leaders of organized crime may gain a measure of respectability or even hero status. Yet group deviance involving only a handful of people with very limited resources can also pose a special threat. This is most obvious in the case of revolutionary sects, such as the Weatherman Underground, whose alleged crimes included robbery and murder. But it is also true of radical groups which are not out to overthrow the government.

The Case of MOVE[1]

Vincent Leaphart dropped out of school after the third grade and was said to be unable to read or write, but that was not true of the people he attracted into his Philadelphia-based sect known as MOVE (not an acronym). They included a woman who was awarded a university scholarship, another who attended college for a time, and an accomplished jazz pianist who performed in places as far away as New Orleans. The man who co-founded MOVE with Leaphart, by then known as John Africa, was a white social worker, though Africa and most of his followers were black.

The rhetoric of the group was often rambling and disjointed, but its basic thrust was rejection of the corruptions of civilization. The members, all of whom adopted the surname "Africa," abstained from alcohol, drugs and meat and subsisted on raw food. A strong family bond united MOVE, which appeared at no point to number more than 25 members, and their child-rearing practices did not include physical punishment. Their values included hard work and self-dependence, and they believed that no person, including founder John Africa, should be considered above any other.

There was another side to this utopian community, one that brought them into conflict with society and led ultimately to their doom. MOVE took in stray animals—not only numerous dogs and cats but also rats. In the inner city neighborhoods the groups inhabited, these creatures and the attendant infestations of insect pests caused major health hazards. In two different locations, MOVE members mounted loudspeakers on the outside of their row homes and blasted their neighbors with obscenities and threats of violence at all hours of day and night.

Neighbors complained to officials and threatened to go to court to force them to deal with MOVE. But a sect like MOVE poses special problems for government authority.

The Official Response

The high visibility and espoused ideology of a group like MOVE raises issues of civil rights that are easier to ignore in the case of individual deviance. For

---

[1]The following account is based on articles appearing in the *Philadelphia Inquirer.*

every neighbor calling for the banishment of the nuisance, there were other voices—more remote from the immediate scene—counseling restraint, for fear of unwarranted official repression. In 1978, a police raid on a MOVE house that resulted in the death of one officer, many injuries and televised coverage of police beating up a MOVE member brought charges of police heavyhandedness. The fact that this action took place under the regime of the Mayor and former Police Commissioner Frank Rizzo, a longtime controversial figure accused of police brutality, especially against blacks, added to the criticism.

When the MOVE issue appeared headed for another confrontation in 1985, Wilson Goode, Philadelphia's first black mayor, was determined to avoid a re-enactment of the 1978 incident. In response to cries for a crackdown, Goode said the city lacked legal grounds for acting, and it was important not to violate one group's civil rights through illegal action on behalf of another's. Meanwhile, the MOVE house was being turned into an armed fortress. Eventually the pressure became too much. Amid complaints of robbery and criminal assault by MOVE members and rumors of possible vigilante action by their neighbors, the police laid seige to the compound in the early hours of May 13, 1985. With fire department water cannons trying to knock down a bunker on the roof, a gun battle between police and MOVE members went on throughout the day. Then at 5:27 P.M., a police helicopter dropped a bomb which touched off a fiery explosion. The firehoses were turned off while the flames spread, eventually killing eleven MOVE members including four children, destroying or severely damaging 60 other homes and leaving 240 persons homeless. The incident seriously damaged the image of Mayor Goode, who up to that time had seemed to live a charmed political life, and led to bitter recrimination between city officials.

The handling of the MOVE incident has been severely criticized, throughout this country and around the world, as a classic case of official overreaction. But attempts to deal with organized deviance always carry that potential—even where attacks on civilians by armed terrorists are involved. Small, dedicated groups have the power to disrupt the society around them, as much by the reactions they provoke as by their own tactics.

THE USES OF SOCIAL CONTROL

The threat of bodily harm or loss of possessions is the clearest reason for social control. In 1978 one out of every 83 homes was equipped with a burglar alarm; by 1985 the figure was one in eleven. There are six million registered handguns in the United States. Private citizens kill more felons with handguns than the police do. American businesses employ a million security guards—about twice the number of police officers (*Philadelphia Inquirer*, 1985). The fear of physical violence, armed robbery and burglary has grown rapidly in recent years, taking on elements of an epidemic.

The official crime rate went up between 1973 and 1975, down between 1975 and 1977, back up until 1980 and then down again from 1980 to 1982. We can anticipate that the trend will be downward in the coming years, not because people are nicer but because of age. About a third of all arrests are of persons between the ages of 18 and 24, and another fifth is accounted for by those under 18. These age groups will be declining as a percentage of total population between now and the year 2,000. The chances of being murdered are less than the probability of committing suicide and less than half the likelihood of dying in an automobile accident. The one exception is black males, who are more likely to be murdered than killed accidentally. Black and low income households are the ones most likely to be robbed. But the fear knows no bounds of race or class, and it keeps growing.

What Is It That Protects?

Placing somebody behind bars has the short-term effect of protecting the community, but most offenders are out on the street within months; even serious crimes may bring sentences running only a few years. Legal processes—necessary if the rights of the majority against arbitrary treatment are to be preserved—may actually place an alleged offender out in the community within hours of being arrested. The ultimate exclusion of an offender—execution—is supported more for its assumed deterrent value than simply removal of an immediate threat.

The issue of deterrence is argued endlessly. The evidence for concluding that punishment of one offender will discourage others from breaking the law is weak—weak enough so that social scientists have looked for other explanations of why societies subject their deviant members to penalties up to and including death. Of particular interest have been the extremes to which we have gone in punishing those who did *not* endanger life and property but simply violated public conceptions of moral behavior.

Protecting Public Morality

About thirty percent of all arrests are for acts that, if they hurt anybody, hurt the willing participants—activities such as prostitution, gambling and vagrancy. In a society that prides itself on defending individual freedom, why is officialdom so involved in people's private lives?

From colonial times forward, co-existing with the liberal concern for individual liberty, has been a belief in right living enforced through laws grounded in religious beliefs. To the Puritans of New England, sin was sin, whether or not it intruded on somebody else's turf. The list of forbidden acts was seemingly endless, and the punishments for even minor infractions were severe (Rothman, 1971, pp. 5-29). Nor were the young to be spared the wages of sin. Said the seventeenth century Calvinist Michael Wigglesworth, all sinners must endure the flames of eternal damnation, though God in his infinite mercy would allow those who died in infancy "the easiest room in hell" (1662). Tough love *in extremis*!

We no longer base most of our morality laws on religion, but the tradition of invading boudoirs and gambling dens and punishing people for what they consume has remained strong. When a practice continues after its original rationale has fallen by the wayside, one must ask what societal purposes it serves.

Basically these laws reaffirm to society that it shares a common set of beliefs, thus they serve as a means of social solidarity. Some sociologists have even claimed that those who violate morality laws, rather than undermining the social order, are necessary to it, for they help to unite the majority in their condemnation of evil (see Durkheim, 1972, pp. 126-127; Schur, 1965). As we saw in the case of drug abuse, the criminal labeling process may serve other, unstated uses. For example, disorderly conduct and vagrancy laws have allowed the police to harass all sorts of nonconformists in ways that the Constitution would ordinarily forbid (Kadish, 1967).

From the beginning, Americans were a bundle of contradictions when it came to morality: oppressive strictures in the settled places and license on the frontier; totalitarianism in the name of freedom; chattel slavery in the land of the free. Selectively enforced, morality laws have allowed us to have our cake and eat it, too.

The Victims of "Victimless" Crime

The real victims of morality offenses are the alleged perpetrators, who are vulnerable to many kinds of abuse. Prostitutes are often kept in a state bordering on servitude. Gamblers mortgage themselves and their property to loan sharks. The cost of drug use is escalated by its illegal status. In the prohibition era the country discovered that legislating against the use of alcohol spawned an epidemic of secondary crimes. Organized crime syndicates worth millions of dollars are dependent on morality laws for their prosperity. Their ability to make sizeable pay-offs, together with the vulnerability of persons who must hide their vices from public view, lead to widespread exploitation and official corruption (Schur, 1965).

Restraining the Majority

One reason for encasing public sentiments in a legal framework is to protect the deviant. Public mortification in a trial and imprisonment, it can be argued, is better than the lynch mob's rope. Whether this restraining function is worth the price in terms of stripping whole classes of people of their dignity and civil rights is another question.

In Denmark following World War II, thousands of persons were imprisoned for activities that were not a crime when they happened and could not be repeated in the foreseeable future. These were the collaborators with the Germans during the occupation. The laws under which they were prosecuted were enacted after the war (Christiansen, 1968). The crimes—including business dealings with the enemy and service on the police force—could only occur again if Denmark were reoccupied by a hostile power, an event the lawmakers were not expecting to happen. So neither protecting the public from tangible harm nor deterring would-be collaborators was involved. But imprisoning the offenders for two, three or in some cases four years symbolized the nation's unity in its outrage while holding the full expression of the outrage in check.

CONTROL OF THE INNOCENT: THE MENTALLY DISABLED

Mental illness as a kind of disease is a twentieth century invention, but since biblical times societies have recognized as a special class those whose behavior could not be explained rationally. Whatever the label—possessed, lunatic, insane, disturbed—it always carried the connotation that one could not be held responsible for one's acts. So the ways of dealing with such persons varied widely. At one time, God might be thought to be speaking through the person, so special powers were attributed. More frequently it was the devil who was believed to be doing the speaking, leading to unspeakable cruelty. Reactions in the American colonies ranged from the persecution of alleged witches to lumping the indigent insane with other indigents, simply in need of care (Dinitz, Dynes & Clarke, 1969, p. 457; Rothman, 1971, pp. 30-56). The exemption from personal responsibility is the basis for the insanity defense, which dates from medieval criminal law and came into wide use in this country during the nineteenth century. Likewise, mental illness makes a person "unemployable," thus outside the standard expectations of work and self-support. Here the labeling process serves a dual purpose: protecting certain classes of people from the full weight of social responsibility, while protecting the integrity of the standards by setting apart from "normal" society those who are so exempted (Smith, 1981).

Unlike criminals, the mentally ill arouse in others the fear that they, too, may succumb. The very unpredictability and abnormality of their behavior sometimes pushes one into a psychotic-like response in trying to communicate. By isolating the mentally ill and viewing them in non-human terms (the early psychiatrists were "alienists"), society has been able to ward off the fear of contamination.

Not surprisingly, the labeling has served a scapegoating function. Witches were women, strange or old women—women, moreover, who had carnal lust in their hearts (Rosen, 1968, p. 13). Thus was a rigidly moralistic, male-dominated society able to evade its darker impulses.

The Labelers

The ways in which the mentally ill have been defined over the centuries have depended very much on who was doing the defining. In colonial America it was the clergy, so the labeling was in religious terms. In the early nineteenth century, as the church began to lose its hold on secular life in America, reformers redefined the problem. Insanity was believed to be among the more curable of human disorders. Isolate the afflicted from the debilitating influences of normal society, place them under firm discipline lovingly administered, keep them busy, and they would readily return to a state of good health (Rothman, 1971, pp. 130-154).

As these facile assumptions gave way to hard reality in the latter part of the nineteenth century, the mentally ill were again seen as aliens to be avoided. Psychiatry at this time was a lowly art within the medical community, concerned mainly with running large institutions. By the turn of the century the mainstream of medicine was moving toward a new level of scientific sophistication and public respect, accentuating psychiatry's second-class status. Psychiatrists began to shift their sights from the large hospital to the private clinic and a more respectable clientele (Grob, 1983).

So the mentally ill came to be looked on as a number of distinct populations. The aging patient wasting away in the back wards of a state hospital had little in common with the middle class young adult suffering from emotional distress. Dissatisfaction with the hospitals was growing, but it was not until mid-century that the chronically disabled would again be seen as fit company for the rest of society. The evolution of care of the mentally ill into and out of the closed institution is traced in Chapter 9.

The Developmentally Disabled

The group of mental casualties whose status has been most marginal has been those labeled feeble-minded, retarded, and now developmentally disabled. Of little interest to psychiatry, they have tended to be written off by a society oriented to solving problems rather than managing them. In recent years professionals trained in behavior modification have introduced new ways of preparing many developmentally disabled persons for life in the normal community.

THE ROLE OF GOVERNMENT IN SOCIAL CONTROL

Given Americans' aversion to big government, it is not surprising that social control was originally looked on as a local responsibility. Only as towns and counties couldn't afford control measures did they turn to the states and finally the federal government.

The first intrusion onto the local turf came in the early nineteenth century, when the reformers were able to convince the public that large asylums held the answer to crime and insanity. It was one thing for a community to operate an almshouse or a jail, but the imposing castles within which the fallen would be rehabilitated required state resources. Thus state-wide and regional penitentiaries and insane asylums signaled a break-through. The federal government proved to be a tougher challenge.

The Pierce Veto

The crusade of Dorothea Lynde Dix to get states to erect mental hospitals is described in Chapter 9. The capstone of her efforts was to be a federal law under which the government would sell ten million acres of public lands and use the proceeds to help states build hospitals. After a number of setbacks both houses of Congress passed the bill, in 1854, only to have it vetoed by President Pierce (Trattner, 1984, pp. 66-67). His argument: Such a move would intrude on the powers of the states and would set a bad precedent; if the federal government supported the care of the indigent insane, what was to prevent it from supporting the indigent who were not insane? It took eighty more years and a Great Depression to overcome his argument.

Pierce's action was full of ironies. The federal government had been *giving* large parcels of land to the railroads and canal builders in the name of economic expansion. There was a more immediate precedent: proceeds from the sale of federal lands had already been earmarked for schools for the deaf. In fact, Dix tried to capitalize on that initiative by adding 2,225,000 acres for services to the deaf, to her own bill (Deutsch, 1949; Tiffany, 1891).

Pierce's veto seemed to settle the issue, and it was another half century before the federal government became involved in regulating the lives of its citizens. Americans have always been most sensitive about the police powers of government, and so the attorney general in Theodore Roosevelt's cabinet waited until Congress had adjourned in 1908 before setting up what was eventually to become the Federal Bureau of Investigation. The occasion was a scandal over fraud in the sale of public lands in the West. In subsequent years the range of interstate activity increased and with it the scope of the FBI's bailiwick (Cook, 1964, pp. 49-52). In the Red scares of the twenties and fifties and civil rights struggles of the sixties, the Bureau's surveillance activities involving private citizens and political organizations made it the center of controversy.

The Harrison Act of 1914, against drug use, and the Volstead Act of 1919, banning alcohol consumption, were occasions for wider involvement of the federal government in personal behavior. Ironically, it has been groups most identified with resistance to "big government" that have pushed the hardest for the expanded police powers of the federal establishment.

The Welfare State and Social Control

After World War II the federal government moved into several new areas involving control of deviant behavior. The large number of psychological casualties in the war and a heightened public awareness of mental health paved the way for passage of the National Mental Health Act of 1947. Grants-in-aid to the states led to rapid expansion of community mental health services, with funding jumping from $5.5 million in 1948 to nearly ten times that amount in the next decade (Kurtz, 1960, p. 386). The movement was greatly accelerated in 1963 with the passage of the Community Mental Health Centers Act.

The mounting concern about juvenile gang violence in the 1950s prompted the Kennedy administration to set up the President's Committee on Juvenile Delinquency in 1961. With strong backing from the top, the professional staff urged action to address the underlying causes of delinquency rather than focus on youth control. A wide-ranging program on New York's Lower East Side called Mobilization for Youth became the prototype for other efforts in cities around the country. The focus shifted from delinquency per se to poverty and barriers to employment and education, culminating in the War on Poverty (Moynihan, 1969).

By the seventies, the momentum for social change had petered out and attention was once again on control. The Juvenile Justice and Delinquency Prevention Act of 1974 was basically an attempt to divert young offenders from the justice system and bring in more enlightened correctional practices. Even more directly focused on the control of crime and delinquency was the Omnibus Crime Control and Safe Streets Act of 1968. Its aim was to make local law enforcement more effective and the judicial process more efficient, but it also sought to reintegrate ex-offenders into the community and prevent crime (Dolgoff & Feldstein, 1984, pp. 216-217).

The rhetoric of safe streets, delinquency and crime prevention made these initiatives palatable to a public increasingly apprehensive about crime, but the programs that emerged under these policies were a mixture of enlightened control measures and attacks on underlying causes such as racism and poverty. It was the welfare state's answer to society's demand for protection. The agency that administered the Omnibus Crime Control Act of 1968 was the Law Enforcement Assistance Administration. It was phased out in 1982, at a time when the country was moving toward more direct confrontation with threatening behavior and away from many of the liberal initiatives in the fields of mental health and corrections.

SOMETIMES THERE ARE MISTAKES[2]

Society can never undo what it did to Charles Daniels. In September, 1978, he was arrested on charges of having sexually assaulted a two-year-old boy and thrown him off the roof of an apartment building. The only witness of the episode was a ten-year-old boy who gave conflicting testimony and it later turned out was under treatment for an emotional disturbance. Other witnesses placed Daniels elsewhere at the time of the attack. But he was convicted and sentenced to prison.

Child molesters are the single most endangered species in prison. Daniels was not aware of that, so when asked what he was in for he told other inmates. From then on he was a marked man. During pre-trial detention his clothes were set

---

[2]The following is based on newspaper accounts.

afire, he was beaten unconscious and scalded with boiling water while he slept. Later, convicted and sentenced to the maximum 18 years imprisonment (the two-year-old had by then recovered from his injuries), Daniels was told by a prison guard that there was a "contract" or death warrant out on him. He was transferred from prison to prison for his own protection, but each time the inmate grapevine followed him. "I'd be in my cell at night and from some place in the tiers I'd hear someone say: 'We got a baby-killer in our midst and someone is going to take care of him.'" He was placed in solitary confinement for his own protection, unable to use the prison library and recreational facilities.

In 1982 an appelate court reversed the original conviction. It was charged that the police had withheld evidence that might have cleared the defendant. There was even question that the two-year-old had been thrown off the roof or had been sexually assaulted by an adult. In 1985 New York City agreed to pay Mr. Daniels $600,000 for damages in an out-of-court settlement. But nobody can ever really pay him back for what happened to him.

The criminal justice system operates on the basis of presumed innocence. The burden of establishing guilt is on the state. When there is sufficient doubt the person is set free. Daniels's punishment began before he was convicted. Society becomes incensed at crimes such as sexually assaulting a baby and throwing him off the roof. Then the legal niceties can get lost, and the informal system of police rage and inmate rage can take over. The legal system probably lets a lot of guilty people go free, or get off with what amounts to a slap on the wrist. Every one of us reacts to such mistaken applications of the presumption of innocence. But then there are the other mistakes, like the case of Charles Daniels.

Chapter 8

Translating Policy Into Practice

A chaplain in a training school for delinquent boys noticed that when an aggressive inmate beat up on a more passive one, it was the victim who was placed in a detention cell. A study of a state mental hospital showed that the ward attendants had more power to decide the course of treatment for the patients than the doctors did. In 1977 a federal judge ordered that an institution for the mentally retarded be closed down. Six years later it was still open.

These are a few of the odd twists one finds as social welfare policies are translated into delivered services. Though policies to control threatening behavior are especially prone to being distorted on the way to the consumer, they are by no means unique in this regard. As we saw in Chapter 5, even as regulations are written by executive departments to carry out legislative intent, new elements are added and old ones changed. This happens every step of the way to the point of actual delivery.

In this chapter we focus on what is at once the most hidden and the most exposed part of the process: the service delivery system itself. Consumers of services are most painfully conscious of the lapses between policy rhetoric and staff behavior, but often they are too weak or intimidated to do anything about them. Meanwhile, the general public is aware of the discrepancies only when a catastrophe occurs and the dirty linen is trotted out on the six o'clock news. But such crises have a way of losing their punch very fast, and then we go back to business as usual and trust officialdom to know what it is about.

Attica Revisited

On September 9, 1971, inmates at Attica State Prison in upstate New York revolted and took a number of hostages. The prisoners complained to outside observers about bad food, lack of medical treatment, lack of recreation, lack of meaningful work assignments, and brutalizing and degrading conditions of life. The facility, intended to house 1,600 inmates, had a population of 2,250. On September 13 state police moved in to take back possession of the prison; 43 persons died in the process. Humbled by the ordeal, state officials vowed to improve conditions at Attica (Wicker, 1975).

Twelve years later Prisoners' Legal Services of New York issued a report declaring that conditions at Attica State Prison had deteriorated to "an emergency situation" and citing a pervasive atmosphere of racism, brutality and institutional indifference. The facility, meant to house 1,700 prisoners, had an inmate population of 2,200. The previous year the U.S. Justice Department, investigating charges of brutality at Attica, gave the prison a clean bill of health (*New York Times*, 1983b).

Death in Queens[1]

What is known is that Roberto Venagas died on March 5, 1984, of asphyxiation due to a crushed throat. He was a patient in the Secure Unit of Creedmoor State Hospital in Queens, New York City. Following the incident a therapeutic aide was indicted on charges of second-degree manslaughter, the Secure Unit was closed, its supervising psychiatrists transferred to jobs involving no patient contact, and federal, state and city investigations of the facility were launched. Venagas had been in a straight jacket for several hours up to the time of death, and a witness claimed to have seen him struck in the neck with a blackjack.

This was not the first time Creedmoor or its high security facilities had been in the news. In July, 1978, the New York State comptroller reported loose controls over the use of psychotherapeutic drugs at Creedmoor and two other state hospitals. Of 5,400 patients surveyed, a fourth had received more than one drug simultaneously in violation of state guidelines. The state mental health commissioner said efforts were underway to tighten the administration of medications at state psychiatric facilities. Earlier that year a court suit had been brought charging that patients in the high-security unit of Creedmoor were not receiving proper care.

In 1980, the director of Creedmoor complained in a letter to the editor of the *New York Times* that dangerous patients were being placed in his facility, which was not equipped to handle them. A few months later the hospital administration was criticized for laxness in allowing dangerous patients to leave the grounds with insufficient supervision. In 1981, New York Governor Hugh Carey backed off of a proposal to use vacant facilities at Creedmoor to house state prison inmates, after protests by the community. However, the Secure Unit for violent males went into operation.

The Secure Unit was closed in March 1984, following the death of Roberto Venagas. State mental health officials said it would be reopened by the end of that summer, after staff were retrained. By that time, presumably, the heat would be off, and everybody would be thinking about other things like the summer Olympics and the vice-presidential campaign of Geraldine Ferraro, the congressperson from Queens, where Creedmoor is located. Everybody, that is, except the people unlucky enough to work or live in the Secure Unit.

Who is to blame for the Secure Unit? The therapy aide alleged to have killed the patient? The supervising psychiatrists in the unit? The executive director of Creedmoor? The state mental health commission? The governor? The legislature? The voters? All of the above? None of the above?

---

[1]The following account is based on newspaper stories.

Why Doesn't Somebody Do Something?

Have you ever wished that just for a few hours you were in charge of some bureaucracy that was complicating your life? What ineptness! Can't they see that the staff is not doing its job? Why do they use all those extra forms when one would do? And why are the people with pull allowed to jump the line instead of being treated like everybody else? Just put us in charge and we'd straighten things out. Or would we? Countless people—some of them very experienced— have accepted the challenge of "straightening out" an organization only to discover that it is not that simple. Every decision, it seems, hinges on three others, and the people who are supposed to make those decisions somehow never do it quite the way you would. Give into the temptation to do everything yourself, and you find you never have time to make all those wonderful changes. This is the world of formal organizations.

Translators or Interpreters?

The title of this chapter, "*Translating* Policy Into Practice," might better have been called "*Interpreting* Policy in Practice." The French boxer, Marcel Cerdan, who later died in an air crash, once visited a New England community with a large French-speaking population. He was interviewed on a local radio station. The interviewer would ask Cerdan a question in French, and the boxer would answer in one or two words, whereupon the announcer would launch into a colorful monologue in English lasting for more than a minute. Next question, next laconic response in French, and again a very long presentation of the answer in English. The announcer was asked why Cerdan had answered the questions so briefly and the English translation had run on and on. "Some people are translators," he said, "I'm an interpreter."

So let us speak of *interpreting*. In order to understand the process, we need to know the language of organizations. And for that we will look at the concept of the social system.

SERVICE DELIVERY ORGANIZATIONS AS SOCIAL SYSTEMS

A system is any set of interrelated parts. A *social* system is a set of social units (individuals, for example) in interaction with one another. As the parts interact over time they become dependent on each other, and the system as a whole interacts with other systems in the same way (See Meehan, 1968; Anderson & Carter, 1974). You can see this in relation to a family. A man and woman decide to live together. Each finds the life together different from the way life was before. They work out ways of doing necessary tasks, each one having primary responsibility for certain tasks, and in the process come to depend on each other. Their mutual expectations help to stabilize their relationship as well as their dealings with the outside world. Each of them has been changed by the experience. They are operating as a social system.

The woman becomes pregnant and gives birth to a daughter. Now we have a system made up of three persons instead of two—not to mention the aunts, uncles and grandmothers. The daughter is strongly influenced by her parents, of course but so are they by her arrival. Where are cause and effect? The daughter is not *the* cause of the parents' behavior, nor are they *the* cause of hers. Instead, each element in the system is both cause and effect, as are their relations with their environment.

A second child is born and now the system shifts again. The family is under severe economic pressure (outside systems impacting) and this, along with the reactions of family members, leads to tension between the man and the woman and eventually he walks out. What was *the* cause of his departure? It was a combination of things, perhaps including his early life experiences in tolerating stress. Family members will try to figure out *the* cause: If only I hadn't complained so much, says the wife. If only I hadn't been born, says the daughter, or if only brother hadn't been born. If only your man were more like us, say the woman's relatives.

Later on the daughter has problems in school. Broken family, says the teacher. Or, what can you expect from their kind? But a better answer will come from considering all the elements in the system, as well as outside influences that affect it. Not only do we want to understand why things have happened, but out of this see what ought to be changed. What are strategic factors that could do most to affect the problem?

The kinds of organizations that deliver social services are also social systems, but they differ from families in several ways. One of the most important differences is that the consumers—the people who receive the services—are not the same as the ones who provide the services. Family members both make the system go and get the benefits of what the family produces. When provider and consumer are separate entities a new element is introduced. The staff person and the client have different ideas about what is needed and how best to provide it. The organization operates under rules—its own and others imposed on it from elsewhere—rules that the consumer has no part in making.

The sheer complexity of service delivery systems—even small ones that provide a limited number of services—affects how staff members and clients deal with each other. Through an intricate set of exchanges with outside systems, the service delivery system obtains the resources it needs in order to function. It also needs internal mechanisms for converting those resources into services.

The system needs resources . . .	. . . which it uses internally . . .	. . . to produce services.
— Social sanction	— Goals	
— Money, etc.	— Roles	

The system needs resources . . .	. . . which it uses internally . . .	. . . to produce services.
— Information — Clientele	— Relationships — Sentiments — Norms	

Resources

In order to get the resources that allow it to function the organization must exchange things with other systems. In this as in all things, there is no free lunch. *Social sanction*—the right to provide services—comes from law or an administrative agency or a board of directors. Aside from the official sanction, the surrounding community may give or withhold the right to function. For instance, neighborhood residents sometimes pressure a traditional social agency to be more responsive to local concerns. In order to earn social sanction, the organization has to show that it is carrying out the expectations of the sanctioners. When two or more sanctioning bodies have different ideas about what is needed, the organization can find itself in a bind.

Money and other material resources are the most obvious requirement for service delivery systems. In theory the organization must show that it is delivering the goods if it hopes to keep the money flowing. In practice that rule is often violated. A counseling agency may be able to convince funding sources that it is providing a useful service without much tangible evidence of success. Conversely, in recent years cutbacks in federal funds have undermined agencies that provide concrete help to many families and individuals in need.

Information includes both content of communication and staff expertise. The *content* may concern money sources, policy changes or consumer needs. The organization must give information to get information. It may also have to show that it can be trusted not to divulge secrets. If it hopes to attract the right kind of *staff expertise*—for example, professional personnel—it must offer enough pay and satisfactory working conditions. It may also need to provide professionally rewarding work.

Clientele may not be thought of as a resource, but without enough of the right kind of consumers the agency would fold up. The "exchange" can be one-sided, however, because clients often have no choice but to take what is offered. That comes through very clearly in both corrections and mental health. But, as we shall see presently, even captive consumers are not without power.

THE TOPSY-TURVEY WORLD OF A STATE MENTAL HOSPITAL

When sociologist Ivan Belknap (1956) went to study a state mental hospital, it had just been through a reorganization. Within a year the old informal ways of operating reasserted themselves. The hospital had been through several reform efforts. Each one had failed. The more Belknap probed into the dynamics of the organization, the more differences he found between the way it was supposed to function and what actually existed. He was discovering the *informal organization*, the unstated part of the system.

Here is the way the system was supposed to operate:

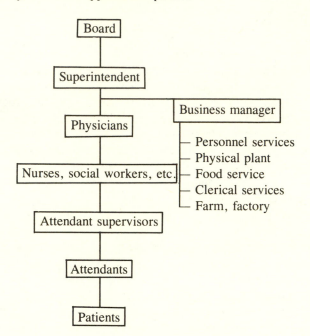

In fact, Belknap found three basic systems that looked like this:

A	B	C
Custodial system:	*Maintenance system:*	*Medical-psychiatric system:*
Attendant supervisors	Business manager	Physicians
Attendants	Physical plant, etc.	Other professionals

Informally, each of these systems had its own direct channel to the superintendent. Furthermore, the most important system was System A and the least important System C. As between keeping order in the institution and rehabilitating patients, it was the former that had primacy. On paper, the attendant supervisors were supposed to go through channels to communicate with the superintendent: Report to the nurse in charge, who will report to the clinical director, etc. In actuality attendant supervisors bypassed this chain of command. This "inappropriate" practice was not only tolerated but encouraged by the superintendent, because what was important to him was learning quickly of potential trouble on the wards.

The group that actually ran the hospital consisted of the superintendent and his assistant, the attendant supervisors, the business manager and the personnel manager. The reason the business manager was part of the ruling coterie is not hard to determine. It was he who helped run the operation on a sound fiscal basis and keep costs down. The personnel manager was important in maintaining a stable staff complement to operate the facility.

This system "worked" in the sense that it was able to keep external resource systems happy. The fact that informal practices may have undermined treatment goals was of concern to the professionals, but treatment was secondary to the survival of the hospital as a system. If patients did or did not get well, who in the general population would know or care? If patients escaped and terrorized the surrounding community or if the hospital showed a deficit, legislators would start asking tough questions.

The Internal System

Inside the organization, goals, roles, relationships, sentiments and norms are the fuel that make things go. Different subgroups in the system may have their own ideas about the *goals* of their efforts. The doctors, nurses and social workers in the state hospital in Belknap's study had one set of priorities while the superintendent, the business manager and the attendants each had their own. Administrators have to strike some kind of balance and get different groups within the organization to submerge their own special interests enough to work together. The power of different subgroups is a major determinant of which goals are at the top of the agenda.

The *roles* of system members are both assigned tasks and unofficial expectations. In Belknap's hospital it was the role of professional staff to make decisions about ward life and release of patients, but informally the attendants had taken over part of this role.

Roles should not be thought of in isolation; system members come to depend on each other, so that my ability to perform my role hinges on the way you perform yours. These *relationships* among roles are what link the parts of the system together and make it a working whole. They are also a major reason why it resists change. If everybody is dependent on everybody else to keep doing the same things in the same way, it takes a powerful force to break up these patterns. Yet there are strains in every relationship. Someone feels left out of important decisions, passed over for promotion or exploited by a co-worker. When people with different attitudes and values come into the system, they don't leave all this baggage at the doorstep. Doctors tend to dominate other staff in hospitals partly because doctors tend to be dominant in the outside world.

So relationships in organizations are a mixed bag. They make it possible for the members to work together but also continually pull at the edges of the organizational fabric. The cement that holds the organization together is shared *sentiments* and *norms*. Sentiments are feelings and attitudes. Norms are feelings and attitudes with a supporting ideology: We *should* feel such-and-such a way about the organization, our work, each other and the clients.

As with roles, the norms are both official and unofficial. The manual says probation officers should respect the dignity of probationers. Old heads in the department may tell the new officer, "Forget that garbage. Those kids won't listen to you unless you take them down a peg and let them know who's boss." Prison guards learn that the rules against use of force are for the orientation class but if they try to follow the book on the cell block they will be punished by their fellow guards.

Rewriting the Rule Book

During one crackdown by state authorities, Creedmoor State Hospital administrators worked out a reform plan in a 14-page memo. Therapy aides were to be trained in self-protective tactics; a crisis-intervention team would be set up to handle outbursts; therapists would organize "anger management" classes to help patients control their behavior; regular outdoor exercise would help drain off patients' tension.

A three-week self-defense seminar for staff was held once. The outdoor exercise didn't happen. The crisis-intervention team wasn't organized. While lower echelon staff tried to cope with the situation, their bosses stayed in their offices, according to reports. In the garrison mentality inside the Secure Unit, aides brought in blackjacks and made their own rule book. Patients became the enemy. A staff member witnessing two aides beating up a patient—one holding him while the other punched him—was told, "If you squeal on us we can always be slow in coming to your aid." Nobody wanted to be abandoned by fellow staffers in that violent atmosphere.

In the hospital studied by Belknap the ward attendants had a major source of power: direct access to the patients. They were with them around the clock and on weekends. They could decide who got to see the doctor or the social worker and were the ones who passed on information to the professionals about different patients' behavior. They had their own system for classifying the people under their charge. The most disruptive or withdrawn were at the bottom of the pecking order, while the most "normal" and cooperative won favored status. Despite their illness, many patients catch on to such informal ranking systems and learn to go along in order to get along. The attendants were operating out of their own priorities; they needed an orderly ward.

It is not just bottom-echelon personnel who informally "rewrite" policy. A juvenile training school, according to Pennsylvania state regulations, is "a twenty-four hour group care facility which provides care, treatment and rehabilitation for children whose patterns of behavior constitute a danger to themselves or to the community." A series of investigations touched off by a fatal fire in a detention cell of a Pennsylvania training school in 1973 revealed conditions that were anything but therapeutic. For such offenses as playing in the dorm, making noise, talking back to staff or spitting on the floor, children were placed in isolation for periods ranging from 24 hours to several weeks. Wrote a graduate student who spent several months at this facility, "Although Pennsylvania law (dating back to 1850) provides that prisoners be kept comfortably warm, our cells have no radiators, and the only heat a youngster has is the heat which seeps through a three-by-twelve-inch hole in the door of his cell" (*Child Abuse at Taxpayers' Expense*, 1974, p. 12).

Such practices are justified with professional jargon. The therapeutic intent of detention cells was described by this school's administration in the following terms:

> . . . the kinds and degree of symptomatic behavior and adjustment patterns associated with the "delinquent" personality dictate the *necessity* for an isolation area. . . . [Inmates] who are unwilling or unable to exercise minimal and appropriate control over themselves . . . can be emotionally and physically *protected* from themselves. . . . [Isolation] can be utilized to confront a student with himself, his behavior, his need for isolation, his need to develop his own limits and controls, and the implication this has for his total development process. (*Child Abuse at Taxpayers' Expense*, 1974, pp. 16-17)

Though some of the most glaring distortions of policy occur behind the walls of closed institutions, they can't be avoided in any service delivery system. The 1963 Mental Retardation and Community Mental Health Construction Act was intended to move away from the medical model of psychiatric treatment, toward community problem-solving and prevention (NIMH, 1966). Here was an attempt to reform practice in mental health facilities that relied for their professional leadership on psychiatrists schooled in traditional techniques.

The vehicle for reform within the community mental health centers was to be the consultation and education (C&E) unit. These units hired social workers and others whose bent was toward prevention, social instead of psychological factors, and political activism. They personified the spirit of the new policy emphasis (Perlmutter, 1980).

Policy in operation was different from policy in theory. First of all, the federal directives were so vague that they could be interpreted in different ways (Adler, 1982). Secondly, while the C&E units were led by activists, they were under the authority of the center directors, who were psychiatrists. C&E directors discovered that they had to modify their reading of policy in order to adjust to their superiors' views. They found themselves being drawn into lengthy struggles for survival. Some quit. Some stayed on to fight for a watered-down version of reform. The psychiatrists who headed up the community centers had an unclear mandate from Washington and the power to resist change. The 1963 law did bring about changes, but the reality of policy at the delivery end was not the abstractions of policy in the original bill.

Specialization of work has been a major factor in advancing the field of mental health, but it also creates conflicts in the workplace. In the psychiatric emergency room of a large city hospital, the clerical staff was making professional decisions and the nursing staff kept getting into fights with secretaries and social workers over issues of turf. Who was responsible for making which decisions regarding the patients? Though supposedly everybody in the unit was there to help patients, the latter often seemed to take a back seat to the rivalries between staff groups. The nurses expressed their concern in terms of medical decisions being made by people who were not qualified to do so, but underneath were other issues. Said one informant,

> To have a good working relationship with all disciplines, a nurse is expected to bend over backwards. . . . We have actually been formally told to hold back and let others—paraprofessionals and clerical people—become more secure in their professions . . . but I don't feel like putting my light under a barrel in order to enhance someone else's prestige. I am competent, I have a contribution to make, and it is both a tremendous professional and personal sacrifice to stand back. (Miller, Mailick & Miller, 1973, p. 29)

Dilemmas of the Individual Worker

In the last analysis, service delivery is what goes on between a worker and a client or group of clients. No policy can dictate that completely, and workers have a lot of leeway in defining policy—usually more than they imagine. This gives the individual worker considerable power. The power is rarely used to influence policy, because most workers don't organize regarding policy issues. They usually react in terms of how a policy affects them personally, not the larger social implications. In Chapter 15 are accounts of cases in which social workers did affect policy by united action.

Sociologist Michael Lipsky (1980) says there are built-in dilemmas for what he calls "street-level bureaucrats"—public servants whose work brings them in direct contact with consumers, for example social workers, teachers, police officers and health care workers. The policy makers send conflicting messages down to the street-level bureaucrat: help/control the client; be humane/punitive; give/withhold public resources. And the policy makers never provide enough resources to do the job. In fact, when the resources expand, the caseload increases, perpetuating the shortage of support (see Richan, 1978, pp. 243-259).

Professional social workers in probation and parole run into conflicts between their professional values and the demands of the job. Trained to work with clients seeking help with problems, in settings with low emphasis on formal authority, they are instead forced to deal with hostile clients who want none of their services and with an agency which is control-oriented (Ohlin, Piven & Pappenfort, 1956).

Street-level bureaucrats find various ways of adapting to these demands. Therapy aides in a high-security psychiatric unit carry blackjacks and wage counter-terror campaigns against the patients. Guards in a prison collaborate with inmate leaders to maintain order. Police officers selectively enforce the law and maintain an impenetrable wall of secrecy around certain aspects of their work. Social workers give ground on the rules when dealing with assertive clients and crack down on the more passive ones. And characteristically the street-level bureaucrats try to avoid trouble with the organization. They try to read the informal as well as the formal rules on how to survive.

All this exacts an enormous cost, as the literature on burnout attests (Edelwich & Brodky, 1980). Several years ago an observer pointed out that police have a higher than average crime rate—and suicide rate (Kempton, 1962). The majority of street-level bureaucrats manage to survive, psychologically as well as materially. To a large extent they do it by redefinition of the situation. Lipsky says they blame themselves and their clients for problems created by the system and more generally by society. In one study public assistance workers were found to feel less stress in administering punitive policies, to the extent that they could justify this to themselves by redefining the situation to make it more acceptable (Richan, 1984).

Add all this to what has been said about service delivery systems as social systems and it becomes clear why social welfare policies never reach the consumer the way they started out. The original policy directives send mixed messages. Agencies must satisfy a number of outside interests if they are to obtain the resources they need to survive. Internally, the different sets of goals and values have to be melded into a working operation. That means making concessions to some people in the organization—not because their views are right but because they have a lot of power.

Let us say you are the executive of an agency. Do you hold firmly to principle and insist on carrying out the letter of policy as it was originally intended? You may be ready to put your own career on the line, but how about the other people whose jobs depend on you? Are you ready to let the agency go down the drain and the staff with it? To say nothing of the clients who may be deprived of service?

If you are the worker at the bottom of the organizational chart your dilemmas will be different. You can provide more resources for a particular client if you get the agency to make an exception, but in doing so you are ignoring basic injustices that affect many other clients. Do you encourage the client to fight for changes in agency practices? What if the agency retaliates against the client in other ways? Or what if the agency threatens to retaliate against you? If you leave or are forced out, who will take your place? Will that person have your same commitment to protecting the clients? Despite what may seem like overwhelming odds against reform, it does happen. It is most likely to happen when people inside and outside the system work together.

System Change: The Case of Juvenile Training Schools

In December, 1973, a fifteen-year-old boy was burned to death in a detention cell of a Pennsylvania training school that had been considered a model institution. When it was learned that the mattress in the cell had fueled the blaze (flammable materials were illegal) and it had taken staff ten minutes to find the key to the cell, people started asking questions.

Under prodding from civic groups the State Department of Public Welfare, which supervised the school, appointed a panel of citizens to investigate. A community organization held public hearings regarding this and other training schools in the area (*Child Abuse at Taxpayers' Expense*, 1974). The investigations revealed that two years before this, at a nearby girls' training school which also had a professional reputation, a girl had died in almost exactly the same circumstances. The difference was that the previous incident had been hidden from public knowledge.

According to written policy, the department was supposed to inspect all training schools once a year and act on any violations. In reality these two schools had been visited only sporadically—and the director of one had to ask for a visit. Quite apart from the investigation of these incidents, the juvenile detention facility of the City of Philadelphia came under fire for abuse of inmates. Not long afterward, the directors of the three facilities resigned, and the two training schools went through major reorganizations designed to make them truly rehabilitative. This was the second such reorganization for one of the schools in the space of a few years. The informal practices in service delivery systems have remarkable resilience, making real reform difficult.

Juvenile training schools, like other systems, respond to pressure. A cell fire or mass runaway will bring the community down on them in a moment. A weak education program or deadening boredom in the living units will not. Custodial staff are outnumbered by inmates, so must rely on inmate leaders to keep order. The inmate leaders are usually more interested in maintaining their power within the facility than being rehabilitated. They believe the outside world will reject them no matter how rehabilitated they are. (See Polsky, 1967.) So everybody, clientele included, may have a stake in keeping an oppressive system going.

Changing a State System

Feeling pressure to reform its entire juvenile justice program in the mid-seventies, Pennsylvania turned to an outside expert for help. His name was Jerome Miller. Miller, a psychiatric social worker, had became a controversial figure, through his work in Massachusetts and Illinois.

In 1969, the Massachusetts juvenile correctional system was a source of public embarrassment to the state administration. In particular, the massive warehouses which passed for training schools required drastic action. The Department of Youth Services (DYS) was given more power and Miller was brought in to head it up. He had several things going for him: a governor who was ready to do what had to be done in order to get the controversy behind him, public support for change, availability of large amounts of federal money, and a gift for capturing public attention. He set to work on a major drive to reform the training schools, bringing in experts, conducting retraining programs and shuffling staff around. This yielded little more than runaways and a dissatisfied work force (Richan, 1980; Rutherford, 1974; Ohlin, Coates & Miller, 1974).

Undaunted, Miller took the more drastic step of closing down training schools and moving their inmates elsewhere. He turned legislative investigations of his tactics to his own advantage. In order to avoid having his efforts frustrated by the resistance of old-line staff he simply hired large numbers of new people oriented to his reform ideas. The approach worked, and when Miller left Massachusetts in 1973, his hand-picked successor took over to continue the reforms.

Miller next went to Illinois to reform its children and youth program, but he was said to antagonize the professionals in that state and eventually lost the backing of the governor who had hired him (Santiestevan, 1975). When he went to Pennsylvania in 1975 few of the people who knew of him were neutral; they were either for or against Jerome Miller. By this time the clamor for juvenile justice reform was ebbing and the spirit of law-and-order had begun to reassert itself. Besides, Pennsylvania was not Massachusetts. County judges and private agencies, not a single state agency, dominated youth services. There was still federal money, but not in the amounts which Miller had used so effectively in Massachusetts. Miller's efforts made the headlines, but the general public was losing interest in juvenile corrections, and the active participants were divided regarding Miller and his methods. As between the activists, who had many social agendas, and the traditionalists who ran the system, it was the former on whom Miller had to rely for his main support.

He was able to make some changes. He managed to remove juvenile offenders from a large adult prison, and the legislature enacted a law which gave counties a financial incentive to place juveniles in community-based programs. But Miller's star was falling, and he began to lose the support of the governor, other state officials and some of his own aides. The reforms which he had initiated would continue, but the time for drastic change had gone by.

The State as Change Agent

In 1972 a freak of nature gave the Pennsylvania Department of Public Welfare an opportunity to reform social services. In June of that year the Wyoming Valley in the northeastern part of the state was devastated by floods. Social agencies in one county were literally under water, their case records being swept downstream, just at the point that flood-ravaged communities needed their help most desperately (United Services Agency Evaluation Project, 1977).

Over the years planners in the Keystone State had designed schemes for services integration, combining several local service systems into an integrated whole. The state welfare secretary now proposed a deal to the stricken agencies in the flooded area: The state would bail them out financially; in return they would place themselves under a state-run integrated system known as the United Services Agency (USA). Having no alternative, the governments of the two affected counties agreed.

For five years public assistance, child welfare, mental health, services to the aging and related public programs were integrated into a single system. There was also some joint work with voluntary agencies. On paper the juvenile probation offices in the two counties were also included, but this never fully came off in practice. And once the state funding was gone, the local agencies reverted to their former status as separate entities. Not that the reform efforts of the state had yielded no gains. The agencies had found new ways of collaborating and had a far more effective information system in place. But, as in most instances, success had to be measured in partial gains rather than the original grand design. So, too, with the advances under Jerome Miller. In both cases the ability to channel funds into the system or withhold them was a critical factor in the ability to bring about change.

In the next chapter we look at how reforms produce changes that were not anticipated by the reformers. One thus ends up with new problems rather than simply going back to square one.

Community-Based Agencies

Many of the illustrations used in this chapter have been from closed institutions, because, being shielded from public view and operating as self-contained communities, they are more given to policy distortion than is true of social agencies in the community. But the basic elements of the social system can be seen in any organization. A neighborhood center bends membership rules in response to community pressure. The new executive director of a family service agency discovers that supervisors are failing to comply with her instructions on case recording and must work out some accommodation to the veteran employees on the staff. An attendance officer in a high school finds that his attempts to enforce the rules with the son of a local politician are undermined by school officials. A new worker in a child welfare agency learns that strict adherence to work standards isolates her from fellow workers who have evolved their own informal rules.

Are these things wrong? Yes, in a real sense they are, because they defeat the original purposes of policy. But in another sense they make it possible for service delivery systems to survive and thus continue to give service. As with most aspects of social welfare policy, the translation (interpretation) of policy into practice is never simple.

Chapter 9

Closed Institutions:
The Solution Becomes the Problem

The *policy cycle* is a pattern in which a social problem leads to enactment of a new policy and then, as the policy is translated into programs, new problems appear. A *cycle* and not a *circle*: the old problems are not simply resurfacing. That is important to remember, because there is a tendency to say that history repeats itself. As numerous observers have pointed out, the only constant is change itself. The policy cycle can be seen in the evolution of care of adult and juvenile offenders and the mentally ill.

Deinstitutionalization means getting people out of the human warehouses called hospitals and prisons and into the community, and it was a rallying cry for a massive movement during the sixties and early seventies. The changes have been nothing short of revolutionary. In 1950 there were 620,000 mental hospital beds in the United States. That meant one bed for every 250 Americans. By 1981 the number of beds had been cut by two-thirds and there was less than one bed for every 1,100 persons (U.S., Bureau of Census, 1962, 1983). In 1975 there were over three thousand juveniles in Pennsylvania jails; today there are none (Allinson, 1983). Meanwhile, there have been active campaigns for stopping the construction of prisons and for moving the developmentally disabled out of institutions and into the community.

The dramatic changes in the handling of offenders and the mentally disabled and the enthusiasm of the reformers are reminiscent of the movement to get threatening people *into* closed institutions in the early nineteenth century.

MENTAL HOSPITALS

The Cult of Curability

This is the term Albert Deutsch (1949) used to describe the quasi-religious movement that swept the country around 1830. Enthusiasts boasted of 90% cure rates and said mental disorders were among the most easily curable of all illnesses. The change from the earlier pessimism was sudden, making it hard for skeptics to challenge the optimistic mood. The panacea was the large mental hospital where the afflicted could be shielded from a rapidly changing social environment. In many ways these havens were like the utopian communities of the day where idealists were also retreating from the secular world (Rothman, 1971, pp. 130-154). Scull (1977) takes issues with Rothman's view that the movement was so idealistic, believing instead that these early institutions served the need of industry to develop a disciplined workforce. One thesis does not necessarily rule out the other. Rothman is talking about conscious intent, while Scull focuses on the effects of the process.

The statistics that were trotted forth to bolster the case for the asylum were probably less a matter of intentional deception than naive enthusiasm. Each time a person was discharged from the hospital it was racked up as a cure. The same person might be "cured" four or five times in this manner (Deutsch, 1949, pp. 132-152).

And what was the magic formula? A fixed schedule, rigid discipline with severe punishment for the transgressor, and hard work. In this way the person could be saved. Seclusion from society was central to the regimen, for society was the villain. In the fluid milieu of urbanization and industrial growth, it was unbounded ambition and resultant frustration that were thought to propel the unwary into madness. Americans looked back longingly on a simpler time.

An Unlikely Revolutionary[1]

By the time she was 39, Dorothea Lynde Dix's life seemed to be behind her. She couldn't remember ever having had a real childhood. After running away from her father, a religious fanatic who made her spend long hours preparing tracts, to her Puritanical grandmother in Boston, she had begun a teaching career at the age of 14. Dressed in long skirts to make her look older, she succeeded in intimidating most of her pupils into quitting. By her early twenties Dorothea was showing signs of TB and growing old fast. For a number of years she did private tutoring and took extended vacations to recuperate from recurrent illnesses. Close to the age of forty, she seemed destined to retreat to the life of a spinster which in those days was tantamount to being a recluse. But underneath the frail exterior was a will of iron—"born to rule," some said.

It all started when a young clergyman who volunteered to teach Sunday school in the East Cambridge House of Correction discovered that he was assigned to the women's section. Most embarrassing, for these women were lunatics who had the disconcerting habit of tearing their clothes off. Asking his mother what he should do, he was told to go see Miss Dix, she usually had sound advice. When he presented his problem to her, she said quietly, "I will take them myself."

What Dorothea Dix found were miserable creatures herded together in a bare room without heat in the frigid New England weather. When she complained to the jailer she was told, "The insane need no heat." It was commonly believed that the insane, being of a different species, were impervious to heat or cold. The

---

[1]The following account is based on Deutsch (1949) and Tiffany (1891).

iron will surfaced. Dorothea went to court and obtained an order to supply heat to the inmates in the house of correction.

Was East Cambridge a special case, or did similar conditions exist elsewhere? Miss Dix determined to find out. She traveled across Massachusetts and discovered that, by comparison, East Cambridge was a model institution. Enlisting such respected figures as the Reverend William Ellery Channing and Charles Sumner, a prominent philanthropist, she presented a "memorial" to the Massachusetts legislature, laying out the scandalous conditions.

The reaction was predictable: Lies—slander—an overwrought imagination. Not just from the keepers of the insane but from the newspapers as well. But Dorothea had three key ingredients for a successful campaign: solid facts, influential friends and, most of all, determination to stay with the fight. The legislature referred her report to a committee headed by Samuel Gridley Howe, who coincidentally was a family friend and supporter of Dorothea. The result was strong endorsement from the committee and eventually enactment of a bill increasing the state hospital at Worcester by 600 beds.

Not bad for a sickly, frail, semi-recluse. But Dorothea Dix had just begun to fight. Her campaign became a national crusade as she went from state to state getting legislatures to build mental hospitals. Her message was simple—and straight out of the cult of curability: mental illness is highly curable, given proper institutional care. She quoted endlessly from medical opinion which said it was so. Under the circumstances, who would presume to argue with her? The expected dollar savings alone were enough to convince tough-minded legislators (Rothman, 1971, pp. 130-154). She then took her cause to Canada and convinced lawmakers in Nova Scotia and Newfoundland to reform their mental institutions. We are not talking about a highly orchestrated program with a large staff but one very dedicated woman.

Dorothea then undertook the campaign that was to end in defeat, the one that President Franklin Pierce stopped with the stroke of a pen. This was the veto of the bill which would have used the proceeds from the sale of public lands to finance mental hospitals across the country, as described in Chapter 7. Time to give up? Not exactly. In response to the urgings of a friend she went to Scotland and lobbied for humane care of that country's mentally ill. Dorothea Dix continued to fight for this and other causes until the age of eighty. Worth remembering the next time you are feeling washed up, burned out, etc.

The Dream Sours

Even as Dorothea Dix battled for federal support of state mental hospitals in the 1850s, doubts were already cropping up regarding the wisdom of housing the mentally ill in large institutions. As chronic patients stayed on to become the majority of inmates, swelling the numbers, the façade of optimism began to give way. The latter half of the nineteenth century witnessed a steady deterioration of standards in mental hospitals across the country. Systems of classification of patients, through which the early leaders had tried to bring a measure of science to the process, were abandoned as harried administrators tried to cope with over-crowded conditions.

The problems of the hospitals were compounded by reform efforts in other facilities. As communities cleaned up local jails and closed almshouses the state hospitals became dumping grounds for all manner of human jetsam. By the end of the century most of the hospital inmates were aged or violent and increasingly poor and foreign-born. What treatment efforts went on were focused on native-born, paying patients; next were the poor and indigent natives; next were the im-migrant poor; at the bottom of the list were blacks (Grob, 1983).

Still the state hospital continued to be the primary means of containing the mentally ill. Gone were the high hopes of the early reformers; the mood was more one of resignation. The belief that the insane were unable to respond to treatment reasserted itself, and the main thrust behind keeping the hospitals in business was simply fear of the inmates (Rothman, 1971, pp. 265-295).

Psychiatric Renaissance

In Chapter 7 the second-class citizenship of psychiatry in the late nineteenth century was described. Mainstream medicine was becoming more scientific, leaving the tenders of the nation's mentally ill behind. Sigmund Freud changed all that. In the early twentieth century psychiatrists found a new respectability. Public concern about the psychological casualties of World War I gave added impetus to the trend. But the new psychiatry's milieu was the outpatient clinic and small, private sanatorium rather than the state hospital (Grob, 1983, pp. 44-45, 70-71).

No one had much to say in favor of the warehousing of the mentally ill. The movement to empty the back wards might have begun in the first half of the century if it hadn't been for two cataclysms: The Depression of the thirties and World War II. For both patients and professional staff, the hospitals were an economic haven during hard times; and in the throes of the global conflict which followed, domestic reforms were on hold. It was in the postwar years that the "snake pit" imagery began to seize the public imagination.

Out of the Snake Pit

Soldiers and veterans, authentic American heroes, suddenly gone berserk. A gifted writer in the grip of delirium tremens. An attractive housewife besieged by tyrants in white coats. Increasingly books and movies were portraying a dif-ferent kind of mental patient from the freaks of American folklore. Now it was the mental hospitals, not their human cargo, that were the object of revulsion, seemingly caught up in their own strain of madness. Whereas the mood before World War II had been to reform the institutions, there was now growing senti-ment behind the quest for alternatives. Some writers—the best known being

Thomas Szasz (1961)—went further and challenged the underlying assumptions behind psychiatry itself. The large hospital is not unlike a prison, said Ervin Goffman (1961), for it degrades and mortifies its inmates, emphasizes their helplessness and demoralizes the more motivated through enforced idleness.

The agent that put the clincher on the move to empty the hospitals was the psychoactive drug. Beginning in the mid-fifties, heavily medicated patients began moving back into the community. The effects weren't immediately visible, because mental hospitals continued to take in more than they discharged. Capacity in nonfederal psychiatric facilities reached a peak of 722,000 in 1960. A decade later the number had declined 27% and by 1980 was less than a third of what it had been twenty years before. The change was most dramatic for the largest age group among mental patients, the elderly. In 1950, there was one mental hospital bed for every 2,000 persons 65 or older; in 1981, the ratio was one per 13,000.

Another Turn of the Cycle

The movement to empty the mental hospitals was part of a more general crusade to restore civil rights to the oppressed. It was not simply the snake pit quality of hospital care but the inmates' captivity itself that fueled the deinstitutionalization cause. The fact that the humane sentiments of reformers coincided with the more cynical outlook of cost-conscious officials didn't hurt. California's 1968 Laterman-Petris-Short Act was typical of the new view: Persons could be hospitalized against their will only if they were dangerous to themselves or others. Funds were provided to spur the development of community-based services (Whitmer, 1980).

The first warnings of trouble in the new approach to the care of the mentally ill came from mental health professionals and unions representing hospital aides (see Santievestan, 1975). The advocates of the movement for emptying the hospitals could write off such statements as self-pleading. But more formidable arguments were coming from the ex-patients themselves. Follow-up studies found them congregating in ghettoes, ghettoes lacking in supporting services; being exploited and physically abused in rooming houses; stopping medication in the belief that it was causing their problems. The supreme irony: having been emancipated from local jails by hospitals a century and a half before, the mentally ill were now being arrested and kept in jails for crimes ranging from disturbing the peace to aggravated assault (Whitmer, 1980). The older ones often ended up in nursing homes which had many of the defects of state hospitals with less control over quality of care (Jansson, 1984, pp. 422-425; Feldman, 1983).

Community services have not been totally lacking, and community agencies have developed many creative programs to help the mentally ill (Nelson, 1982; Bloom, 1977). By no means are things back to where they were in the early nineteenth century. Most important, those suffering from mental disabilities have powerful allies in the political arena. But this has not protected mental health services from drastic cuts. In 1981 mental health funds were reduced sharply, and further cuts were likely as ways were sought to lower the federal deficit. These economy moves showed up in more walking wounded in the streets of American cities and more pressure on a host of social agencies to pick up the slack (Jamieson, 1982; McQuaide, 1983; SPIGOT, 1982, 1983). Meanwhile, Americans were learning a new vocabulary: bag ladies—street people—the homeless. In terms of public attitudes, the biggest problem facing these social victims is neglect. For those labeled as criminals, the reactions are more often fear, outrage and a wish to punish.

PRISONS

Gangster movies. Jimmy Cagney and Edward G. Robinson paying their debt to society behind prison walls. Prison life on the silver screen was full of glamor and high adventure a generation ago. In time we learned that prison life is anything but glamorous—that it is dehumanizing, degrading and cruel. But in the early nineteenth century prisons were viewed as a benign and humane setting where criminals could be rehabilitated.

The Secular Monastery

When compared with traditional treatment of law violators—the gallows, mutilation, branding, whipping—imprisonment was a great leap forward. To the reformers it wasn't just the lesser of several evils but a positive and benign action. The earliest prisons in the Old and New Worlds were modeled after monasteries—places for penitence (''penitentiaries''), away from the influences of the outside world, the inhabitants housed in cells. Meditation was aided by enforced silence.

Two kinds of prisons evolved in the early decades of the nineteenth century—the Pennsylvania and the Auburn models. In the Pennsylvania system the inmates stayed in their cells, cut off from corrupting associations within as well as outside. This was a major departure from the old congregate arrangement where all the prisoners mingled together. The prison at Auburn, New York, kept inmates in separate cells at night but brought them together during the day to work. But there, too, interaction among prisoners was avoided (Barnes, 1930, pp. 138-144; McKelvey, 1936, pp. 8-13).

All American prisons of that period used the same three principles in one form or another: separation, strict obedience and labor. Because the periods of confinement in local lock-ups had always been temporary, there had never been need for much in the way of disciplinary measures. But prisons devised new forms of control for their long-term inmates, such as whipping, reduced diet and more extreme isolation (Rothman, 1971, pp. 79-108).

Mounting Criticism

By the post-Civil War years, prisons, originally conceived as progressive and humane, were losing their luster. Charles Dickens, after visiting the "model" Eastern State Penitentiary in Philadelphia, wrote,

> The system here is rigid, strict, and hopeless *solitary confinement*. I believe it, in its effects, to be cruel and wrong. . . . I hold this slow and daily tampering with the mysteries of the brain, to be immeasurably worse than any torture of the body. . . . (1867, p. 54)

As immigrants were shunted into the criminal justice system, the prisons became more and more overcrowded. There were calls for reform, but the initial focus was less on treatment of the inmates than on state oversight to guard against mismanagement and corruption. It had long since become obvious that imprisonment was not the panacea originally envisioned. This led some states to experiment with flexible prison terms and parole, the idea being that a person should be released as soon as he was rehabilitated (Lewis, 1922; McKelvey, 1936, pp. 68-91; Barnes, 1930, pp. 210-213).

A Captive Labor Supply

Work had always been part of prison life. In the latter part of the nineteenth century new ways were found to exploit its full potential. In Northern states, work and education were seen as tools of rehabilitation. Correctional authorities contracted with private industries—either for goods produced in prison shops or for leasing inmates directly to them (Barnes, 1930, pp. 219-221; McKelvey, 1936, pp. 93-125; Rothman, 1971, pp. 246-247). This system had the appeal of providing low-cost products and shaving prison costs, and fit in with the work ethic and the belief that inmates owed something to society.

Exploitation of prison labor did not sit well with one segment of American society: organized labor. It was clear that a captive labor force served to undercut working conditions for the country's workers. Most galling of all was the use of prisoners as strikebreakers. As the unions gained strength in Northeastern states they and others were able to shift the focus of prison work to training for later employment rather than sheer exploitation. Non-economic production was a reasonable investment in the future value of the discharged prisoner, it was argued.

Convict labor in the South was something else again. The Emancipation Proclamation had freed the slaves on paper, but in the aftermath of the Civil War new forms of servitude rapidly emerged. The one which came closest to a literal revival of the old slavery system was that which took place in the prisons of the region (McKelvey, 1936, pp. 172-189).

None of the reform efforts in Northern states were evident below the Mason-Dixon Line. In the post-Reconstruction era, blacks soon made up more than 90% of the prison population. The chain gang became an effective means of literally shackling convicts to menial work. Railroads, built on the backs of the re-enslaved, were a major factor in the revival of the Southern economy. When the railroad boom ended, there was the "more wholesome" toil on plantations. There was one difference between this slavery system and the old one: The slave owners had had a stake in conserving their labor supply, but there was no such restraint on the prison system. In 1882, the death rate in Southern prisons was 41 per thousand, as compared with 15 per thousand in Northern prisons (McKelvey, 1936, p. 183). Whereas the states sought control of penal systems in the North, Southern states frequently turned their captive labor force over to the counties, which were far more brutal.

Individualize the Prisoner

Not that Northern policies were particularly enlightened. As penitentiaries got to be more and more overcrowded, public agitation became more vocal. By the end of the century, prison reform was part of the Progressive agenda. Enforced silence was abandoned, and prisons experimented with a variety of humanizing measures: cottage systems to make life behind bars more homelike and education and training to prepare the inmates for a useful life. Prisoners were writing books, exposing the injustices they endured. Central to the reforms was the individualization of offenders and wide use of early release and parole (AFSC, 1971, pp. 34-47; Barnes, 1930, pp. 201-230; McKelvey, 1936, pp. 213-231).

By the early decades of the twentieth century, penology was becoming corrections and prison guards were called "correctional officers." Psychiatry moved inside the walls (Barnes, 1930, pp. 270-281; Stutsman, 1926). Prisoner self-government and other experiments appeared to herald a new day of enlightenment (Barnes, 1930, pp. 213-218). But prison was still prison, and by mid-century critics were asking whether true reform was possible as long as offenders were penned up for long periods of time (Martin, 1954).

The Crime of Captivity

For some the issue of treatment versus punishment has become a non-issue, since the fact of imprisonment is punishment (AFSC, 1971; Mitford, 1973). Ervin Goffman (1961) has pointed to the similarities among all *total institutions*—so called because the person's total life goes on within them under constant surveillance—regardless of their avowed purpose. It is worth noting that, just as Quakers were in the vanguard of the penitentiary movement 150 years ago, Quaker groups have been leading proponents of closing prisons down. Unlike some critics of long-term incarceration, they also question the value of community-based alternatives which mandate participation.

> Many proposals that seem to urge the abolition of prisons are really exercises in label switching. Call them "community treatment centers" or what you will, if human beings are involuntarily confined in them they are prisons. . . . There is an easy test that can be applied to any purported abolition of punishment or imprisonment. Is the proposed alternative program voluntary? Can the subject take it or leave it? If he takes it, can he leave it any time he wants? If the answer to any of these questions is "no," then the wolf is still under the sheepskin. (AFSC, 1971, pp. 23-24)

As with most social movements, the anti-prison forces have included diverse agenda. They range from outright abolition of all vestiges of imprisonment to creation of model institutions for the most hardened convicts (Garrity, 1961; Hawkins, 1976; Morris, 1974). But since the sixties there has been a visible toughening of attitudes toward crime and criminals.

The Eclipse of Reform

The arguments between liberalized penal practices and total abolition have become largely academic in recent years. Tougher juries, greater readiness of judges to commit offenders and widespread use of mandatory minimum sentencing have caused serious overcrowding in the nation's prisons (Galvin, 1983; Levine, 1983). The resultant unrest and periodic flare-ups merely serve to confirm the public's apprehension. In the 1980s, prison reform has seemed further away than ever.

JUVENILE TRAINING SCHOOLS

As is discussed in the next section of the book, children personified at once the best hopes and worst fears of early nineteenth century America. Failure to train them properly would visit untold disaster on society, but being more malleable than adults they were the more amenable to reform. So the establishment of houses of refuge for wayward children was high on the reformers' agenda.

Houses of Refuge

The regimen in children's institutions was closely akin to that in adult prisons and insane asylums—isolation from the outside world, strict discipline, hard work and a mind-deadening routine—but it had its own rationale. The central tenet in child rearing generally, but especially in houses of refuge, was obedience to adult authority. The ideal inmate population resembled nothing so much as a row of automatons, and the child who sought to test the limits was subjected to the whip, lovingly administered of course. The children's own parents assumed to be among the more baleful of influences in their lives, total isolation from family contact was the rule (Rothman, 1971, pp. 206-236; Zatz, 1982).

The purpose of work, far more than keeping idle hands occupied, was to prepare the young for useful careers. For many the period of incarceration was brief, to be followed by placement out as an apprentice. Serious offenders were written off as poor candidates for reform and tended to remain in the institution longer (Rothman, 1971, pp. 206-236; Zatz, 1982).

Just as with adult institutions, the houses of refuge began to feel the effects of overcrowding in the latter half of the century, and the typical home for wayward children came to look more and more like a poorly run prison. As the definition of wayward expanded to embrace the incorrigible, stubborn, ungovernable and runaway, the numbers of inmates rose. If courts resisted consigning children to such places, legislatures were ready to alter the definitions. Needless to say, immigrant children were a special object of concern (Garlock, 1979; Rothman, 1971, pp. 237-264).

Yet the rhetoric of child-saving persisted, and when a new public outcry arose toward the end of the century, it was directed, not at the houses of refuge per se, but at the entire way in which the criminal justice system dealt with minors. Beginning in the 1890s, reformers agitated for diversion of youthful offenders from the legalism and harshness which surrounded the adult system. The result was the establishment of juvenile courts, beginning in 1899.

Treatment, Not Punishment

The juvenile court introduced a number of reforms intended to humanize the adjudication process. Get away from the formality of the courtroom. Emphasize treatment instead of a strict reading of the law. Don't allow attorneys to obscure the true needs of the child. Replace the rules of evidence with the principles of social diagnosis. Avoid the stigma of a public trial and a criminal record. Keep the child in custody for as long as help is needed. The court was the ultimate expression of the idealism of the early twentieth century, the century of the child (Empey, 1979; Zatz, 1982).

Such reforms were benign only insofar as the underlying function of the juvenile court was benign. In subsequent years critics began to question that assumption. In imposing the forms of a social welfare agency on what was still an adversary process, the reformers had stripped juvenile offenders of historic protections of the accused.

Public trials prevent secret inquisitions. A criminal record is the basis for appealing a conviction; for the juvenile there was no appeal. Attorneys are an essential means of asserting one's rights before the law. Surrendering the rules of evidence subjects the defendant to the tyranny of professional wisdom, which by definition is beyond the ken of ordinary people, thus not open to external scrutiny. The indeterminate sentence can imprison a child for a longer period of time than would be possible for an adult convicted of the same act.

In the sixties and early seventies came a series of Supreme Court decisions that sought to restore some balance to this one-sided contest between the juvenile justice system and the defendent. *Kent v. United States* (383 US 541, 1966) overruled a juvenile court decision on the grounds that the child's due process rights had been violated. *In re Gault* (387 US 1, 1967) set forth procedural guarantees for those subject to juvenile court commitment powers. *Wyatt v. Stickney* (325 F Suppl 781, 1971) challenged the right of the state to incarcerate youthful offenders without providing treatment and called for appropriate services in the least restrictive setting. This last ruling struck at the trump card in the hands of juvenile judges: the threat of commitment to a closed institution.

The Attack on the Training Schools

The fifties and sixties were a time of growing panic over two related phenomena: a rapid increase in the adolescent population, as the graduates of the baby boom began entering their teens, and a wave of highly publicized gang violence in American cities. The fact that racial minorities were prominent in the latter trend only heightened the public reaction. The impact on the country's juvenile correctional facilities was predictable: overcrowding and deteriorating conditions.

Now they were training schools—or in some cases simply "schools." But the realities of life behind the locked gate overtook each attempt to change the image of the old houses of refuge by relabeling. Jerome Miller's campaign to overhaul the system in Massachusetts, described in the previous chapter, was an outgrowth of a series of scandals in that state. There, as elsewhere, liberal activists were finding common cause with fiscal conservatives: training schools were costly, both in dollars and in human potential (Zatz, 1982). It was futile to try to fix up what was a bankrupt system, said the critics, the solution was to get young offenders into community settings (Bakal, 1973; Miller & Ohlin, 1976).

As the abolition movement spread, two views began to emerge. There were those who rejected institutionalization and saw community-based programs as the standard prescription for most youths. But more and more the issue became one of "status offenders" versus "delinquents."

Status offenders are those who commit an act which is illegal only because of their status as minors. Adults are not arrested for running away from home, drinking under the legal age or playing hookey from school. Interest in doing away with training schools gradually shifted to wanting to divert status offenders out of the justice system altogether, allowing the correctional authorities to concentrate on work with the youthful criminal (Arnaud & Mack, 1982).

It is in relation to status offenders that a genuine reform has taken place. Most states now accept the idea of keeping them out of the courts and the training schools, and the practice of incarcerating them for extended periods has virtually ceased (Handler et al., 1982; Bartollas & Sieverdes, 1982). A series of federal and state laws has further helped to change the position of status offenders (Allison, 1983; Zatz, 1982).

The separation of juvenile offenders into two populations has raised a number of new questions. Many law enforcement officials question the reality of the distinction between status offenders and delinquents, as do some scholars (Arthur D. Little, 1977; Erickson, 1979; Kobrin & Klein, 1981; Thomas, 1976). More disturbing is the race and sex discimination inherent in the new practices. Females are processed by the juvenile justice system more readily than males and, once inside, are more likely to be detained for longer periods (Chesney-Lind, 1977). Black offenders are more likely than whites to be arrested; if arrested, more likely to be processed as delinquents and incarcerated (Thornberry, 1973; Liska & Taussig, 1979). And for those who remain in the throes of the correctional system, things are getting worse.

Getting Tough

The outpouring of support across the country for private citizens who have gunned down juveniles assumed to be threatening them reflects a more general association of crime, violence and social disorder with teenagers, particularly minority teenagers, in the public's mind. The crackdown on youthful offenders has if anything been more severe than what their older counterparts have experienced. Though the rates of serious law violations by minors have been relatively stable over the past decade, the justice system has been getting tougher with delinquents, especially the more violent and chronic cases (Galvin & Polk, 1983). Increasingly, juveniles are being redefined as adults—by judges and legislatures—so they may be dealt with in the regular criminal justice system (*Corrections Magazine*, 1983).

LOOKING FOR PATTERNS

Why did the asylum come to be seen as a panacea in the 1830s, an anathema in the 1970s, and now once again as a wise alternative to allowing threatening people to roam the streets? The rationales for these shifts in the policy cycle have been different, as the target population is defined as intentionally deviant or mentally disordered. Particularly in the most recent sequence of *de*institutionalization and *re*institutionalization, practice seems to be based on diverse theories. So we must look deeper for explanations. In doing this we should avoid imposing too much order on events which were overlapping and often contradictory.

The first drive to build closed institutions in the early nineteenth century came amidst rapid technological change, the rise of an industrial order and challenges to the rule of the old aristocracy. The reformers spoke to the anxieties of a society in turmoil. The socially deviant—adult and youthful offenders and the mentally ill—played back to the majority the extreme expression of their own darker impulses. Hiding them behind institutional walls would protect both the inmates and the rest of society.

The uses of asylums in subsequent decades hinged not only on the concern for preserving social order, but also the labor value of the respective inmate populations. The prime workforce candidates, adult prisoners, were systematically exploited as a source of productive energy—in the North to fuel a burgeoning industrial complex; in the South to rebuild a devastated agrarian economy. Juvenile offenders were viewed in terms of their future as well as present value to the productive systems. The idea was to hold and remold them for a few years, then release them to the labor market. Mental patients were the least relevant to the work force, so were warehoused at the lowest possible cost.

Just as in the Jacksonian era, the 1960s witnessed the unleashing of new political forces. The move to close down state hospitals, prisons and training schools grew out of a generally expanded notion of civil rights and personal liberty. The current agitation to return to the closed institution is in part a reaction to the more radical elements in that liberalizing trend. But more fundamentally, the tendency to once again lock people up comes at a time of heightened anxiety about a multitude of concerns—nuclear war and breathtaking technological change being the most dramatic. There are thus close parallels between the current period and that from which the earlier reforms emerged a century and a half ago.

THE POLICY CYCLE

What does this tell us about the evolution of a policy? To start with, the original *problem* was determined by perceptions as much as by events. A general uneasiness was translated into "the problem" which—in characteristic American fashion—concerned deviant subgroups. In another milieu "the problem" might have been capitalism, or moral sickness curable only by Armageddon.

Someone then had to translate this problem into *policy* implications. The reformers who said the solution was to wall people off from the rest of society were articulate and respected. Dorothea Lynde Dix, for example, had good connections. Her friends and supporters were among the intellectual elite in the country: William Ellery Channing, a celebrated preacher, Samuel Gridley Howe and Charles Sumner, big-name philanthropists. Dix herself was an imposing figure, effective in the use of language, and absolutely tireless. Her frail appearance was probably an added advantage; a stranger wouldn't expect her to be so dynamic, so would find her burning message all the more persuasive. It is striking how quickly a few articulate spokespersons can seize the terrain, so to speak, and become the definers.

Once the policy direction has been set, it picks up its own momentum. The policy-in-fact never quite measures up to the promise, but we adjust our sights to fit the original rhetoric. Converting policy into *program* often begins with a few high-visibility applications. The "model" program is assumed to represent *the* program. Whether this leads to a program epidemic, in which a fad leads to rapid expansion to the whole country, or is simply the good idea that churlish policy makers refuse to recognize, the commitment to the model is strong enough to push criticisms out of the line of vision. In the case of asylum, the model was bought by the policy makers.

The widespread application of any model is enough to show up defects in it, because *no* model can live up to the hype (Bernard, 1975). Closed institutions were trying to cope with a changing environment. The explosive industrial growth and inundation by waves of immigrants created a new situation unknown to the original definers. But it's hard to give up on a good idea, once one is thoroughly committed to it. Critics' questions are defined as petty carping or ideological wrong-think. The loyalists very soon find themselves doing exactly what the majority did when they, the loyalists, first broached their own critique of the status quo.

In time a new definition of "the problem" captures the public imagination. It is not simply that the original design had defects nor that events overtook it. Many elements of it may be sound; with some modification it may still serve a useful purpose. But at some point the balance shifts and the good idea becomes a bad idea. Two analogies at the personal level come to mind: divorce and job change. A married couple block out the negatives in their relationship, deal with problems on a piece-meal basis and let minor irritants pass without a confrontation as long as they are committed to making the thing work. At some point, one or both decide it is a lost cause and become committed to ending things, whether or not they acknowledge it to themselves. Then all those little hurts are magnified and it is the good moments that get ignored. The other person can do nothing right. This oversimplifies what is often much more complex but basically the definition changes and with it the readiness to act. The same thing happens in a decision to leave a job—or fire an employee. Up to a point we redefine things as all right, to the extent that we are committed to the status quo. But then we reach the end of our rope and no amount of fixing up can salvage the situation.

There is nothing inevitable about divorce or quitting a job. Nor is it inevitable that a basic policy conception must be trashed. Adjusted, yes, because times change and public acceptance changes. The experience with closed institutions illustrates this point very well. In the sixties and seventies there was an attempt to dispense with the asylum as a means of caring for the chronically mentally ill because of major flaws in that system. Already we are seeing that there are large numbers of people who need something other than simply to be "set free," and some form of asylum care seems inevitable. It is to be hoped that as we revive that notion we can avoid the worst elements of the snake pit.

PART 4

Preparing the Good Citizen

Newcomers present a special problem to any society. The fact that newcomers and the children of newcomers have made up a major part of this country's population has meant that preparing people to assume useful roles and fit in with their surroundings has been a major preoccupation since early in our history. Slaves were so thoroughly excluded from ante-bellum society that they were to all intents and purposes newcomers after Emancipation. And internal migration from the rural South to Northern cities and from Puerto Rico to the mainland have had much in common with the arrival of foreign immigrants on our shores.

But this section of the book, while touching on role-preparation of people who move into new surroundings, is mainly concerned with another kind of "new arrival," the child. Underneath the sentimentality that surrounds children has been hard-nosed pragmatism. In the name of protecting them from sin, early Americans brutalized them and demanded slavish obedience. In the name of character-building we exploited them in factory and field. And in the name of self-expression we have turned them into a market for everything from clothes and music to drugs and liquor.

Through it all, the contradictions: Americans were horrified by tales of parental abuse in the 1870s but saw nothing wrong in the more widespread abuse in sweat shops. Today we recoil at the rates of teenage pregnancy while we bombard teenagers with sex in our advertising. In part the contradictions spring from the fact that children represent at once our darkest fears and our highest hopes. Not only can the newborn infant rise to great heights or become a social menace, but historically Americans have believed in their own power to make it happen. Needless to say, children have been the focus of a broad range of social welfare policies and programs.

Chapter 10 surveys the policies through which we have sought to mold the citizens of the future. Public education, a distinctive American institution, has had the major role in this endeavor, along with social services aimed at shoring up the family or replacing some of its functions.

Chapter 11 examines the voluntary and commercial sectors of social welfare and their relationship to the changing role of government. Children's services are an excellent vehicle for this exploration because of the complexity of the rela-

tions between the public and private sectors, the preoccupation with children in this country and the role of religion in this field.

In Chapter 12, we look at how a phenomenon comes to be defined as a crisis, the nature of the crisis varying with who is doing the defining. Our case in point is a cluster of trends in teenage sexuality, pregnancy and parenthood.

Chapter 10

The Investment in Children

To say that a society gets what it asks for in the way its children grow up implies a degree of control over events that is not warranted. For example, no society in its right mind would claim credit for No Name Maddox. So named on his birth certificate because he was the result of his 16-year-old mother's being raped. He bounced around among relatives, lived with his mother and various "uncles" who were as drunk as she was most of the time. When he was 13 she tried to have him placed in a foster home but none was available so they put him in an institution that kept order by laying the children over a wooden rack and beating them with heavy leather straps. Beatings like that put him in the hospital a few times. He graduated from there and went on to become an experienced criminal. His last escapade was the one that brought him the most publicity. By then his name was Charles Manson and he supervised the murders of actress Sharon Tate and 40 other persons (Wooden, 1976, pp. 47-57).

But in a way societies do get what they ask for. Child-rearing practices are shaped by the needs of society. Just as relief policies are more responsive to the economic order than to humanitarian sentiments, child-rearing—that object of so much sentimentality—can be a pretty tough-minded business at times. Take our colonial forebears, for instance. Both the Massachusetts and Connecticut colonies had laws on their books which called for the death penalty in cases of certain forms of disrespect toward parents. Not that this sentence was actually carried out, but public whippings and sentences of hard labor in the workhouse were (Bremner, 1970, pp. 28, 38). More was at stake than obedience within the family. The Reverend John Cotton wrote in 1662,

> Question: What is the 5th Commandment?
> Answer: Honor thy father and thy mother, that thy days may be long in the land which the Lord thy God giveth thee.
> Question: Who are here meant by father and mother?
> Answer: All our supervisors, whether in family, school, church and commonwealth. (Bremner, 1970, p. 32)

Rescuing Children

Do we wish to get Americans to feed starving Africans? We show the picture of a dying child, better yet a mother and a dying child. One of the best war photos ever taken showed a crying infant sitting alone amidst the rubble of a Chinese city. We have already seen how the early nineteenth century reformers sought to shield wayward children from the influence of their parents by sealing them off in houses of refuge. But the movement to rescue children also involved orphans and those whose parents lacked the means to provide for them. Orphanages were established in some of the large towns in the colonial period. Elsewhere children were cared for in almshouses. The settlements too small for either facility placed orphans in private homes. There were even instances of children being sold at auction (Abbott, 1938, p. 4).

The motives behind child rescue included both physical protection and setting the young on the path to right living. A select committee of the New York State Senate reported in 1856 that young almshouse residents were exposed to "filth, nakedness, licentiousness, generally bad morals, and disregard of religion and the common religious observances, as well as of gross neglect of the most ordinary comforts and decencies of life . . ." (Thurston, 1930, p. 29).

By this time some progressive minds had begun to question the wisdom of institutional care per se. They claimed that many municipal orphanages were little better than segregated almshouses. In midcentury came a movement to abandon aggregate care entirely, as well as the corrupting influences of city life, by placing homeless children with families in rural America.

Where Life Is Better

As a boy, Charles Loring Brace used to ramble across the woods and fields near his Connecticut home and trace countless trout streams with his father. When he founded the New York Children's Aid Society in 1853, he was struck by the contrast between his own happy childhood and the misery of the street urchins who were sent to his agency. It was thus natural for Brace to look to the countryside to provide decent homes for the children he called "the dangerous classes" (1880). His idealized view of rural life was shared by many Americans, who saw the city as a place of smoke, filth and evil influences.

Brace sent his agents to small towns throughout the East and Midwest to recruit free foster homes for his wards. The magnitude of this operation was nothing short of remarkable. From the 1850s to the late 1920s the Society sent children numbering in the tens of thousands to farms and small towns across the country. After Brace died in 1890 his son carried on the work (Thurston, 1930, pp. 121, 131).

In time Brace's approach came under growing criticism, largely because after placement the Society did not keep track of what happened to a child. In 1884 the head of the Minnesota State Board of Charities made a study of Brace's children who had been placed in that state. Of 340 children who went there in a three year period, no trace could be found of 76. A third of those he obtained information on had moved at least once. Two-thirds were reported doing well and about a sixth were said to be doing badly (Thurston, 1930, p. 115). Other assessments were less encouraging (see Friedlander & Apte, 1980, p. 79).

Brace launched a movement which has had an enduring impact on child welfare practice. Previously the model of private family care was that of indenture, in which the children earned their keep. Today, foster family care—in which the foster parents are screened, supervised on an ongoing basis and paid for their services—is the predominant form of substitute care of children.

Rescue the Family

By the twentieth century, child welfare advocates were coming to question both institutional and substitute family care. Even the best-run orphanages created an abnormal environment and distorted models of "parents." Mere economic necessity was not proper grounds for taking children away from their own parents, said the 1909 White House Conference on Dependent Children (White House Conference, 1933, p. 59). Professionals began to emphasize the need to strengthen the family rather than dismember it. Accordingly, foster family care was seen as a temporary measure while the child's own family was helped to straighten itself out. But later research showed that "temporary" care often turned into a progression of unsatisfactory placements—for the child, life "in limbo" (see Sherman, Newman & Shyne, 1973; Wiltse & Gambrill, 1974).

The charity organization societies of the late nineteenth century had always seen the enhancement of family life as a major focus of their work, and as their economic security function ebbed they evolved quite naturally into family service agencies. This was the core field with which the emerging social work profession was identified. But child welfare had traditionally been imbued with a mission of rescuing children from their evil surroundings, and it took some adjusting to shift the focus to work with children in their natural families.

In recent decades child welfare agencies have developed a range of approaches to family support: preventive services to children in their own homes (SCOH), day care, and family life education or parent effectiveness training. In the process, the field has had to broaden its conception of "family" from the traditional model of father-as-breadwinner, mother-as-primary-nurturer and children in an enduring nuclear system, to include working mothers, less-predictable marriages, and intergenerational families.

Day Care

The middle of a revolution is probably the worst vantage point for seeing what is happening in historical perspective, and we are in the middle of a revolution. In the early seventies President Richard Nixon vetoed a bill for providing funding for a range of services for children, including day care, because it would "commit the vast moral authority of the federal government on the side of communal approaches to child-rearing as against the family-centered approach" (Jansson, 1984, p. 337). The statement was in keeping with a popular view that young children should be cared for by their mothers.

By 1983, as many mothers of children under the age of six were in the labor force as were out of it. The most dramatic increase has been among mothers whose youngest child was less than two years old: from less than a quarter in 1970 to 45% in 1983. The country is fast approaching the point where the majority of children under six will have mothers who are in the workforce (Waldman, 1983; Kamerman, 1983a). Under the circumstances, one can no longer look on care of young children by persons other than their mothers as an aberration, as President Nixon did in 1971.

In 1958, 27% of all under-six children of mothers employed full-time were being cared for outside of their own home for a substantial part of the day. By 1977, the figure had jumped to 47%. The percentage in group care facilities had gone from 4.5% to nearly 15% (Lueck, Orr & O'Connell, 1982, p. 6). Clearly the central factor in this shift has been the entry of women into the workforce in unprecedented numbers. This trend has compounded the problems of child care, because women who once might have been available to care for other people's children are now gaining access to other, higher-paying occupations.

For many years child care experts have been calling attention to the growing need for adequate day care resources. The professionals in the field reacted strongly to Nixon's 1971 veto, but the population at large had not yet begun to define the support of day care as "a social problem." Two developments in the early 1980s transformed this latent issue into a public crisis. One was the Reagan administration's targeting of day care, a "controllable" item in the federal budget, for severe cutbacks. This helped to mobilize the constituencies with the most vital direct concern—child care professionals and working mothers. The other was a series of exposés of alleged sexual abuse of children in day care centers in 1984, which had the potential for igniting the powder of public concern.

In and of itself, the trigger incident of child sexual abuse—with its potential for stirring strong emotions surrounding sex, violence and exploitation of young children—might fade from the public consciousness fairly rapidly. Scandals are like roman candles: they burn brightly for a brief time and then go out almost as quickly as they appeared. But this particular trigger has special meaning to a large and growing population which is articulate and politically aware. Furthermore, the issue of day care cuts across racial and class lines, adding to its impact. The definition of the issue goes beyond the relative rarity of sexual abuse to the more general concern about poor standards, low salaries and high ratios of children to caretakers.

In the mid-seventies, the U.S. Children's Bureau asked the Child Welfare League of America to sponsor a series of policy papers on the vital issues facing the field in the coming years. Twelve experts were engaged to write the policy papers, which appeared under the title *Child Welfare Strategy in the Coming Years* (Kadushin, 1978). Significantly, day care was not one of the dozen topics, nor was it a primary focus of any of the papers. It is likely that if such a project had been undertaken in the mid-eighties, day care would indeed be a major focus of attention.

Custody v. Socialization

The quality of day care has become a key issue. While protection of the young against physical harm and exploitation is the rock-bottom concern for all parents, those with the financial means are seeking more than purely custodial care. Is there a low enough child-to-adult ratio to allow for individualized attention? Do children sit glued to a TV set all day or are they involved in activities designed to enhance their school-readiness?

One of the central issues is cost. Even mediocre programs are expensive for families of modest means, yet the field as a whole has difficulty attracting qualified personnel because its salaries do not compete with those in other fields. In the eighties, cutbacks in government support of day care have aggravated this situation. The upshot is a major confrontation between the proponents of quality day care and those whose priority is reducing government spending. At the very time that the day care issue was emerging in the public consciousness, the fall of 1984, both major presidential candidates were saying they would need to trim back spending for most social programs, day care included. One of them—Walter Mondale—had long been identified with expansion of social programs, child care in particular.

The issue promises to become sharper in the years to come. The day care forces argue from the standpoint of self-interest—*my* child's development and protection—and in terms of the inability of AFDC parents to become self-supporting if they cannot find adequate child care resources. The respective parties to the debate appeal to the broad constituency with less direct stake in the question. Typically, the ability to maintain wide public interest in an issue of this kind is time-limited. The news media begin to relegate it to the back pages and drop it from TV talk shows, in response to what they see as ebbing audience interest. The task of those who wish to stir significant majorities to action or at least acquiescence in the development and funding of programs is to capitalize on the attention while it lasts.

A new element has entered the day care arena in recent years: commercial firms offering to provide quality care to children whose parents can pay the price. Just as in the cases of insurance protection against unanticipated medical expenses and the care of elderly persons, commercial day care firms must find a balance between costs and fees which will yield a profit. To the extent that this does not meet the need, government will be asked to step in to pick up the slack.

Unlike many industrial societies, the United States has not come to view day care as a basic right. Predictably, we will see two worlds of day care, as in other social welfare areas. Those who can pay the price or throw their weight around in the political arena will be able to provide an enriching preschool experience for their children; those who cannot will settle for custodial care. But society will undoubtedly provide some level of care for the majority of children, because the society needs the labor of mothers in the post-industrial workforce.

Adoption: Creation of a New Family

Laws of adoption have followed changes in the functions of families in society. To the ancients the family was a means of passing property from one generation to the next, and adoption was created to deal with interruptions in the blood line. In like manner, rulers adopted sons in order to keep the royal family in power.

Historically children born out of wedlock have been an anomaly. The social stigma attached to this status is not just a matter of frowning on unwed mothers for their behavior. In ages past when private inheritance was central to the economy, *bastards* (the legal term) were dysfunctional. Little wonder that society has punished "illegitimacy" in inverse ratio to the party's role in it: the male parent, ordinarily the initiator of the event, has tended to escape unscathed; the female parent has been the object of public scorn, exile from her family and all sorts of discrimination. But the greatest punishment has been visited on the one least involved in the proceedings: the child. Courts have been particularly reluctant to force heads of intact families to assume responsibility for their extra-marital children partly because of the confusion this creates in determining inheritance rights of their various off-spring (Krause, 1969). The issue of teenage unwed parents is discussed in Chapter 12.

The child welfare field has traditionally been concerned with the social and psychological consequences of illegitimacy: This has led to a preference for surrender of the out-of-wedlock child by the mother and placement of the child with an adoptive couple. Because of the legal and social import of such a step, adoption is treated as a specialty demanding the best professional talents. Informal adoptions arranged by attorneys, medical personnel or close friends are frowned upon by professional social workers.

Two trends have emerged in recent years. One is the readiness of more women to keep their babies instead of surrendering them. The other is acceptance by the professionals of a wider range of adoptive choices than the classic placement of the healthy infant with the middle-class childless couple. Adoption by poor parents who require a subsidy in order to care for the child, adoption of older children with physical and mental disabilities and adoption by single parents are increasingly seen as reasonable options. In Chapter 11 we explore the role religion has played in adoption policies.

ABUSE OF A VULNERABLE POPULATION

We think of labeling of people as being based on *their* behavior or characteristics, but one set of labels for children is really a way of categorizing parental behavior. Children may be *dependent*, in need of care and support because of parents' inability to provide for them; *neglected*, in need of protection because of willful failure of a parent or caretaker to provide; or *abused*, in need of protection against overtly harmful behavior by a parent or caretaker. Just as with other kinds of labeling, these designations can be a convenient way of classifying a population in order to exercise public authority, but they can also interfere with flexible responses to need.

Professional social workers have tended to shun such labels, in the belief that they ignore the subtleties of parent-child dynamics and get in the way of good working relationships with clients. This outlook grew quite naturally out of a clinical approach to problems that sought to be non-judgmental and non-authoritarian. In recent years, however, child abuse has been thrust into the limelight, for both the lay public and child welfare professionals, just as other forms of domestic abuse have. It is recognized that children, being physically weak and lacking in mature judgment, are prime targets of adults' baser and more violent tendencies, in as well as out of the home.

Child abuse as a recognized social problem is only a little more than a hundred years old. Before that, society accepted the principle of total obedience to parental authority and the admonition that to spare the rod was to spoil the child.

The Discovery of Child Abuse

When New York state senators reporting on almshouse conditions in 1856 wrote, "Common domestic animals are usually more humanely provided for," they could not know just how prophetic their words were. Eighteen years later the state's laws against cruelty to animals were invoked in the first court action against child abuse. The facts of Mary Ellen Wilson's six-year existence were shocking enough: battered almost daily, slashed with a pair of scissors, tied to a bed, allowed out only for brief walks at night, poorly fed, exposed to the elements in the middle of winter. What made it worse was that the presumed protectors of New York's children had allowed it to happen (Sloan, 1983, pp. 145-146).

Mary Ellen had been placed with the couple soon after birth by the superintendent of the Department of Charities. According to the foster mother, he had asked no questions nor investigated the home. And when the abuse was uncovered six years later, none of the institutions to which the case was referred was willing to touch it. It was then that the Society for Prevention of Cruelty to Animals was brought in. Mrs. Connolly, who was charged with abuse, was sentenced to a year in prison at hard labor. Her husband had disappeared. If there were any consequences for the child welfare system, they went unrecorded.

The case of Mary Ellen led to the founding of the Society for the Prevention to Cruelty to Children (SPCC), which investigated child abuse for the City as well as responding to other calls for help. In time SPCCs sprang up in other cities. But it was not until the middle of the twentieth century that overt physical abuse of children became a major focus of concern, and it was physicians rather than social workers who first brought it to public attention. In 1946 a physician named John Caffey noticed a pattern in many young children he was asked to treat: long-bone fractures and bruises that didn't make sense as accidental occurrences. He suspected that what he was seeing was the result of deliberate action by adults. Investigations by other physicians confirmed Caffey's suspicions. In 1961 Dr. Charles Kempe of Denver coined the phrase, "the battered child syndrome" (Shepherd, 1965).

As the statistics on child abuse mounted, so did public agitation, culminating in the Child Abuse Prevention Act of 1973. This legislation provided for research and local demonstration projects but no general funding to support protective services (Jansson, 1984, p. 335). This prompted states and territories to pass their own child abuse legislation. The centerpiece of most of these laws was required reporting of suspected abuse cases by professionals such as teachers, health care providers and social workers. Not surprisingly the statistics on child abuse climbed after that. For some professionals, the mandatory reporting laws raised the spectre of unfounded accusations against parents and concern about violations of the confidentiality of worker-client relationships (Stein, 1984).

In the eighties, attention has shifted from physical abuse to sexual exploitation of children. One estimate placed the number of girls who were sexually abused before their eighteenth birthday at one in five; 47% of these cases were said to involve family members and in another 42% the perpetrator was known to the family (Conte, 1984). Missing children became an object of concern in the mid-eighties. A few highly publicized cases of youngsters being snatched off the streets, their mutilated bodies turning up later, touched off widespread fears. It turned out that the great majority of children reported missing were either taken away by one of their parents in a custody battle or were teenagers running away from home.

Child Abuse in the Workplace

At the time that the case of Mary Ellen Wilson shocked the public, between 750,000 and a million children aged 10 to 15 were gainfully employed in the United States, about one out of every seven children in that age cohort.[1] They worked in cotton mills and coal mines, hawked newpapers in the city streets and worked the fields in rural areas. Wages were uniformly low. For many the hours were long, the conditions of work hazardous and unhealthful. Factories were equipped with whipping rooms to deal with discipline problems (Trattner, 1970). This army of the employed included children as young as six, seven and eight. The number of 10-15-year-old workers peaked at 1.75 million in 1900.

The child welfare system, geared as it was to teaching children the value of work, paid little attention at first to child abuse in the workplace. The annual proceedings of the National Conference of Charities and Correction, the major

---

[1]Figures based on tables in U.S. Bureau of Census (1975).

social welfare organization, had little to say about child labor until after 1900, when the numbers of employed children had already begun to recede.

In the 1870s it was fringe political parties that began calling public attention to the issue. In 1892 the Democratic Party climbed aboard. The unions, generally averse to getting caught up in political issues, stayed aloof. Finally, in 1897, the American Federation of Labor joined the ranks of the protestors (Trattner, 1970, pp. 32-33). Labor might not have gotten involved then if it had not had a direct stake in removing low-wage competition from the labor market.

The major organization which fought the battle against child labor was the National Child Labor Committee (NCLC) which first met in 1904. In the following years, the exploitation of children in the workplace drew increasing attention. Progressive states with strong labor movements were passing legislation to protect children, but until the federal government established national policies many states with the worst records of abuse did not act.

It took the Depression, with plummeting demand for workers and unions fully aroused, to bring about change. Child labor provisions under the Fair Labor Standards Act were finally enacted in 1938. Still relatively untouched was agriculture. Organized labor had little direct involvement in farm work at that time.

Although the young are no longer the integral part of the workforce they were 100 years ago, preparing children for future work roles is a central function of the child welfare system, just as it has always been. From the beginning there was an obsessive fear that children born into poverty would grow up to be indolent unless steps were taken to avoid this. In Elizabethan England and later in the colonies, the basic system was indenture, under which the child was bound out under contract to a master to learn a trade and, as soon as possible, earn his keep. Private contributors would set up a rotating fund to compensate those who took in children too young to pay their own way. In time, it was expected, the child would become productive enough not only to relieve the master of further burden but also to allow him to pay his original advance back into the fund (Thurston, 1930, pp. 10-11).

In the early seventeenth century, Virginia colonists imported pauper children who had been kidnapped on the streets of London and placed them in unpaid indentured status. It was, they said, in order to educate them to honest and profitable toil and avoid the ways of sloth and idleness (Trattner, 1970, p. 25). In the North, the Society for Encouraging Industry and Employing the Poor, founded in 1751, had the dual purpose of utilizing the labor of women and children and teaching the value of work. But the main task of preparing American youth for the world of work fell to the public schools.

PUBLIC EDUCATION

The Protestant Reformation brought with it two principles: that the laity should read and interpret the scriptures and that honest toil was the center of life.

In the theocratic societies of colonial New England these precepts were translated into a need for literacy and inculcation of the work ethic, and the major instrument for these tasks was public education. The first step toward the establishment of public schools in this country was the 1642 law in Massachusetts Bay Colony which required that children be educated, either by their parents or a master. Five years later came the Old Deluder Act, which required towns to set up schools (see Butts, 1947, pp. 295-300). The "old deluder" was Satan, and the object of the law was to keep children out of his clutches.

This was a clear break from the European roots, where formal schooling had always been the preserve of the well-to-do. The South followed that tradition; private schools were established for those who could afford them or by churches so inclined. Not that the New England colonies themselves moved into the business of education. Rather they placed that obligation on localities. State public school systems did not come into being until the nineteenth century (Crary & Petrone, 1971; Church & Sedlak, 1976).

Public Schools and Child Labor

The workforce needs of society have had a major role in shaping the evolving public education system. Initially, compulsory school attendance laws were resisted because these would interfere with child labor, both in industry and agriculture (Crary & Petrone, 1971). In particular, high schools did not become a universal phenomenon until this century; prior to that they were primarily an urban institution (Church & Sedlak, 1976). A two-to-three month hiatus in the summer might seem strange in a society obsessed with the fear of prolonged idleness, especially among the young. This pattern originated in the fact that July and August was the period of maximum farm work (Ellena, 1974; Gillette, 1912).

As industry came to need a technically more sophisticated kind of worker, education became an important resource. The first entry of the federal government into provision of social welfare for the general population, in fact, was in the field of vocational education, with the passage of the Smith-Hughes Act in 1917.

Making Good Americans

The other major role of public schools was to Americanize the children of immigrants and through them their parents. The melting pot—a common culture for all Americans—was a widely held article of faith in the nineteenth century. It was much later that the cost, in terms of cultural diversity and enrichment, would be recognized.

Character-building organizations such as the YMCA and social settlements sought to integrate the newcomers into the national fabric. They were also teaching people of peasant backgrounds to become part of an industrial order, where punctuality, ability to follow instructions and facility with the English language were essential ingredients. The workforce functions of all these institutions are clearly seen in the segment of the population which for a long time was excluded, then became a special object of attention: the blacks.

THE SOCIAL EDUCATION OF BLACK CHILDREN

Slavery, like feudalism, provided a built-in means of maintaining order and managing the workforce. A free labor system relies on expected rewards and internalized work values to get people to work. A slave system is based on forced participation and docility. The outlook that fits in best with this system is fatalism, a belief that one's destiny is ruled by luck or an all-powerful other, not by one's efforts. But slavery also taught survival skills. Black children learned to rely on their own community for protection and support, even in its powerlessness.

Chapter 9 described how the South used convict labor to re-enslave black men after the Civil War. Black children were also caught up in this process. In 1865 Mississippi decreed that orphaned or dependent black children were available as apprentices, with preference given to former slave owners. Other states soon followed suit (Axinn & Levin, 1982, p. 93). So a slave-like system for managing black labor continued. There was no need, therefore, for the kind of social education to which native and immigrant white children were exposed.

For decades after Emancipation, black children were virtually ignored by organized child welfare. Those few institutions open to blacks were operated by whites. Meanwhile an informal system of child care developed within the black community (Billingsley & Giovannoni, 1972).

It was as blacks began moving into the white-dominated workforce that black children became a target of child welfare work. Blacks were drawn to northern industrial centers in great numbers by war jobs in World War II. In the post-war years, public child welfare began to expand. Private agencies were continuing to serve mainly white children, and it fell to the public sector to deal with the needs of black children. In the seventies, 80% of the children under the care of the New York City Department of Welfare were from minority backgrounds, the majority of them black (Fanshel & Grundy, 1975). But the development of foster care resources lagged behind the perceived need. More and more it was the child's own family which was seen as the primary resource.

"As a result of family disorganization," wrote black sociologist E. Franklin Frazier in 1950, "a large proportion of Negro children and youth have not undergone the socialization which only the family can provide. . . . Because the disorganized family has failed in its function as a socializing agency, it has handicapped the children in their relations to the institutions in the community" (Frazier, 1950, p. 54). To this failure of the black family Frazier attributed crime and many other social ills in the black community. It was in 1965—a year of increasing black pressure on the white power structure—that this same theme was put forth as national policy. Daniel P. Moynihan, writing a widely circulated policy paper for the U.S. Labor Department, asserted that the deterioration of the black family was a "case for national action." Black leaders, meeting at Fisk University in 1984, also raised concern about the state of the black family. But whereas Moynihan had seen the federal goernment as the solution—the white society repairing the failed black society—the conferees in 1984 said the black community must be its own salvation (*New York Times*, 1984b). This was, after all, the way the needs of black children had been met under slavery and in the years when white America excluded them from its organized systems.

The underlying question was one of control. Who was to determine how black children were to be socialized? One of the ways in which this issue crystallized in the 1970s was in relation to the adoption of black children. Should whites adopt black children? For most of the country's history, white America had answered the question in the negative: racial mixing was to be avoided. In the 1960s white attitudes began to soften on the issue, and the more liberal elements said race was less important than other factors. By the 1970s it was blacks who were saying "no" to interracial adoption (Chestang, 1972; Chimezie, 1975).

It was not a new issue in American child welfare. As is discussed in Chapter 11, similar controversies have raged for many decades between religious groups. They underscore the import which has always been attached to the social education of children.

Chapter 11

The Voluntary and Commercial Sectors

Now I am not suggesting that we stop welfare tomorrow. . . . I just have faith in the American people that, if through some set of circumstances welfare did disappear tomorrow, no one would miss a meal. The people in this country, in every community all over, would get together, form emergency committees, and take up the slack. (Witcover, 1977, p. 98)

That was what Ronald Reagan told a reporter during his unsuccessful bid for the Republican presidential nomination in 1976. It spoke of an unbounded faith in the voluntary way, a faith which has deep roots in our society. A century and a half earlier the French philosopher, Alexis de Tocqueville, wrote,

In no country of the world has the principle of association been more suc- cessfully used, or applied to a greater multitude of objectives, than in America. . . . In the United States, associations are established to pro- mote the public safety, commerce, industry, morality, and religion. There is no end which the human will despairs of attaining through the combined power of individuals combined in a society. (Tocqueville, 1835)

The free-standing, nonprofit, social service organization, while not an Amer- ican invention, is distinctively American in its evolution. Caught between its fear of government regimentation and the excesses of private market exploitation, the country was fertile ground for "the principle of association," as Tocqueville put it. Some observers feel the designation of a separate voluntary sector of social welfare is misleading, in view of the complex mix of governmental, gov- ernment supported, charitable and profit-making systems that now dispense social services (see Kamerman, 1983b). But one can understand these respective systems in their historical context only by making such a distinction. For the pur- pose of definition, the formal auspices of a program will be used as the determi- nant of the sector to which it belongs. Thus *public* services are those that are of- fered by a governmental agency. *Voluntary* services are those which are offered by a sectarian or nonsectarian organization with its own governing body, regard- less of the degree to which it depends on tax money and is accountable to govern- mental bodies. Admittedly an arbitrary division, but necessary for our purposes.

As of the mid-seventies it was estimated that 37 million Americans—a fourth of the adult population—were engaged in some sort of volunteer activity (Sieder & Kirschbaum, 1977). The trend had been upward for several years, a period marked by expanded scope and magnitude of government social welfare programs. This seems to challenge the conventional wisdom that increased government welfare activity discourages volunteer efforts. Government revenues for welfare dwarf money raised from voluntary contributions—the ratio is nearly 20:1 if we exclude contributions for purely religious activity. But the significance of the voluntary sector cannot be measured in dollars.

CHILDREN AND CHARITY

From what has been said so far about the place of children in society, it should not come as a surprise that they have been the object of vast outpourings of money and effort. Nor should the fact that government intervention has been particularly controversial, considering the concern about central control of people. Nor the fact that services to children have been a major battleground among religious groups.

The very early entry of the state into public education was noted in the last chapter. The Old Deluder Act came just 27 years after the landing of the Pilgrims. But this was a theocratic state enforcing local responsibility, an expression of religious dominance as much as governmental. It would be two more centuries before the states could be said to have become serious actors in public education. Aside from schooling, the earliest organized efforts in relation to children were in child care, mainly private. By the end of the eighteenth century four orphanages had been established in this country, three of them under religious auspices (Abbott, 1938, p. 7).

Sectarianism

Each of the major faiths approached child welfare services differently, based on different conceptions of the relationship of humans to God. The ruling elites were Protestant, and so "Protestantism" was easily translated into "Christianity" which was easily translated into "faith." The sectarian splits among Protestants, and the view that social welfare was the province of the laity as well as the clergy, led to a high degree of autonomy of agencies and institutions (Reid, 1971). There was not *a* Protestant mindset. The Calvinists of New England were more remote from the Episcopalians of Virginia than the latter were from the Catholics in Maryland. But all the Protestant sects had a fierce commitment to instilling in children an appreciation of religious values; it was incumbent on anybody responsible for child-rearing, be it parent or asylum matron, to provide religious training.

Catholic social welfare was highly integrated within the church structure, not only a set of tenets guided by religious values but a worldly expression of what was at base otherworldly. The earliest Catholic social welfare institutions were orphanages, beginning in 1727 with a New Orleans convent operated by the Ursuline Sisters. The nuns simply continued practices that were well established in Europe. The spiritual needs of children were a primary concern, spirituality being defined in precise doctrinal terms. This was an approach to child care which continued well into the twentieth century (O'Grady, 1930).

These two traditions—the Protestant and the Catholic—collided head-on in mid-nineteenth century. The conflict was typical of a basic pattern: naive assumptions by the majority that they *were* America, bumping up against senstivity of a minority, not only about its religious beliefs but about its place in the American pecking order.

In the last chapter we met Charles Loring Brace, the man who transplanted thousands of children from the slums of New York City to the farmlands of the Midwest. The families with whom Brace placed them were God-fearing Christians. Also Protestants. That last fact may have escaped Brace's attention, so strong was his zeal to rescue "the dangerous classes," but it did not escape the notice of the New York Catholic Protectory, a child-care institution. The majority of the street urchins, from immigrant backgrounds, were nominal members of the Catholic faith. In the eyes of the protectory, they were being lured away from their religious roots. Brace reacted to the criticism defensively; and like most arguments over religion, this one was never resolved (Thurston, 1930, pp. 126-127).

This issue has persisted down to the present, though with far less virulence than in Brace's day. Adoptive placements across religious lines have been banned in many states, and even foster family care by a person of a different faith can cause repercussions.

In the nineteenth and early twentieth centuries there was a good deal of mutual misperception on this issue, each side sure that the other was bent on mass conversions. But while some Protestants were active evangelizers, others were basically insensitive to the issue—at most guilty of a kind of presumptive Protestantism. Meanwhile, Catholic social service providers were mainly preoccupied with ministering to the needs of their immigrant constituents.

Jewish social services were specifically designed to meet the needs of Jews who began to arrive in large numbers at the turn of the century. Unlike Catholicism, which was doctrinal unity in cultural diversity, Judaism provided a strong cultural base but allowed differences of doctrinal interpretation. Given this cultural emphasis and the pressing needs of a population which left one form of persecution in the Old World to encounter new forms in the New, it is not surprising that Jewish social welfare was largely secular in nature. The strong emphasis on education in the Jewish community led quite naturally to a high degree of professionalization of its social services, further secularizing Jewish social welfare. Rather than seeking to win converts, the Jewish community has struggled with the problem of the religious and cultural identity of its own youth.

Religious differences in this country were historically compounded by class differences. As Catholics and Jews have moved increasingly into the middle-class mainstream, the acrimony that marked earlier sectarian encounters has largely dissipated. Even abortion, the issue that used to separate Catholics and Protestants, has become muddied as Protestant fundamentalists have come to be among the most vocal pro-lifers. This trend is part of a more general resurgence of religious activism among born-again Christians and a variety of smaller sects.

BANKROLLING THE VOLUNTARY SECTOR

The most powerful lever for unifying the voluntary sector is control over the money on which it depends. Voluntary social welfare is still a confusing patch-work of autonomous programs, but since early in the twentieth century there have been two developments with the potential for bringing a degree of unity and order out of the chaos. One has been united fundraising. The other has been the growing role of the federal government in supporting voluntary social welfare.

United Fundraising

The charity organization society (COS) of the nineteenth century lacked an important weapon in its efforts to coordinate charities: the power to control funding. As long as the COS provided useful services to the agencies, they sup-ported it, but they were less willing to give up their autonomy for the sake of scientific philanthropy. In time the COS evolved into the family service agency, one more specialized social welfare organization.

In the early part of the twentieth century a few cities experimented with joint fundraising, but the practice did not become widespread until World War I. The heightened need for relief led to the establishment of war chests, many of which began raising funds for non-emergency social welfare activities as well as war-related work. At war's end many communities converted their war chests into community chests with major responsibility for funding local nonprofit agen-cies. An important force behind federated funding was the business community, which saw it as a way of reducing the pressure from multiple drives. In the early years of the Depression, united fundraising was an important element in local communities' attempts to handle the escalating need for charity. World War II gave further impetus to the movement, much as had happened in World War I.

A major source of resistance to the federated funding concept was large na-tional agencies, such as the American Red Cross, which had the means to generate their own funds independently, and new special appeal agencies which emerged in the postwar years. Sectarian federations of agencies have also con-ducted their own independent fundraising activities.

In the sixties and seventies new sources of tension emerged for the United Way organizations. A perennial issue over the years was birth control and abor-tion: Would inclusion of a family planning agency lead to the withdrawal of sup-port by the local church hierarchy and with it a large number of contributions? That question has recently become much sharper as women's groups threatened to set up their own fund drives if family planning organizations were excluded.

Since the mid-sixties local United Ways have been under pressure to become more activist in their orientation and take a more dynamic approach to social policy issues, lest they alienate assertive new elements in the political spectrum (Institute of Community Studies, 1970). But responding to this kind of pressure can bring on counter-pressure. In the late sixties the Philadelphia police commissioner threatened to advise personnel not to contribute to the United Way because it was funding organizations which were viewed as "the enemy." The threat was one factor leading to a reconsideration of funding priorities (Love, 1969).

Historically, united fundraising was supposed to foster coordination of social agency activities. This was most likely to happen in communities in which a local council of agencies and organizations was organically linked to the fundraising structure. Rarely did such councils have much impact on agencies and their programs beyond offering research and other forms of technical assistance. Beginning in the sixties, however, a new element entered the picture: government, more specifically the federal government, as a major source of financial support for voluntary social services.

Government Financing of Voluntary Services

In the past twenty years the meaning of "voluntary" has changed radically. The notion of independent nonprofit organizations relying solely on contributions from foundations, corporations and private individuals for their income is a thing of the past. Of $116.4 billion in revenue which voluntary agencies received in 1980, 35% came from the federal government, the largest single source, while only 22% came from private individuals, foundations, and corporations (Salamon & Abramson, 1982). Add to this $8.4 billion in indirect support through tax exemptions (U.S., OMB, 1980, p. 323). The economic realities of voluntary social welfare give the federal government tremendous leverage over the nature and scope of these nongovernmental services.

There are three basic routes through which federal funds are channeled to voluntary agencies—*direct allocation* (example: special demonstration and research grant); *grants to state and local governments* (example: Title XX funds); and *in-kind benefits to individuals* (example: Medicare). Of the 40.4 billion in federal funds which went to voluntary agencies in 1980, more than half was channeled through in-kind benefits to individuals (Salamon & Abramson, 1982, p. 45). It is the 20% in direct grants to agencies that gives the federal government the greatest impact on the nature of services.

Federal money has influenced the voluntary sector in several ways. In the old days, health and welfare "planning" consisted mainly of managing interagency relations and accommodating to the local power structure. But with federal funds targeted to specific purposes, the voluntary sector has had to become more disciplined in defining needs and objectives. Similarly, a demand for accountability regarding the use of government funds has stimulated an expansion and upgrading of evaluative research. The conscious identification of target populations and problems in federal programs has been a major factor in shaping the thrust of voluntary agency services. The attempt to get voluntary agencies and planning bodies to assure representation of consumers and the poor in their decision-making structures has been less successful.

Historically, the voluntary sector viewed itself as the "growing edge" of social welfare. While public agencies were saddled with meeting mass needs and required to serve any and all with basic supports, so the theory went, the voluntary agencies were free to experiment and challenge traditional ways. But in reality professionalization tended to create its own kinds of orthodoxy in many agencies. Thus in recent years it has been the federal government which has injected new blood into social service practices (Beck, 1970; Kramer, 1981). Another powerful force for generating new ideas has been private foundations.

Foundations

Eighty percent of all private philanthropic contributions come from individuals. Only about five percent is from foundations, and a like amount from business corporations (U.S., Bureau of the Census, Statistical Abstract, 1983, p. 399). But individual contributors rarely have much impact on agency programs, so the foundations and corporations carry more weight in program decisions than the dollars would suggest. The corporations may influence agency practices, though generally they take little interest in the substance of the programs they are helping to finance. Their main business is business, and the tax write-off is probably more important to them than the effects of the services that are delivered with their donations.

The foundations, on the other hand, are in the business of making contributions and they deliberately try to mold social welfare and other programs. In particular they see themselves as helping social services, education and health to break out of orthodox patterns. With assets totaling $48.2 billion and grants totaling $3.4 billion (1981), they are in a position to influence social welfare. They are tax exempt, thus vulnerable to government pressure—which fact was brought home to them rather abruptly in the late forties and early fifties. This was the period when Senator Joseph McCarthy launched his witchhunt in the name of anti-communism which added a new word to our vocabulary: McCarthyism. Senator McCarthy didn't focus his attacks on foundations, but other members of the Senate and House did. They charged that the foundations were funding projects which were not only directed by persons of questionable loyalty but whose very purposes were inimical to national security (Andrews, 1973, pp. 131-147; Bremner, 1960; p. 195).

The tangible effect of one series of hearings in the Senate was new restrictions on tax exempt status by the Internal Revenue Service. The hearings, in 1948, 1952 and 1954, made the foundations more gunshy regarding controversial issues.

The Tax Reform Act of 1969 had a major impact on foundation finances. It was inspired more by an effort to crack down on the use of foundations as tax dodges for private gain than on ideological grounds, though support of voter registration and other "political" activities also proved embarrassing to the funds (Smith & Chiechi, 1974). The 1969 act slapped new limits on the kinds of functions which could be written off for tax purposes. It is impossible to measure the exact impact of the act, but it is worth noting that from that point on, foundation gifts leveled off while individual charity, business donations and bequests continued to climb (U.S., Bureau of Census, 1983).

The experience of the foundations reflects basic problems of private initiative in a democracy. By conferring tax exempt status the electorate is underwriting activities over which it has no direct control—activities, moreover, which involve the use of large amounts of money to carry out somebody's agenda. To give private funds free rein risks abuses of the public trust. To clamp down limits the kind of creativity needed to solve the country's problems.

REAGANOMICS AND THE VOLUNTARY SECTOR

Upon assuming office in 1981, the Reagan administration made its priorities clear: Military spending was to be increased sharply, taxes would be slashed to stimulate the economy, the federal government's role in regulating commerce and industry would be pared to the minimum. With economic security programs among the less controllable budget items, it stood to reason that the voluntary sector of the human services would be expected to bear a major share of the burden of the defense build-up.

Budget projections released by the Office of Management and Budget confirmed the administration's game plan. Over a five-year period, federal funds for social welfare programs other than income assistance would be reduced by precisely the same percentage as Pentagon spending would be increased: 57% (Salamon & Abramson, 1982, p. 29). Other than environmental resources, social welfare would be hardest hit of any budgetary category. It was estimated that if all the Reagan proposals through 1985 were enacted, voluntary social service agencies and community organizations would lose from a fourth to a third of their *total* revenues.

Congress went along with the first year's stage of Reagan's plan with only minor modifications, then balked in subsequent years, forcing the administration to compromise. Not, however, before serious damage had been done to many programs. Local surveys of agencies showed that among the casualties of the cuts were total social service programs, professional and nonprofessional staff positions, free staff resources which had been made available under the Comprehensive Employment and Training Act (CETA), and preventive as opposed to emergency services. One of the primary casualties was staff morale. (See Bernard, 1983; SPIGOT, 1982, 1983; Turem & Born, 1983.)

The 1984 presidential election may have been as much a verdict on the man as his policies, but Ronald Reagan correctly interpreted his victory as a mandate to move ahead. For a president to do less is to abdicate responsibility, however much one may disagree with the agenda. Hanging over all budgetary decisions was a monumental federal deficit. Leaders of both major parties were looking for ways to trim controllable expenditures. Being among the most controllable, funds for voluntary social welfare appeared to be a prime target.

COMMERCIAL ESTABLISHMENTS

At the beginning of this book, social welfare was described as being outside of the market system because the normal relations of exchange in the marketplace do not apply. The provider of a social service does not exact a price from the consumer based on cost plus a reasonable profit. We now have to revise that original distinction to an extent because of the ambiguous nature of some service provisions. Where the transaction is entirely between producer and consumer—such as in commercial recreation—the difference between welfare and non-welfare spheres is clearest. What about private schooling or physicians' services? Insofar as these are profit-making ventures and there is no government subsidy involved, one can still refer to them as non-welfare. They become welfare as the society—either through the use of tax funds or voluntary charity (which indirectly involves tax money)—supports the activity.

Commercial enterprises are very much a part of social welfare today. Although it is the Reagan administration which has become identified with the "privatization" of human services, the trend predated the Reagan years. In reality there have been two kinds of trends—more government involvement, through direct allocation and tax exemption, in activities which were historically private, and entry of profit-making firms into areas previously dominated by voluntary and governmental systems. The result has been a bewildering complexity of relations among government, voluntary and commercial sectors (Kamerman, 1983b).

The largest field of for-profit welfare is nursing home care. With the advent of Medicare and Medicaid in the mid-sixties, this field expanded rapidly. By 1980, four out of five nursing homes were privately run. In contrast, 27% of mental hospitals and 12% of general hospitals were run as profit-making establishments. In child day care, over half of all establishments are operated on a for-profit basis (U.S., Bureau of Census, 1983).

PRIVATIZATION: ISSUES AND PROSPECTS

There is nothing sacrosanct about using either government or the private sector to provide human services. Discussions which emphasize the mixing of public, voluntary and commercial components in a "public-private sector" blur an important distinction: between the auspices under which services are delivered and the sources of funding. As to auspices, there are two basic questions: Under what circumstances are services *better* (i.e., more effective and efficient)? And under what circumstances are they *more equitable* (i.e., available on the basis of need rather than the ability to pay)?

On the first of these questions, the evidence is mixed (see Kamerman, 1983; Ostrander, 1985). Gibelman (1981) points out that the use of public funds to subsidize voluntary agencies stretches tax dollars further by drawing upon matching funds from private sources. But often the case for privatization is based on speculation: It stands to reason that competition for the public dollar should yield better quality for less money. This argument is also used in support of the use of vouchers, with which consumers can go shopping for services (see Schultze, 1977).

That brings us to the question of equity. Cloward and Epstein (1967) claim that private agencies have abandoned poor people because their professional staffs prefer to work with middle-class clients. If that is true, competition could work to the disadvantage of the poor, since agencies would be more inclined to go after the clients with whom they felt they could have the greatest success. Regardless of whether the Cloward-Epstein thesis is correct, voluntary agencies that serve predominantly middle-class clientele should not be compared with public agencies that deal with the most intractable problems of the underclass. The typical public assistance office is indeed bureaucratic, unresponsive and mired in mediocrity. It is doubtful that privately run public assistances offices would be any less so.

The source of funding is a different question. Cloward and Epstein wrote their essay on the disengagement of private family agencies prior to a revolution in social service financing. The large scale support of the private sector by government subsidies dates from the late sixties. Federal funding—with rules calling for the extension of services to low-income families—brought about the transformation in private providers to which Bibelman (1981) refers. She points to outreach activities and a broadened clientele in family service agencies as indicators of this trend. Yet according to Ostrander (1985) there is still evidence of screening out of poor people and, with the reduction of federal funds, shifting to services that are reimbursable by Blue Cross-Blue Shield and Medicare. The cutbacks have also led to an increase in fee-charging, another way in which people at the bottom get screened out (SPIGOT, 1982, 1983).

Without federal money, coupled with requirements that services be accessible to all, there is little prospect that the private sector would continue to extend its services to those at the bottom. Certainly commercial enterprises would quickly lose interest in that population. *True* privatization of human services—that is, abandonment of the field by the federal government—would most certainly mean abandonment of the poor by the private sector.

The Wave of the Future?

It is risky to make long-term predictions on the basis of rapidly changing events. Privatization of the auspices of human services dates from the late sixties. The massive federal deficits that have precipitated cutbacks in funding of services date from the early eighties. In terms of auspices, the best bet is that they will continue to be the public-private mix described by Kamerman (1983). That issue can be expected to become less ideological and more pragmatic, as different kinds of service systems appear to be most successful at certain tasks. As for the federal role in funding: for reasons advanced earlier, it is the thesis of this book that in the long run the national government will continue to support a range of social services in addition to economic security.

Chapter 12

Case History of a Crisis: The Child as Parent

We have seen how the way a problem is defined determines what policies will be created to deal with it. Calling somebody criminal or mentally ill may make all the difference in the world as to how that person is treated. Whether a child is labeled dependent or neglected or abused has major consequences for both the child and its parent. But definition also determines when something is even viewed as a problem. We see that very clearly in the case of teenage pregnancy.

In this chapter we shall look at a crisis that occurred in the late seventies in the United States. A crisis is a turning point. We speak of a medical crisis as the time when an illness takes a decisive turn for better or worse. A revolution is a crisis in government. Social workers frequently get involved with clients when their personal lives are in crisis, for example when a marriage is breaking up. In each instance, we are most conscious of outside events intruding on the life of a person or society. But a crisis is also the point when old definitions no longer apply to what is happening. That adds another dimension: the way social definitions help to determine when a crisis exists.

When a society is in turmoil, revolutionary elements may create disruptive incidents as a way of showing that the official government is no longer in control—that is, that the state is in crisis. When Fidel Castro was trying to overthrow the Batista regime in Cuba in the 1950s, Castro's men were alleged to be setting fire to the sugar cane fields. Clearly this would not win the minds and hearts of Cuban farmers, but it could show that the Batista forces no longer ran the country and that in effect they had already been overthrown.

A married couple define their relationship as being intact. At some point one or both may acknowledge that the marriage is in trouble. The quality of the relationship has not suddenly deteriorated, that has probably been going on for a long time. But now the marriage is in crisis because the couple have redefined their relationship as no longer stable.

Teenage pregnancy had been around for a long time before the late seventies, but the public suddenly "discovered" it around 1978. Professional journals and popular magazines began using words like "crisis" and "epidemic" whereas previously those terms had rarely been used to describe what was going on. Why did the crisis in public perception occur when it did, and how did different groups' ways of defining the situation affect their ways of responding to it?

157

THE CHILD AS PARENT

Parents have always been seen as the primary agents for preparing children for life. When this role is thrust on children themselves—in other words, when people supposedly still being prepared now have to do the preparing—that presents society with a problem. The problem may not be defined in that way. Instead we may talk about immorality, fatherless families, dependency on welfare, infant deprivation or blighted dreams.

There is a chain of events that runs like this: An adolescent female engages in sexual activity. She may or may not get pregnant. If she becomes pregnant she may have an abortion, miscarry or give birth. She may marry before or after pregnancy or after giving birth. If she gives birth she may care for the child, with or without help from her family, or turn the child over to somebody else to raise.

How often some or all of this chain takes place depends on many factors: the number of adolescent females, both absolutely and as a percentage of all females; the age at which females reach puberty; the age span that is considered "adolescent"; the amount of sexual activity engaged in by adolescent females; the use of contraceptives; the use of abortion by pregnant females; attitudes about keeping or giving up babies for adoption; attitudes toward forced marriage and unwed parenthood. Since the sixties every one of these factors has been going through major changes. That helps explain why a crisis occurred but not the way it came about.

Discovery of an "Epidemic"

In the years 1970 through 1976, a standard index of magazine articles listed an average of between one and two articles a year on teenage pregnancy.[1] In 1977 there were a total of five and in 1978 there were eighteen. In 1978 there were eleven articles on teenage sexual behavior as compared with an average of three a year before that. In contrast, there was no such sudden increase in articles on teenage parents at that time, though an underlying concern expressed in many of the articles on pregnancy was the problem of teenage unmarried motherhood (see chart). For some reason the mass media "discovered" a problem in the late seventies and defined it mainly in terms of one aspect of the problem: pregnancy.

A similar trend can be seen in articles of special interest to social workers. *Social Work Research and Abstracts for Social Workers* publishes abstracts of articles appearing in many professional journals. From 1973 through 1977, there were fewer than five articles on teenage sexuality, pregnancy and parenthood cited in any one year. In 1978 there were ten, in 1979 fourteen and in 1980 seventeen.

---

[1] *Reader's Guide to Periodical Literature*. Actual date of volumes is March of one year through February of the next.

Articles on teenage pregnancy, sexuality, and parenthood, 1970-1984.
Source: Reader's Guide and Index to Periodical Literature.

Not only was 1978 the year when teenage pregnancy suddenly became big news in the media, but this was also the point at which the term "epidemic" came into vogue as a way of describing what was happening. TEEN-AGE PREGNANCY: GLOBAL EPIDEMIC . . . AMERICA'S TEEN PREGNAN-CY EPIDEMIC . . . THE TEENAGE PREGNANCY EPIDEMIC . . . EPI-DEMIC: TEENAGE PREGNANCY. The problem "has reached dimensions of a national disaster, comparable to a flood, epidemic or famine," wrote a Harvard University biologist (Konner, 1977). Archbishop Joseph L. Bernardin was quoted as saying teenage pregnancy was "reaching epidemic proportions" (Lincoln, 1978). The dictionary defines an epidemic as, "A contagious disease that spreads rapidly. . . . A rapid spread, growth, or development" (*American Heritage Dictionary*, 1969).

But teenage pregnancy had not suddenly exploded in the mid-seventies. Clearly the objective reality was not a rapidly spreading disease but rather a longterm trend which had largely been ignored by the general population. What had touched off the epidemic of public concern?

11 Million Teenagers

The Alan Guttmacher Institute (AGI) is a nonprofit organization for research, policy analysis and public education on pregnancy and childbearing. Originally set up as a quasi-autonomous affiliate of Planned Parenthood Foundation of America (PPFA), the Institute has been an independent organization since 1977. Of particular concern to AGI are unwanted pregnancies, and it supports sex education and the availability of contraception and termination of unwanted pregnancies through abortion.

In 1976 AGI released a report entitled *11 Million Teenagers: What Can Be Done About the Epidemic of Adolescent Pregnancies in the United States.* The attractive 65-page booklet, replete with photographs and multi-color charts, documented trends in teenage sexual activity, pregnancy and parenthood. Through it, the reader could learn, for instance, that the United States had one of the highest rates of births to teenagers in the world; that eleven million persons between the ages of 15 and 19—more than half the U.S. population in that age bracket—were estimated to be sexually active (hence the title of the booklet); that a million teenagers became pregnant each year; that 600,000 of these gave birth; and that nine out of ten who gave birth elected to keep their babies.

According to AGI staff, the timing of the report had more to do with the availability of new data about teenage pregnancy and childbirth than anything else, but the intent was clearly more than simply to inform (Murray, 1985; Parks, 1985). The booklet served not only to escalate public awareness of the issue but also to shape the emerging debate about what should be done. In newspaper and magazine articles and congressional hearings, the numbers from the report were cited over and over again until they became accepted truth—part of the presumption with which different parties entered the discussion.

Zelnick and Kantner are not household words. They are the names of two researchers whose studies helped to precipitate the epidemic of public concern. Their national surveys of teenage sexuality and pregnancy, beginning in 1971, were reported in professional journals and special monographs (see Kantner & Zelnik, 1972, 1973; Zelnik & Kantner, 1978). Studies such as these, along with reports from the U.S. Bureau of the Census and other government agencies, were the information base for *11 Million Teenagers* and testimony in congressional hearings. Writers of news features and magazine articles would in turn draw on these more accessible sources in transmitting the message to the general public.

The degree to which researchers have done major studies on teenage pregnancy is not itself accidental. Research takes money. Social scientists must interest government agencies or private foundations in funding certain kinds of investigations. Similarly, funds are allocated to universities and social agencies to operate demonstration projects in pregnancy prevention, maternal and infant care and parent effectiveness training. Reports on such projects also find their way into the mass media, further adding to public awareness and interest.

The Carter Administration's Dilemma

The policy-makers in Washington were also pushing teenage pregnancy to center stage in the late seventies and giving shape to the public's view of it. The issue of abortion hung over the 1976 presidential campaign like a sword. Three years earlier, the Supreme Court had set sharp limits on states' ability to restrict abortions in its historic *Roe v. Wade* decision (410 US 113, 1973). This had brought various constituencies out in force, determined to make candidates for office in the 1976 election stand or fall on this question. Jimmy Carter's strong opposition to abortion was in line with his Southern fundamentalist background. His choice for secretary of Health, Education and Welfare, Joseph Califano, a Roman Catholic, was equally adamant on the issue.

Upon assuming office, Califano saw the statistics on teenage pregnancy for the first time. According to one aide, he was "dazzled" by what he saw. Not only was Califano getting political pressure to act, but as the father of adolescents he had a personal stake in the issue (*New York Times*, 1978a). The administration's solution was to lobby hard for services to help prevent teenage pregnancies as an alternative to abortion. During 1978, several congressional committees held public hearings on these proposals. The hearings made good copy, so newspapers and weekly news magazines were full of articles on the subject.

News generates news, and a particular subject takes on more significance in the eyes of reporters and editors as more stories are written about it. In time the excitement begins to fade, but for a time the public interest in an issue feeds on itself. Not that the concern about teenage pregnancy was manufactured. Long term trends had in fact produced a major problem, one with consequences for infants' health and social welfare, the health and future prospects of their teenage parents, and the public purse.

A CONCERN WITH A REALITY BASE

The chance that a baby born to a teenager will survive the first year of life is about half that of a baby born to a woman in her twenties. Mothers under the age of sixteen are twice as likely to have babies with low birth weight—a major cause of infant mortality—as are mothers aged 20-24 (New York State, 1980, Table 6). Girls under the age of fifteen are more likely to die while giving birth than are 15-19 year olds, who are more likely to die than women in their early twenties. The risk of anemia and toxemia associated with pregnancy and birth is higher for teenage mothers than for those in their twenties (AGI, 1976, p. 23).

One has to be careful in citing such evidence. Mothers in their teens are also more likely to come from low-income backgrounds and have health risks not related to age. Teenage mothers are more likely to have babies out of wedlock than are older mothers. There is no question that giving birth sharply changes the future lives of teenage women. It used to be that schools would expel students as soon as their pregnancy was discovered. That has changed for the better in recent years, and many high schools have developed special programs to help young mothers complete their education. Yet a national study which was able to rule out factors such as race, economic level, academic aptitude and earlier aspirations found that women who had given birth before age 18 were twice as likely to have dropped out before graduation as those who did not give birth until after age 20 (Card & Wise, 1978, Tables 5, 6). This in turn affects later earning capacity and the need to turn to public assistance. The problem is not simply one of unmarried teen parents. Marriages of teenage parents are far more likely to end in separation or divorce than when child-bearing begins after age 20 (McCarthy & Menken, 1979).

The Rising Tide of Teenage Pregnancy

Unlike births, pregnancies are not routinely recorded in census statistics. So it was not until researchers began conducting special surveys of the adolescent population in the early seventies that the nature of what was happening came to light. What these studies revealed was that teenagers were more sexually active, and more females among them were becoming pregnant at an earlier age, than anyone had imagined. On top of this, successive surveys showed that the numbers were continuing to rise (AGI, 1976; Zelnik & Kantner, 1977):

— A thirty percent increase in sexual activity among never-married American teenagers between 1971 and 1976.
— A million teenagers—one in ten of that age group—getting pregnant every year. For those under the age of 15, it was 30,000.
— Six out of ten pregnancies resulting in births to child-parents, most of whom were electing to keep and raise their offspring.
— Three hundred thousand abortions a year.

What gave the news special urgency was the fact that for many years Americans had been able to deny that it was happening. The blindness had a racial component. Traditionally a black teenager who became pregnant gave birth and then the family raised the child. If there was no family, friends or neighbors raised the child. The dismal prospects of employment for young black males made forced marriage an option of limited value for many pregnant black teenagers. In contrast, a pregnant white teenager's parents might pressure the man into marrying her, or send their daughter into exile until the baby could be put up for adoption or consigned to life in an orphanage. In the seventies, the most dramatic increase in births was happening among *white* teenagers. More jarring still, these young women were rejecting forced marriages and electing to raise their babies on their own. In fact, at the point that Americans were becoming alarmed about the epidemic in teenage pregnancy and parenthood, the rates for blacks and other minorities were going down, while the rate for whites continued to rise.

Births Per 1,000 Unmarried Females, Aged 15-19,
By Race, 1940-1978, Selected Years

Year	Whites	Other Races	Blacks Only
1940	3.3	42.5	*
1960	6.6	76.5	*
1972	10.5	92.7	98.8
1976	12.4	84.6	91.6
1978	13.8	83.9	90.3

* No separate figures reported
Source: U.S., Public Health Service (1982), Table 1-52.

Biological and Social Changes

The trends which so alarmed Americans in the late seventies had their roots in underlying changes in teenagers' physiology as well as norms of behavior. Since 1850 the onset of puberty among females has been getting younger by four months per decade. Thus the average female in the mid-nineteenth century was not capable of becoming pregnant until she was seventeen, whereas now the age is around eleven or twelve (Tanner, 1970). Meanwhile, the average first marriage is happening later, leaving a wider and wider gap between the biological age of parenthood and the socially defined age of parenthood.

Add to this the revolution in sexual attitudes in recent decades, ranging from greater openness with young children about their sexuality, to greater acceptance of a variety of lifestyles among young adults, to removal of most restraints on the mass media. There are persuasive arguments to the effect that many of these trends have been for the good, leading to a healthier and more honest approach to a basic component of life. But a byproduct has been greater freedom to experiment among children now capable of becoming parents without having been taught how to be parents.

The changing role of women has also had its impact. The refusal of pregnant teenagers to be forced into marriages of convenience, their sense of their own adequacy as parents and of their right to make decisions are part of a more general emancipation of American women. But when the woman is a child still struggling with her own transition to adulthood, and when the decisions concern the care of a newborn infant, the results can be costly—for the teenager's own aspirations and even more so for the infant.

A Cultural Lag

Social changes are never orderly and uniform. The revolution in sexual attitudes and the emancipation of women have occurred alongside widespread adherence to old ways and in some cases counter-revolution. Sex education programs in the public schools have been growing rapidly but many school systems either oppose such content or restrict the kinds of material which can be included. Despite the fact that a majority of Americans believe sex education—including contraceptive information—should be taught in schools, fewer than a fourth of all states require or even encourage it (Gallup, 1978; AGI, 1981, p. 39).

A majority of sexually active teenagers fail to use contraceptives or else use them sporadically. One reason for this is ignorance. Another is the magical belief that they can somehow escape negative consequences of what they do: It is not unlike the mindset with which some teenagers get behind the wheel of an automobile while under the influence of alcohol or drugs. Another, ironically, is the belief that sex is wrong. If I have intercourse on impulse, the reasoning goes, I am a good person. If instead I plan ahead in order to protect myself, I have started out intending to have sex and am therefore a bad person. This attitude is a vestige of a time when nice girls were expected to wait until the wedding night to have their first encounter with sex, as contrasted with the expectation that nice boys would experiment (Zelnick & Kantner, 1979).

One result of this cultural lag is that the Unites States has a higher rate of births to unmarried teenagers *and* of teenage abortions than the rest of the industrialized world. Even when limited to whites, the American rates are way above those in comparable countries. Are American teenagers simply more sexually active than their counterparts in other countries? Not according to researchers, who have concluded that the patterns of sexual behavior are similar among teenagers in all these nations. The major distinguishing factor is the greater use of contraceptives in the other countries (*New York Times*, 1985c).

WHAT IS THE PROBLEM?

A social problem is both a set of circumstances and a social definition of those circumstances as something to be solved. At different times "the problem" of teenage pregnancy has assumed different shapes, and the way it has been defined has depended on which constituency was doing the defining.

Personal Adjustment

Long before the epidemic of public awareness in the late seventies, social workers and health care professionals were involved with the problem of adolescent pregnancy. The concern about the "unwed mother" included older women as well, but a major part of the target population was in its teens. Many situations were "resolved" by forced marriage or, in the case of most blacks, by having the girl and her baby cared for within the family. But for those white adolescents who would not or could not marry the baby's father, the standard solution was delivery in a maternity home and then surrender for adoption or institutional care.

Among social workers, the problem was defined mainly in terms of the prevailing psychiatric outlook of the profession. A girl became pregnant as a conscious or unconscious way to get back at her parents or to deal with other personal adjustment problems. The task, then, was not only to get her through the crisis with as little damage as possible but also find a more effective way of coping with internal conflicts (see Young, 1954). For the baby, the goal was placement for adoption with a couple who met agency standards and whose own personal needs meshed with those of the child. For the sake of all concerned, the natural mother broke off any further contact with the child and her identity was kept secret from the adoptive couple.

Welfare Dependency

As the welfare system became the chief support for more unmarried teenagers and their offspring in the fifties and sixties, the attention of the child welfare field turned more and more to this population. While the problem was cast in terms of maternal and child health, social adjustment and development of human potential, the prospect of welfare dependency for ever larger numbers of female-headed families was at the bottom of much of the concern.

During the sixties and early seventies, several school-based programs were set up, primarily for low-income minority pregnant teenagers. As the AFDC rolls blossomed, the high rates of unmarried parenthood in this population became the center of attention. Revelation that by the midseventies half the $9.4 billion in AFDC payments was going to families in which the woman had first given birth as a teenager and a fourth of all teenage mothers were receiving such payments added fuel to the fire (Moore, 1978; U.S. Social Security Administration, 1980).

The "crisis" of adolescent pregnancy became two crises: the defiance of adult norms by increasing numbers of girls from the mainstream in terms of both sexual behavior and single parenthood, and the growing numbers of low-income minority families dependent on the state.

This dual view of the problem can be seen in the way it has been treated in the mass media. Articles about sexual behavior and the threat to traditional family values tend to be illustrated with photographs of white teenagers and feature case histories of girls from middle-class backgrounds. Articles focused on the other end of the spectrum—unmarried parenthood and economic dependency—are more likely to show pictures of minority mothers and their children and cite racial differences in the statistics (see *U.S. News*, 1978).

Unwanted Children

For some the biggest problem of teenage pregnancy is the birth of children to teenagers who do not want them and are unprepared to care for them adequately. The issue is not the desirability of the babies but rather their right to be wanted and cared for, and the mother's right to control her own life. Accordingly, the central task is to prevent the birth of children under the wrong circumstances, and whatever serves that end should be considered among the solutions.

In this point of view, the increase in teenage sexual activity is simply a fact of life. Regardless of how one may feel about it personally, it is not the critical issue. Instead the focus is on preventing unwanted pregnancies and making various birth control techniques more accessible. While abortion is a less desirable remedy, it is seen as a suitable option. For those teenagers who decide to carry their babies to term, there should be adequate health care before, during and after birth, and supportive services should continue for the young mother and her child. There is an underlying presumption that teenagers need special help in being adequate parents, regardless of their desires (Murray, 1985; Parks, 1985).

Family Values

Another school of thought holds that the foregoing view is too narrowly focused on the biological aspects of teenage pregnancy. The rising statistics point to a general decline in traditional values and social institutions. Thus remedies which appear simply to get young people off the hook and possibly make it easier to experiment sexually without facing the consequences are frowned upon. But while abortion is ruled out as an option, many contraceptive techniques are not. Typically the focus in relation to the latter is on preventing subsequent pregnancies after the initial one.

Adolescents should be helped to make responsible choices about sexual behavior, reproduction and parenting. Once pregnant, they should be given maximum support to assure a healthy and well-adjusted mother and child. This approach places great emphasis on spiritual and moral values and family solidarity (Shriver, 1977; Kramer, 1985). It appears to have been the approach favored by President Jimmy Carter and his secretary of Health, Education and Welfare, Joseph Califano.

Teenage Chastity

A more extreme form of the family values position sees the problem of teenage pregnancy as primarily one of sexual license. Whereas the previous approach stresses the need for teenagers to take responsibility for their actions, this one seeks to curb the actions more directly. The solution to the increase in adolescent pregnancy and parenthood is abstinence from sex by unmarried teenagers. The way to achieve this is to provide moral education with a religious emphasis and require that teenagers using family planning services involve their parents (see U.S., Congress, Senate, 1981).

What Crisis?

Finally, there is the view that the "epidemic" of teenage pregnancy is actually the result of a well-orchestrated scare campaign promoted by family planning and abortion interests, and that the problem, rather than being one of too many unwanted babies, is the general decline in the birth rate in the United States. The intent of the scare tactics: to pave the way for genetic engineering and elimination of undesirables from society, much as the Nazis massacred the Jews in Germany. The Planned Parenthood Federation of America is seen as the main villain, but manufacturers of birth control devices are also viewed as part of the conspiracy (Kasun, 1978; U.S., Congress, House of Representatives, 1981, pp. 329-338).

Teenage Pregnancy and Oppression

All of the above definitions start by presuming that the locus of the problem is the teenager and/or her family. Once we do that, we move naturally to "solutions" that focus on doing something to or about them. Instead, the problem can be cast in terms of the social structure—specifically, systematic oppression based on sex, race or class, or some combination of the three. The fact that women are the only ones who *can* become pregnant may blind us to the implicit sexism in unwanted pregnancies.

Likewise, a society that excludes large numbers of young black males from the workforce and more generally spawns a large underclass of people with little prospect of leaving it is likely to see a high incidence of births to young persons unprepared to take on the burdens of parenthood. Looked at in this way, teenage pregnancy can be defined as a symptoms rather than *the* problem.

Oppression may be involved in a more direct way. Implicitly, discussions of teenage pregnancy have assumed willing if not willful participation of the young woman. Yet it is estimated that as many as one in five women have been sexually abused before reaching adulthood. The figures are speculative, and there are no good estimates of the number of cases in which coitus takes place, but it stands to reason that some teenage pregnancy is the result of rape or incest.

SOCIAL DEFINITIONS AND SOCIAL WELFARE POLICY

The critical importance of problem definition for the proposed remedies can be seen in the history of policy changes regarding teenage pregnancy. Our historic reluctance as a country to face it, its emergence as a crisis in the late seventies and the conflicting views about it have all helped to shape the policies for dealing with the problem.

Early federal programs to deal with adolescent pregnancy and parenthood were buried in other programs or given innocuous titles as a way of protecting them from political opposition. By the early seventies the genie was beginning to get out of the bottle and the problem could no longer be ignored. Medicaid funds were already being used for abortions for teenagers in many states and an array of special programs for school age parents were appearing.

The Supreme Court decision of 1973, which curtailed states' ability to restrict abortions for teenagers, set in motion conflicting forces. Now family planning agencies, hospitals and private physicians were freer to provide legal abortions, and the number involving adolescents shot up. But the decision also galvanized anti-abortion groups into action, leading to clashes between so-called pro-life and pro-choice factions. Though abortion was the red flag that evoked the strongest passions, the antagonists became polarized around a cluster of issues including the kind of sex education, if any, that should be offered, the role of parental authority and acceptable means of birth control.

The conflict can be seen in the ambiguity of federal policies. In 1977, Congress slapped limits on the use of Medicaid funds for abortion. That same year the Supreme Court ruled that agencies could not require teenagers to get parental consent for abortions (*CQ Almanac*, 1984). The Carter administration sought to steer a course between the shoals. Reflecting this approach, the Adolescent Health Services and Pregnancy Prevention and Care Act of 1978 included sex education, broadly defined; birth control; and a requirement that grantee agencies advise their teenage clients of the availability of abortion. Funded agencies were to encourage teenagers to inform their parents of their request for family planning help, but they could not mandate parental consent for abortions. The modest funding for the program—$60 million—led some critics to call it a hoax. In order to get even this program, administration forces had to buck not only pro-life forces but also strong resistance to spending money on any social programs (*New York Times*, 1978a; Cherlin, 1978).

The pro-choice groups that chided the Carter administration for being half-hearted in its support of services to pregnant teenagers discovered an active opponent in the succeeding Reagan administration. As a price for continuing the 1978 program in 1981 they had to accept a parental consent stipulation and agree to funding of teenage chastity education (*CQ Almanac*, 1982). The agency which administered the 1978 act, the Office of Adolescent Pregnancy Programs (OAPP) in the Department of Health, Education and Welfare, had originally been directed by Dr. Lulu Mae Nix, whose philosophy was generally consistent with the Carter-Califano view. The Reagan administration replaced Nix with Marjorie Mecklenburg, a pro-life activist whose views were closer to those of Senators Jeremiah Denton, Alabama Republican, and Orrin Hatch, Republican of Utah. Denton was the main champion of chastity education, and Hatch had authored the 1977 amendment which restricted the use of Medicaid funds for abortion (*New York Times*, 1984c; Murray, 1985; Nix, 1985).

By the end of 1984, the policy restrictions passed by Congress in 1981 had percolated down through the policy machinery to influence the delivery of services to pregnant teenagers. Limits on the use of Medicaid funds for abortions were arousing fears that low-income teenagers would again resort to illegal means to end their pregnancies, with attendant dangers to themselves. The religious auspices of many of the federally funded chastity education programs provoked charges that they violated the principle of separation between church and state (*New York Times*, 1984c).

In early 1985, the Alan Guttmacher Institute released its report showing that the United States now led the industrial nations of the world in teenage pregnancy and abortion (*New York Times*, 1985c). It appeared that the battle over definition and redefinition of the problem of the child as parent was far from over.

PART 5

Social Work and the Social Fabric

It is remarkable that this country has had only one serious insurrection (the Civil War) in its more than two hundred year history and that was not to overthrow the Republic as much as to be left alone. Violence we have had aplenty, including attempts on the lives of almost every president in the last sixty years and a murder rate several times those of most countries of Western Europe. But throughout it all we have maintained a basic national unity if not consensus, notwithstanding occasional periods of unrest such as occurred in the sixties. Our labor movement's distinctive hallmark has been militancy toward foreign threats more than toward our own privileged classes. This has all happened, furthermore, without overt repression of the majority by a police state. But it has not just happened.

It is the contention of this book that American social welfare has been one of several institutions which have helped to maintain the fabric of our society. Others include the mass media and organized religion. Peace has been bought at a high price. As compared with other industrial countries, this society has been particularly slow to respond to human misery in an organized way. Its worst injustice, slavery, has left a deep residue of bitterness and blighted hopes that still defies solution. Social welfare must also share responsibility for this.

In this final section of the book we look at the profession that has been most closely identified with American social welfare: social work. There is evidence that most people who enter this field do so out of a sincere desire to help their fellow beings. Not that the motives are pure, nor that social work has a monopoly on altruism. But social workers as a group probably spend more time wrestling with issues of social justice than do most other professions.

Chapter 13 asks what is the mission of social work. It is a question that social workers themselves have a hard time answering; certainly they don't speak in unison on the subject.

Chapter 14 is a debate on the question of social work licensure. It serves the dual purpose of throwing light on an issue that is by no means resolved among those who call themselves "social workers" and illustrating use of argument on a policy issue.

Chapter 15 brings us full circle by examining the role of social work professionals in influencing social welfare policy. Their potential impact on decisions is probably greater than most people, including social workers, realize.

Chapter 13

Social Workers as Social Integrators

Ask five people what physicians do and you will probably get similar answers. "They treat people who are sick," or some such thing. Ask the same five people what lawyers do, and the answers will be some variant on, "They represent people in court." Accordingly, architects design buildings, professors teach in universities and dentists fix teeth. The answers distort the full range of occupational activities, but they will come with little hesitation. Ask the same five people what social workers do, and you will get some interesting reactions. "Let's see, they investigate welfare cases, I guess." "They're sociologists, aren't they?" "My aunt used to work in a mental health clinic, but I'm not sure what she did." "Them? They're the bleeding hearts that want to let the crooks out of prison."

Well, maybe not surprising. Many people have never had any dealings with professional social workers—or least that they knew were social workers. But you get almost as much confusion from social workers as from non-social workers. Even more hesitation, and then often a lengthy lecture in abstract language or else a long list of special fields.

A major problem in defining social work and its mission is its scope—from *A* for alcohol and drug counseling to *Z* for zoning and land use planning. The diversity of social work roles goes back to its earliest history.

THE ROOTS OF SOCIAL WORK

Although the kinds of helping activities associated with social work are as old as civilization, the identification of a distinct occupational field came about in the latter part of the nineteenth century. Earlier chapters have discussed the charity organization societies (COS) which sprang up in many American cities in the 1870s and 1880s. In addition to efficient administration of charity, the COS was dedicated to moral uplift of the destitute. Volunteers known as *friendly visitors* went to the homes of the poor to determine their needs and inspire them to help themselves.

In time, reliance on volunteers gave way to hiring of paid staff who were called *case workers*. The COS was dedicated to *scientific* charity, and science meant training. Around the turn of the century, COSs in the largest cities set up training schools for their workers. These schools eventually broke away from their COS moorings and became professional schools in universities.

In the 1890s, another movement in social welfare appeared: the social settlement movement. University students, clergymen and wealthy individuals *settled* in the slums of big cities (hence the name) to work and live with the poor. Contrary to the COS mission of charity to other people, the settlement volunteers saw this as a two-way street—they would learn from the immigrant neighbors as they helped them deal with a strange and often hostile environment. That difference in outlook—helping *them* versus helping *one another*—was fundamental to the way COS and settlement workers defined the poor and their problems, and ultimately the kind of help they gave. The settlement workers couldn't hope to match the material resources the COS workers could channel to the slums, but relied more on education, innovation and agitation for social reform.

Meanwhile, other institutions were coming to see the value of workers who specialized in fact-gathering, knew how to work with people and were familiar with community resources. Hospitals began to use social workers to assist patients in making the transition from hospital to home care. The public schools were becoming aware of the impact of home life on school work and hired social workers as visiting teachers. Psychiatric hospitals and clinics used social workers to take social histories.

This initial diversity was reflected in the growth of separate professional associations and specialized social work education. Group work, rooted in settlement houses and other community services, was originally identified with the field of education. It became a recognized professional social work field in the late thirties. It was not until 1955 that the seven major social work professional organizations merged to form the National Association of Social Workers. Little wonder that few people, including social workers, have an easy time saying what "social workers" do.

SOCIAL WORK AND SOCIETAL TASKS

Social workers are involved in every one of the societal tasks described in this book: providing the means of survival, getting work done, controlling threatening behavior, preparing people for useful roles and building social solidarity. It is the last that gives social work its distinctive character.

Survival Tasks

For many persons, the image of the social worker is that of the almsgiver. It is an image social work professionals have been trying to shake off, though social work grew out of charity work. Not that social workers are against giving alms to the needy. As an organized professional community they have been in the vanguard of the fight for adequate social insurance and relief standards. (A notable exception was the opposition of COS leaders to state mothers' aid, the forerunner of AFDC.) But social workers have feared that being seen as doing what anybody could do without extensive training would spoil their professional image. Also the stigma of the poor might rub off on them.

During the late sixties and early seventies some social workers were active in organizing the poor in their own behalf to make demands on community resource systems for material benefits. Advocacy for those in need became an accepted role for social workers, regardless of their official duties. But these thrusts never involved the majority of members of the social work profession.

As services to the aging and the permanently disabled have grown in importance, the profession has been reassessing its involvement in survival functions. Traditionally, social work was identified with optimism about changing people's circumstances. From the COS visitors forward, social workers have been bent on moving people from their current mode of life to something more productive and rewarding. This "cure" mentality may be increasingly irrelevant, says Morris (1977), as social services are directed more and more to maintenance of the chronically impaired.

Workforce Tasks

Galper (1975) has concluded that the social work profession's primary function is to aid in the management of the workforce in order to supply the capitalist system with labor resources. Atherton's (1969) assertion that society has assigned to social work the task of controlling dependency could also be interpreted in these terms.

The task of the COS friendly visitors was not to distribute relief but to inspire people to become self-dependent. The slogan of COS, "Not alms but a friend," meant moral suasion was a more important part of the agenda than giving material aid. In the early sixties social work professionals moved into public assistance agencies to mobilize clients' personal resources through counseling. The focus became more avowedly work-related with the inauguration in 1967 of the Work Incentive (WIN) program. Social work professionals were also heavily involved in Lyndon Johnson's War on Poverty, an important focus of which was making low-income youths work-ready.

In recent years, increasing numbers of professional social workers have been employed by private industry, to provide services to employees whose personal problems, such as alcoholism and drug abuse, interfere with their productivity. More generally, integration of their clients in the world of work has always been a significant concern of social workers, regardless of setting, except where the client population was obviously excluded from work roles.

Control of Threatening Behavior

Social workers have been identified with some fields of behavioral control more than others. In corrections, it has been juvenile rather than adult offenders who have attracted the interest of social work professionals. The mentally ill have been a major target population, but until recently there was little involvement with the developmentally disabled (mentally retarded). There are two reasons why mental illness but not behavior labeled as criminal attracted social workers. First, social work professionals have traditionally had difficulty with the police function, a basic ingredient of the criminal justice system. The disaffection was probably mutual, those charged with responsibility for corrections viewing social work professionals as too naive and permissive to deal with hardened criminals. Mental health, on the other hand, has had a benign image, where control measures as well as treatment have been cast in terms of helping. From the establishment of the first juvenile court in 1899, juvenile justice had a more positive and therapeutic orientation than adult corrections, and it has overlapped with child welfare, a major social work field.

A more important reason for social work's attraction to mental health has been that field's domination by the medical profession. Since early in its history social work has measured its own professionalism against that of medicine. A landmark statement on whether social work was, indeed, a profession was delivered in 1915 by Abraham Flexner. His claim to fame was that he had done an exhaustive study of medical education a few years before (Flexner, 1910). Using the model from medicine, Flexner said no, social work was not yet a profession. Why not? Because, among things, it lacked a communicable body of theory (1915). This caused no little amount of consternation among the social workers, whose drive for recognition as a technically competent field in subsequent years was said to be accelerated by Flexner's assessment (Bruno, 1947).

Preparing People for Useful Roles

Social workers' facility for teaching life skills and implanting values made the induction of children and immigrants into American life natural foci of the social work profession's activities. In no field is social work dominance clearer than in child welfare and family service: child protection, foster family and institutional care, and adoptions and family counseling. Even where the direct activity is with adult family members, concern about the effects of marital discord and personal malfunctioning on the children is a constant theme. Social workers tend to view families much more in terms of their socializing potential than as economic resource systems.

It was the response to the waves of European immigrants that gave birth to social work as a distinct occupation. The charity organization societies came into being to help cities cope with the flood of humanity, and the immigrant ghettoes were the soil from which settlement houses grew. When internal migration supplanted that from Europe as the major population movement in this country, social workers turned their attention to work with the newcomers from the rural South and more recently, Latin American and Asian immigrants.

Social Workers as Integrators

In each of the foregoing societal tasks, social workers have played a unique role in seeking to reconcile differences among segments of the society. They have urged compassion for the poor, at the same time preaching to the poor the prevailing values of work and self-improvement. They have sought humane treatment of offenders and the mentally disabled while trying to bring the socially deviant into the mainstream. They have worked to protect children against abuse and exploitation and worked to prepare them to fit into society as adults. In short, they have interpreted their clients to society and to themselves in such a way as to create an integrated whole. This role of social integrator has placed social workers at the center of most of the conflicts of American society, and in so doing has created tensions within the field.

SOCIAL INTEGRATOR OR GADFLY?

If social work contented itself with merely integrating, smoothing the way for entry of dissident elements into the existing social order, it would be helping to perpetuate the social injustices that are endemic to society—softening their harshest effects, but perpetuating them nonetheless. Yet social workers have always felt uncomfortable with the role of integrator. Along with it has come a gadfly function—sometimes strident, sometimes muffled, but always there.

In the folklore of the profession, the two competing impulses have been identified with the two institutions from which social work sprang: the charity organization movement and the social settlement movement. The charity organization societies were the integrators, seeking to get the immigrant poor to adjust to American society, while the settlement residents agitated for reform and made common cause with the newcomers against an oppressive system. In reality the charity organization movement fought for better housing and public health measures, and a major function of the settlement houses was to Americanize the immigrants and help them become integrated into society.

On the eve of the Depression, Porter R. Lee (1929) identified the dilemma in social work as being between cause and function. The first of these was action against entrenched evil; the second was rehabilitative services. He saw these as complementing each other, rather than a source of conflict. But the economic collapse of the thirties put social work's unity to the test. At a time when casework services were beginning to come under the influence of psychiatry, whose basic mission was adjustment of the individual to society, other elements in social work were becoming radicalized.

In the forties and fifties, the integrative side of social work was dominant, identified mainly with clinical services, but the activist side of the coin was still evident in community work. Events of the late sixties again exacerbated the differences, as many young social workers became swept up in the politics of urban unrest. In the seventies and eighties the pendulum seems to have swung back toward the integrator role and a lessening of the internal tensions in social work. While these shifts in social work mirror changes in the general political climate, the relationship between the two is not simple and direct. One complicating factor has been the professionalizing of the field.

PROFESSIONALISM IN SOCIAL WORK

Social work aspires to be considered a profession but some people have called it a "semi-profession" (Etzioni, 1969). What is a profession, and how do occupations make it into the winner's circle? While the answer lies partly in a field's ability to sell itself and wield political power, there are real differences between professions and non-professions, and if they didn't exist we would probably have to invent them. We are talking here about *learned* professions, which involve trained judgments applied to practical problems. All sorts of people who are not considered professionals are trained to deal with practical problems. In fact, most jobs require some training. Secretaries and drill press operators and flight attendants all need training, and their work is eminently practical, but we don't think of them as being professional in the sense it is being used here.

The difference lies in the kind of training and that word *judgment*. You can go only so far in using detailed instructions to guide decisions, and the more complex the subject matter the less you can rely on set formulas. That means taking risks, often in matters that have monumental consequences for people. Those two factors—complexity of the subject matter and the risks involved for the person using the services—set professions apart from other occupations.

Sociologist William Goode (1969) has developed a model of professions, based on two central qualities: a body of knowledge and a service ideal.

Professional knowledge is abstract and organized into a codified set of principles that can be applied to concrete problems of living. Society believes in the efficacy of the knowledge, accepts as proper that such problems be given over to the designated occupational group for solution, and accepts the profession as the final arbiter in any dispute over technical solutions within its area of competence. There is an air of mystery surrounding the expertise of the professional community, and the profession itself helps to create, organize and transmit the knowledge.

The *service ideal*, in Goode's conception, is such that the practitioner rather than the client decides what is best for the client; there is a selfless quality to the sacrifice one goes through to become professional; the professional community contributes to the development of professional knowledge and is committed to the recruitment of talented people to the field even though this means increased competition for clientele. The professional community sets up a reward and punishment system such that "virtue pays"; that is, the practitioner who lives by the service ideal is more successful than the practitioner who does not. The society believes the profession accepts its own precepts and follows them to some extent. This is how it is in theory at least. The reality may be something else.

One of the earliest fields to gain official protection of its professional status was the legal profession. Yet up until a few decades ago it was still possible to prepare for the bar examination in many states by reading in somebody's law office, with no formal education required. Even today, principles of argument and social science theory are virtually ignored in many law schools, which are presumably transmitting abstract principles to those preparing for a field of practice in which argumentation skills and social science issues are central. Medicine gained a professional monopoly before it developed the kind of technical expertise we associate with that field today.

In recent years the public image of these established professions has been tarnished by revelations of unethical practices and social irresponsibility. In medicine, malpractice suits—a sign of public disenchantment—have become so common that a major cost of private practice these days is the premium for malpractice insurance. Major professions have spawned allied fields through which much of the hands-on work takes place. This trend, together with the growing use of computers to guide decision-making, has further weakened professional claims of exclusive competence.

But even though the professional reality does not always live up to the theory, the underlying rationale for professions is still sound. Ethical codes set a standard against which professional behavior can be measured. And no matter how sophisticated computers become, there will always be major areas where they will be no match for human judgments tempered by human values, human interaction and human experience. It is in those fields involving people-changing and people-processing that the complexities and value issues make trained judgment and professional commitment so vital.

In fact, the more our lives become intertwined with computers the greater will be the need for the human element. People understand this intuitively, as John Naisbitt points out in his bestseller, *Megatrends* (1984). Even as our infatuation with Atari games and word processors and microchips grows, says Naisbitt, there is a resurgent interest in human-to-human contact. Not just in the delivery process, either. The Orwellian implications of high-touch specialists being wired to all-wise machines aside, decision-making about work with humans must be vested ultimately in other humans. And so far the best means of assuring both the competence and social responsibility of such decision-making has been through professionalization.

In a 1957 article which has been widely quoted in the social work literature ever since, Ernest Greenwood set down the attributes of a profession: systematic theory, authority, community sanction, ethical codes and a culture. Such a list is useful as a starting point, but it tells us very little about why these and not other attributes. Why should a profession have a code of ethics, for instance?

We need to step back for a moment and consider what professions are all about and where they came from. The original meaning of ''profession'' was profession of faith, of adherence to religious vows, and the church dominated the original fields of medicine, law, and university teaching as well as the clergy. Law and then medicine and teaching broke away from church domination, beginning in the fourteenth century, and ''profess'' took on a different meaning: to profess that one was qualified to engage in certain activities

(Hughes, 1965; Larson, 1977). These learned fields held a status not afforded other occupational specialties which grew out of the medieval guilds.

The abstract nature of professional knowledge is what gives practitioners their distinctive capacity to analyze and intervene. Once you are cut free from dependence on rote formulas you can interpret new and unanticipated situations. In its pre-professional days, social work labored under fixed rules for gathering information. If some facts were useful, then twice as many facts were twice as useful, so the task was to amass as many facts as possible. But just as a student who approaches a term paper assignment by simply accumulating every available scrap of information without a design is soon mired in confusion, the early practitioners could make little use of much of the social evidence they collected. The great contribution of Freudian theory was that it provided a set of abstract principles with which to make sense out of the data. One could then be more selective in the kinds of questions asked of the client.

A physician is called in to interview a patient who is complaining of a sore leg. This sore leg resembles a lot of other sore legs, but each one may be the result of very different disorders, ranging from arthritis to circulatory problems to malignancy. Without a system of abstract principles with which to interpret symptoms and test results, the physician is helpless to know how to proceed.

The engineer must know whether the degree of sway in a bridge is within normal range or is a sign of imminent collapse. Nonprofessional technicians may be aware that the readings on their instruments are outside the normal range, but it is the professional engineer with abstract principles who can make the expert judgment as to what to do. Likewise, a lawyer could quickly be overwhelmed by the millions of pages of legal lore if she did not have a set of principles for choosing among legal precedents and applying them to the case at hand.

Professional expertise is based on a body of knowledge that is not shared by the general population, creating problems of accountability. Clients are not customers. Not only must they allow the professional to invade their privacy, but they don't have the expertise to challenge what is being done to them. Often their questions are treated as part of the data on which the practitioner bases her diagnosis. The problem is compounded by the fact that most human service clients are already vulnerable due to illness or personal crisis. On the societal level, the public is not expected to second-guess the special wisdom of professions. This means the usual kinds of external scrutiny and market control are absent.

If the professional community is to develop a sound knowledge base and the individual practitioner is to apply abstract principles effectively, both must be able to think and act objectively, unswayed by public pressure, client wishes or practitioner bias and self-interest.

For all these reasons, professions are afforded a high degree of autonomy. The practitioner is subject to control by her professional community, but this must not interfere with her use of her own trained judgment in work with her clients, or else the practice is no longer "professional." Over the years professions have developed mechanisms for assuring responsible use of this power and autonomy. Prolonged training under professional auspices is intended not only for mastering complex principles of practice and foundation knowledge but also learning the values and behavioral standards of the profession. Codes of ethics and licensure also help to assure responsible, ethical behavior of practitioners.

"Old" versus "New" Professionalism

Not only is the preceding model a picture of what takes place in theory, it is also derived from the oldest fields, medicine, law and the clergy. It is the model which sociologists have relied on in describing all professionalism (Perrucci & Gerstl, 1969, p. 7). Even those established fields deviate from the model in significant ways. Science-based? The knowledge base of law is more accurately scholarship than science per se. Some theology strays very far from the usual meaning of science. The model is based on the notion of an autonomous practitioner who either operates outside of any formal organization or who dominates the organizational base. But this does not fit the case of many members of the clergy. Meanwhile, all professions, including medicine and law, are becoming increasingly bureaucratized (see Zola & Miller, 1973; Etheridge, 1973).

But the professional reality has outrun this model in even more basic ways in this century. Technological change has created a large number of emerging professions which depart from the classic image in basic ways. They include fields like journalism, clinical psychology, occupational therapy, library science and engineering. Some of these may be considered "semi-professions" by the sociologists, but they consider themselves professions in every sense of the word. Social work is one of these newer fields.

Professional Knowledge in Social Work

Expertise is the core of professionalism. The evolution of social work's knowledge base has made great strides in recent years. The debate over the scientific validity of this knowledge and social work effectiveness goes on, as it will continue to in the future. (See, for example, Brown, 1968; Fischer, 1976; Reid & Hanrahan, 1982.) We should welcome the dialogue rather than try to quash it, for it can only lead to a better product.

The Service Ideal in Social Work

Social workers worry more as a rule about their social mission than do members of most professions. Every social work student, regardless of specialty, must be exposed to content on social welfare policy, poverty, racism and sexism—*must*, according to mandates of the Council on Social Work Education.

A social work code of ethics and enforcement machinery have been in effect since 1962, but these cover only members of the National Association of Social Workers, which does not include all social workers. Lack of public recognition of social work as a profession has meant that membership in a professional association is not necessary to being hired as a professional social worker. So the dominant social work association lacks the clout available to such bodies as the American Bar Association.

EDUCATIONAL CREDENTIALS IN SOCIAL WORK

Lacking a clear line of demarcation between "professional" and "nonprofessional" activities such as exists in medicine or law, social workers have focused on the level of professional education as the primary status base. By 1940, the two-year master's degree was firmly established as the minimum credential for professional status in social work. Thus, contrary to the pattern in the legal profession, a standard of university-based graduate education was erected long before the social workers were able to obtain legal regulation. This made a distinction between professionals, with their graduate credentials, and the other 80% of persons holding "social work" jobs, some with no more than a high school education.

In 1970 the National Association of Social Workers opened its membership to persons with a bachelor of social work degree. The baccalaureate programs were growing rapidly at that time, a result of an explosive growth of social work jobs fueled by federal anti-poverty funds. At the same time the Council on Social Work Education moved to bring bachelor's degree programs under its accrediting standards. In addition, it became possible for persons with a bachelor of social work degree to complete requirements for the master's degree in as little as one academic year.

The expectation at the time was that baccalaureate programs would be the growth sector of social work, allowing an extension of professional standards to a large proportion of the uncredentialed majority of social work positions (see Specht, 1972, p. 485). Some observers saw the two-year master's degree as a twilight zone between the bachelor's degree and the expanding number of social work doctorates.

Events did not go according to this scenario. The shortage of social workers turned into a shortage of positions. Particularly vulnerable were graduates of baccalaureate social work programs, since professional, private agencies tended to prefer workers with a master's degree, and many public agencies were recruiting staff with other professional backgrounds or no professional background. In addition, holders of the bachelor's degree in social work did not flock to the ranks of the National Association of Social Workers, so it remained predominantly a community of graduate social workers (see Attinson & Glassberg, 1983).

Agency-Based Practice

A key difference between "old" professions and "new" professions is the fact that the latter by and large are practiced under the auspices of bureaucratic organizations. This is probably a major reason why social work has been slow to develop internal control mechanisms such as licensure and an ethical code with teeth. While increasing numbers of social workers are moving into private practice, it is still a field mainly of employees. In the vast majority of cases these are employed by governmental or private, non-profit agencies. The priorities for social agencies are dictated largely by available funding; and increasingly, as we saw in Chapter 6, this has been governmental funding. The influence of financial resources on the service delivery system, described in Chapter 8, is translated into the availability of social work positions, who gets hired to fill those positions, and the pressures on their incumbents.

The official vehicles of the social work professional culture in turn respond to these influences. Schools of social work need to be able to convince potential students that there is a career at the end of the tunnel. Professional associations must respond to the priorities of their members or lose membership, and the members' priorities are strongly influenced by their agency identification. The fit between professional and agency priorities is not exact. Senior staff members in professional associations have great influence on decisions which guide the affairs of those associations, because unlike the volunteer leadership they can devote full time to the enterprise. Professors in schools of social work are insulated against direct pressure from social agencies and funding sources. So the political system influences social agencies and they in turn influence the social work profession, but there are lapses in the chain of influence.

Penny, Jenny, and Denny are classmates in a graduate social work program, where they all major in "micro practice" (direct service to clients) with a specialty in family service. Their professional training is identical, but what they do after graduation is not. Penny goes to work in a private family service agency in the suburbs, Jenny becomes a probation officer in the criminal court of a large metropolitan county, and Denny takes a job with a community center serving a low-income urban neighborhood.

It is not just the formal duties of these three that are different. They quickly learn that there are many expectations—formal and informal—attached to their jobs. In time their own views of their role and of their clients are affected by the daily exposure to the working environments. Penny's clients come asking for her help; their problems and the task of helping are defined in terms of personal adjustment and family relationships. Her biggest challenge is often zeroing in on exactly what the problem is, and often work on one problem evolves into work on others.

Jenny's clients come to see her because they are required to. Many have problems with drugs and alcohol. She goes through a period of deep disillusionment, as the behavior of some of her clients seems to confirm the advice from older staff members that these guys are not to be trusted, that they will steal from their grandmother to get drugs, that they interpret kindness as weakness. One of her biggest problems is keeping up with the mass of paper work she must complete on all cases. She gradually develops a style which allows her to survive in the system—getting tough with clients who break the rules, shaping her reports to satisfy her supervisor, and juggling a set of conflicting expectations.

Denny has to learn to adapt his concept of "professional" to an informal system in which it's hard sometimes to tell the staff from the clientele, some people make impossible demands on his time and energy, and he must work a crazy schedule. In school he had what he thought of as a balanced view of social welfare agencies and social work professionals. In the agency he begins to hear tale after tale of how these supposedly benign institutions are really punitive and dehumanizing. Having little opportunity to check out what he is told against any objective standard, he gradually comes to believe the worst about organized human services.

Three professionals, each strongly influenced by the work setting. Not that any of them have abandoned their professional principles nor forgotten their technical training. Penny is more aware of environmental factors in her cases than the clinical psychologist who acts as the agency's consultant; at times she has had to fight for a client's rights in relation to the school system, when "wiser heads" in the agency counseled against it. Jenny has been able to help one of her clients develop a strong self-image and mobilize his resources to return to school. She has also found ways to run interference for clients when the chief probation officer or a judge was ready to throw the book at them. Denny has been alert to mental health problems in some of the men who frequent the center and refer them to appropriate help. He's also been working with the secretary in relation to her snap judgments and unsolicited advice to clients.

The importance of a work setting in molding the behavior and attitudes of professional social workers is underscored by research (see Billingsley, 1964; Piven, 1961; Scott, 1969). Nor should this be surprising, since one's career is so dependent on one's employing organization. In recognition of this fact, the National Association of Social Workers has developed machinery to protect workers' right to behave professionally, including sanctions against the offending agency and a legal defense fund for members subjected to retaliatory measures.

To return to the societal tasks. Society develops means of carrying out essential tasks, but changing circumstances constantly lead to tension between what is needed and what can be delivered. So society creates special mechanisms for filling the gaps and reducing the tensions. Social welfare institutions are one kind of mechanism. In this age of technical specialization, trained cadres of experts are needed to run the social welfare machinery. These experts are not machines but humans, with their own needs and aspirations. So their interests, including career interests, impact on the social welfare system.

Professions are more than simply occupational groups and they introduce ad-

ditional concerns beyond material self-interest. The intrinsic satisfaction in doing the work rates very high for all professions. There is a service commitment
in all professions, though in some it seems rather far down the list of priorities.
The service commitment ranks high in social work, as compared with other
fields. This has helped to inject into this field the tension between activism and
integration cited earlier.

The internal tension between the integrator and the gadfly in social work is
what gives the profession its vitality. Though the differences are sometimes intense, they have never reached the point of dismembering the profession. Some
individuals have left the field, called themselves other things, but the main body
of social workers goes on struggling with diversity. Neither integrator nor gadfly
has ever "won" in the sense of defining social work entirely in its own image.

Ironically, each has believed at times that the other side *has* won. One is told,
for example, that the schools of social work don't teach "practice" any more
because they're too busy changing the world. And a common complaint of activists is that social work professionals are nothing more than junior psychiatrists.

Both claims are wrong. Social work education continues to emphasize theory
and skills in interpersonal intervention as it prods students to grapple with the
larger issues of social justice. A number of years ago a group of writers proposed the establishment of a new profession—psychotherapy—out of four related fields, including psychiatric social work. In studying these fields, they
found that the social workers were distinctive in one way: It was they who were
most politically involved, and in a liberal direction (Henry, Sims & Spray,
1971).

This book is written at a time when the profession seems to be having trouble
finding its voice. The cutbacks in social service programs and the conservative
political climate have taken their toll. Racism and poverty no longer evoke the
kind of anger that they did in the past. But this has happened to social work
before. It happened in the twenties, then came the Depression and with it a
rekindling of the fires of outrage. It happened in the fifties, but then in the sixties
the spirit of activism reappeared. There is little question that it will assert itself
again. The shape it takes will be dictated largely by social work's identification
with liberalism. Social workers are involved with people who have been labeled
by society as failures; the temptation to override the principle of self-determination is strong.

The internal conflicts between the integrators and the activists in social work
reflect the dilemmas within liberalism. They will continue into the future,
because the liberal agenda is an evolving process, not a fixed doctrine.

SOCIAL WORK AND THE LIBERAL TRADITION

Social work professional ideals lie squarely in the tradition of twentieth century liberalism. Individual freedom is basic to everything else in the field. The
concept of "client self-determination" is about the first lesson the social work
student learns. The right to privacy is to be protected by holding personal infor-

mation confidential. Tolerance of difference, a historic part of liberalism, has been translated into appreciation of difference. Social work is committed to maximum equality of opportunity, and many of the struggles within the profession revolved around the way equality is to be defined and promoted.

But social work must constantly struggle against illiberal tendencies, in professionalism, in agency policies, and within itself. The special expertise of professionalism brings with it the danger of arrogance and domination of the client. Social workers are frequently called upon by their agencies to exercise authority in a demeaning and punitive way. And as a socially concerned field, social work has a tendency to want to make people over to fit a predetermined role.

Chapter 14

A Policy Debate:
Should Social Workers Be Licensed?

The purpose of a debate is not just to score a victory over an opponent but also to shed light on an issue. The use of arguments to persuade an audience has led some people to wonder about the integrity of the whole process. But integrity can be protected in different ways. The researcher does this by observing canons of scientific investigation and inviting critical examination from colleagues. The clinician does it by exercising professional discipline and self-insight. In debates —for example in a legislative body or the courtroom—integrity is protected by the presentation of opposing views in an atmosphere of free expression.

That having been said, we are aware that each side in a debate will try to maximize its case and undermine the opponent's by deliberately emphasizing points which favor its position and selectively using information to its advantage.

Pro and Con are social workers who disagree on the question of social work licensure. Pro believes that all states should have licensing laws while Con believes just as strongly that social work licensure is bad. The reader is invited to render the verdict.

PRO'S CASE

Defining "Professional"

Let's begin by defining terms. The dictionary says a license is official or legal permission to do something. Professional licensure is the legally sanctioned right to engage in professional practice. The literature on professionalism is unequivocal on the point that professions have publicly and legally recognized control over their own territory. I'll address the question of whether professionalism is desirable in social work in a moment; but if we are to be a profession, we need legal sanction through licensure.

A critical distinction between professions and semi-professions, according to Etzioni (1969), is that the latter have less legitimate status, their right to privileged communication is less established and they have less autonomy from the supervision of society (p. v). Elliott (1972) states, ". . . society has accepted in whole or in part some claims for separation and autonomy made by various occupational groups. . . . This . . . provides the main basis for a distinct professional type'' (p. 2). Goode (1969) asserts that for an occupational group to be considered a profession, society must accept as proper that certain problems be turned over to that group for solution, and it is accepted as the final arbiter over technical disputes in its area of competence (pp. 277-278). Greenwood (1957), speaking specifically to social workers, declared that community sanction was an essential attribute of a profession. (See also Barber, 1965; Wilensky, 1964.) Without licensure, the social work professional community cannot hold persons calling themselves social workers accountable.

The Need for Professional Control

Is professional control desirable? Yes it is, for the consumer of services, for the community at large and for the profession itself. What are the consequences for the consumer of not having licensure? Without it the client lacks protection against shoddy, incompetent and outright unethical behavior. In the 1979 revision of the code of ethics, NASW added a principle that is not found in earlier versions: "The social worker should under no circumstances engage in sexual activities with clients." Why was this new language added? Obviously because such behavior had come to the attention of the social work community. But as of today, there is no way the profession can prevent the sexual exploitation of clients by persons calling themselves social workers unless there is legal regulation. The client is thus put in the same position as the customer of a traveling salesman—only more vulnerable, since clients cannot shop around. Similarly, the profession cannot prevent racism and sexism on the part of its members.

Well, why not rely on the agency to prevent exploitation and abuse of clients? In the first place, growing numbers of social workers are practicing as free agents, outside of agency auspices. But trusting the agency to protect the client is often tantamount to putting the fox in charge of the henhouse. Some of the worst abuses of clients' rights are perpetrated by agencies themselves—dehumanizing policies, red tape and bureaucratic indifference. Earlier chapters in this book have detailed instances where children were snatched from their parents, shunted around among foster homes, locked up in training schools that were little better than adult prisons. Mental patients have been dumped on the community, elderly persons have been tied to beds and physically abused. These are *agency*-sanctioned abuses. Far from relying on agencies to protect clients against abusive social workers, we should give professional social workers legal status in order that they can protect clients against abusive agencies. As Cloward and Piven (1977) point out, social workers' acquiescence to dominant professions and employing agencies is the major culprit in the abuse of clients: "Resistance is necessary in every social service setting." Richan (1973) asserts that social workers need control over social work practice and education in order to shift the lopsided balance of power between the agencies and the profession (p. 164), and that requires legal regulation.

As important as protection against outright abuse is protection against incompetence. A dedicated but inept worker can do as much damage as a person bent on exploitation. Under the pressure of tight funds, agencies have been downgrading social work positions, relying on untrained personnel to handle tasks which call for professional expertise. This trend has been most flagrant in public agencies, but it has also gone on in the voluntary sector. Meanwhile, a variety of persons calling themselves social workers but with dubious training or none at all are being placed in positions of critical responsibility.

The 1981 Delegate Assembly of NASW took note of this problem, citing the widespread practice of placing undifferentiated "human service" staff in positions formerly filled by professional social workers, relying on in-service training or simply experience on the job to make up for advanced social work training (NASW, 1983, p. PI 1.1). The Reagan Administration has taken the lead in shortchanging the consumers of social services by undermining professional standards (see *NASW News*, 1984a). This is a clear demonstration of their lack of appreciation of human services and the attitude that cutting costs is more important than meeting the needs of people. It's the perfect fulfillment of Gresham's Law: cheaper services driving out quality services.

There is no more compelling evidence than this to show that the consumers of services need the protection of enlightened policies at all levels of government. To their credit, social workers have been getting more involved in policy making in recent years—as consultants, as political activists, and even as candidates for office (see Mahaffey & Hanks, 1982). But if we are to be listened to as an authoritative voice we will have to become a *profession* in the eyes of the public, and right now we lack the public perception. It is no accident that third-party vendor payments for services under health insurance specify licensed practitioners. That's the only kind of professional the public understands. And, let's face it, the public respects and listens to the advice of professionals, whether it's in the clinic or the legislative corridors.

Unlike some professions, social work doesn't lobby just to advance its own interests. NASW's agenda of social policy issues covers fields in which there are few professional social workers involved—for example, income maintenance (see NASW, 1983). But the effect on social work careers of being an unlicensed occupation is a fair question. Social workers get uncomfortable about this one—we're probably distinctive among all occupational fields in that respect. But allowing everybody to claim the mantle of "social worker" and cheapen the product does discourage young people from spending years and hard-earned money on social work education. Undermining the economic viability and public respect of social work as a career will serve nobody's interest.

Licensure as the Answer

How does licensing deal with the problem? It's not a cure-all but it does accomplish several important things. First, let's see what we mean by social work licensure. Licensure, as opposed to title registration, regulates social work practice—that is, determines who may engage in certain activities. The model of licensure supported by NASW recognizes that there are different levels of competence in the field, based on professional education, and these should be addressed by multi-level licensure. Generally, the greater the complexity of the task to be performed and the greater the autonomy of the worker, the higher the necessary level of education (*NASW News*, 1974).

Persons qualify for licensure by attaining certain educational credentials and passing an examination. As is true of just about any licensing legislation, social work licensing bills normally include a limited period for "grandfathering in" persons already working in the field.

Aside from demonstrated competence, licensure assures adherence to a professional code of ethics. And in protection of both the client and the worker, licensure protects confidentiality of information.

The licensing authority should be under the direction of a board on which the dominant group is social workers, so that the professional community can take appropriate responsibility for the behavior of its members. I propose representation of an additional constituency on licensure boards: the consumers of social services. This would help to assure that licensing protected the clientele, not just the professionals.

Is Licensure Feasible?

Feasibility can be thought of in terms of politics, economics and administrative efficiency. The political feasibility of licensure is clearly demonstrated by the way the movement has spread from state to state during the very period when social workers were supposedly out of favor. As of 1984, legislators in 34 states had been persuaded of the need for legal regulation. Eighteen of those states have licensure, while the remainder have title registration only (*NASW News*, 1984b, p. 3). But in some jurisdictions, registration has been a precursor to licensing. Clearly, social work licensure is not just a flash in the pan.

Economically feasible? Some opponents charge that, once social workers have established a "monopoly" over the field, they will drive the price of services up and out of the reach of poor people. The fact is that the costs of social welfare are born primarily by taxpayers and voluntary contributors, and these costs are the result of complex forces in society, not manipulation by a small elite. If indeed the spending for social services were to go up in the wake of licensure—something the opponents have failed to demonstrate in those states which have passed licensing laws—it would most likely be because at last we had the political clout to have an impact on social welfare policy. Not a bad reason to support social work licensure!

Administrative feasibility has been demonstrated in those states which have enacted licensing laws. In recent years some states have conducted reviews of their social work regulatory machinery under so-called "sunset" legislation. Not one such review has resulted in repeal of social work legal regulation.

The fact is states license a wide range of occupations, not just professions. Your hairdresser has to be licensed, so does your plumber, but not the person who meddles in your personal affairs. Isn't it ironic that the disposition of your corpse after death requires a license in every state in the union, but in many states anybody can claim the title of social worker and be authorized to make life-determining decisions about you and your family while you're still alive?

CON'S CASE

I want to congratulate you, Pro, for making a very good statement of your position. You might even have me persuaded if I bought some of your basic assumptions. But there are a few points which trouble me. Let's start with the concept of professionalism.

Taking Another Look at Professionalism

I'm inclined to agree that professions seek to control their own turf, but sad to say this is not motivated by concern for the client or any other altruistic impulse. From the beginning, professionhood was an opportunity to gain status through work (Larson, 1977, p. 5), and it has continued to serve this function ever since. According to Haug and Sussman (1969), "professionals discovered that being too other-oriented could be costly in relation to satisfactions of economic, status and power needs. Like others in competitive societies professionals have organized around a common interest in order to maintain and enlarge their privileged position in society" (p. 154). Wilensky's (1964) survey of professionals in different fields found an inverse relationship between professionalism and client orientation (p. 154).

But this is *other* professions, not the "professional altruists," right? In Billingsley's (1964) study of 110 professional social workers he found that both agency and professional considerations took precedence over client needs. Lubove's (1965) influential history of the development of social work points out that "to the degree that social work developed a professional subculture, controlling career opportunities and personality, it erected another formidable barrier between the spontaneous will to serve and those in need of help" (pp. 118-119).

Specht (1972) raised the spectre of deprofessionalization in a widely quoted article in which he drew a sharp distinction between political activism and professionalization. Activism for social justice, he says, "is not what the profession prepares one to do, nor should it" (p. 6).

Pro tells us that social workers need licensure in order to protect clients against agency abuses. Talk about putting the foxes in charge of the henhouse! In Chapter 8 we read about the abusive treatment of juvenile offenders in training schools. Some of those training schools have been run by professional social workers—people Pro wants us to give legal sanction to continue their "good works."

There are other instances of agencies, headed by professional social workers, in which shoddy staff practices have been implicated in the abuse and even death of children. Well, you may say, licensure would give the professional community the power to prevent such things from happening. That suggests a misunderstanding of the real purpose of professional monopolies. They protect the members of the profession, not the clientele. Notice, for instance, that most professional codes of ethics prohibit the public criticism of one member by another. Incidentally, Wilensky's (1964) study of a range of professional fields revealed that in the process of professionalization licensure typically *precedes* the adoption of a code of ethics (p. 146).

Even where the professionals dominate the organization, as in medicine, says Freidson (1970), "rather less influence over performance is exercised than the organization of practice allows. . . ." In his study of physicians he found that "each practitioner tended to keep his complaints about others to himself, so that what he could observe of other's performance in the division of labor was not transmitted to other colleagues." The physicians were aware of the looseness of the control system but felt it was adequate (p. 93-94).

But doesn't professionalization affect the way workers view clients and their plight? In studies of professional and nonprofessional workers in probation (Piven, 1961) and child welfare (Richan, 1965), the orientation toward clients and their plight was no different for professionals and nonprofessionals, once other factors such as agency setting were held constant.

Sometimes the professional code of ethics has been used *against* social workers who had the guts to support social work values. Take the famous case of Mrs. B who was fired as being "incompetent" from her job as director of a planning organization because she belonged (as a private citizen) to a civic group working against racism. She filed a grievance with NASW, which ruled,

> Mrs. B was obligated to choose between resigning from her position and resigning from the antisegregation organization. . . . The ethical pledge of social workers states: "I regard as my primary obligation the welfare of the individual or group served which includes action for improving social conditions." The group served in this instance was the board of the planning council. . . . (*Personnel Information*, 1962)

Just so the point wouldn't be lost on social workers, this decision was prominently featured in the NASW periodical which listed job openings in the field. At times NASW has taken the worker's side in similar situations, usually at times when it was trendy to be brave. But who's to say which way the professional weathervane will turn in these reactionary times?

The 1979 revision of the NASW ethics code is not encouraging in this regard. Article IV-L declares, "The social worker should adhere to commitments made to the employing organization.'' If those commitments include not embarrassing the agency and then said agency engages in abuse of clients, so be it.

A social worker named Irwin Levin went to work for the New York City Office of Special Services for children in 1979. He uncovered eleven instances in which children died because of abuse while under the care of the OSSC. When he could get no response from his superiors, Levin took to writing anonymous letters to public officials and community organizations and enclosed sample material from case files as evidence. When the city brought charges against him for violating a confidentiality ordinance, he turned to NASW for legal assistance. His local chapter refused to support him, and it was only on appeal to NASW national that he was able to obtain $600. The association was careful to point out this was ''chiefly so that the principle of confidentiality could be tested in the court'' (*NASW News*, 1984c). Lost in the flap over Levin's ''unethical'' behavior was the fact that, but for this, agency neglect in the deaths of eleven children might have been successfully covered up. Whistleblowers beware!

Professional Competence

Licensure is usually granted on the assumption that the insiders bring a special set of knowledge and skills which outsiders lack. The first problem is to figure out what the special competence of social work professionals is. We should start by defining social work practice—that about which there is special competence. According to the Kansas social work licensure law, typical of most,

> ''Social work practice'' means the professional activity of helping individuals, groups or communities enhance or restore their capacity for physical, social and economic functioning and the professional application of social work values, principles and techniques in areas such as psychotherapy, social service administration, social planning, social work consultation and social work research to one of the following ends: Helping people obtain tangible services; counseling with individuals, families and groups; helping communities or groups provide or improve social and health services; and participating in relevant social action. . . . Social work practice includes the teaching of relevant subject matter and of conducting research into problems of human behavior and conflict. (Kansas, Senate, 1974)

What is a person other than a professional social worker prohibited from doing? Teaching ''relevant subject matter'' or ''conducting research into problems of human behavior and conflict''? That could knock off a lot of social scientists.

According to the Kentucky licensing law, social work practice is ''the professional activity of helping for remuneration individuals, groups or communities enhance or restore their capacity for social functioning and create societal conditions favorable to this goal'' (*Commonwealth of Kentucky*, 1975). Does a Kentucky state legislator engaged in creating favorable societal conditions need a social work license? And how about all those psychiatrists and psychologists and clergy members who, for remuneration, help individuals restore their capacity for social functioning? Kentucky's concern for the protection of its citizens is selective: Certified employees of boards of education and employees of the Commonwealth of Kentucky are exempt from the social work licensing provisions. Many states' laws explicitly exempt members of allied professions performing similar functions.

But the holes in the cheese do not reduce its odor. In fact, the vagueness with which the regulated practice is defined allows for exclusion of many persons engaged in helping activities, without any grounds for declaring that they are any less competent at what they do than are persons with professional social work education. That is a central issue in the licensing debate and one to which I'll return in a moment.

Even supposing one could define social work practice, what evidence is there that professionally trained social workers are better at it than persons without the training? The evidence is mixed, to say the least. Fischer's (1973) survey of eleven empirical studies of the effectiveness of social work practice found that in nine out of eleven cases, professional social workers were unable to bring about any positive changes that could not have been accomplished by nonprofessionals, and in a substantial number of studies clients actually deteriorated. The methodology in some of these studies has been criticized, but for there to be no more positive outcome than this in eleven different studies conducted under conditions of scientific research is a sorry track record indeed.

Reid and Hanrahan (1982) did another survey of studies, nine years later. Their conclusion was less than a resounding vote of confidence for social work's effectiveness.

> Perhaps the most striking point is that the outcomes of most of the studies were positive. That is, clients in experimental groups *tended* to show more gains than their counterparts did in the control groups. . . . All but two or three of the twenty-two studies yielded findings *that could on balance be regarded as positive.* (pp. 330-331. Italics added)

They acknowledge that in several studies the "success" was limited to performance in role-play tests or related to restricted areas of clients' lives. And typically the data were gathered immediately at the cessation of the experiment, so no follow-up information was available.

Well, surely the educational credentials which are to separate the sheep from the goats must be clearly delineated and grounded in something more than in-group consensus. The NASW licensure policy calls for multi-level laws which recognize the difference between the baccalaureate and the master of social work degree. This is what the Council of Social Work Education, the accrediting body of social work schools, says in relation to curricula in master's and bachelor's social work education programs: "In keeping with the tradition of academic freedom, the philosophy, objectives and organization of the social work curriculum are left to the discretion of the individual program" (CSWE, 1984b, Appendix 1). In other words, the magic formula which will determine whether you are allowed to hold a certain job in the social services is left up to the respective schools to define.

With an urgency seldom seen in relation to other social issues, social workers are rushing to encase the field in licensing laws, ostensibly to protect clients against having persons engage in an ill-defined and weakly validated set of practices unless they have completed an educational curriculum whose content depends on who is teaching it.

Whose Protection?

Apparently the clients of social agencies are not aware of the dangers to which they are exposed. At least it is not they who are clamoring for social work licensure. Instead, this is a campaign of, by and for social workers. If we are concerned about clients' vulnerability to abuse and incompetence, we should be setting standards for practice in those agencies serving the most vulnerable, for example public agencies which impact on the lives of many poor people. But many state laws have explicitly excluded public sector jobs from licensure, leaving those clients unprotected against abuse and incompetence. In some states, the only legal regulation is title registration, which offers no protection to clients. Some states restrict legal regulation to holders of the master of social work degree, which leaves many vulnerable clients without the alleged protection of licensure.

The big drive for social work licensure began in the 1970s, *after* the height of the social ferment and "activism" in social work had died down. The explanation is not hard to find. This was the period when social work jobs were shrinking, when there were second thoughts among the holders of master of social work degrees about the wisdom of having admitted baccalaureate workers to the fold (see Lewis, 1982). More specifically, this is when social work professionals saw themselves being excluded from third-party payments in favor of licensed professionals. The drive for licensure has been spearheaded in many states by private practitioners; for them it is clearly a bread and butter issue.

Who Is It Hurting?

So why should we be concerned about this misguided drive to set up barriers around social work? Isn't it enough that social workers simply own up to their stake in gaining professional prestige? Unfortunately there are harmful effects—for consumers of services, particular groups of practitioners and for the field as a whole.

Legal regulation of the kind under discussion hits directly at minority group members who wish to work in the social services. The percentage of blacks and other minorities in social work student bodies has dropped off sharply from what it was a decade ago (CSWE, 1973, 1974, 1984a). Tightened academic standards in the name of "excellence" and cutbacks in support of social work education are excluding many minority candidates. This is not just a question of career opportunities for aspiring minority group members. If the "excellence" being pushed by social work schools and their parent institutions were really relevant to social work practice with the disadvantaged, it would be hard to quarrel with this emphasis. But we are talking about traditional academic competencies which are quite different from the hands-on skills of working with people.

Professionalism has its place, but it should not be used to exclude people from helping people or, as Lubove (1965) puts it, "erect another formidable barrier between the spontaneous will to serve and those in need of help" (p. 119). It is not just minority group members per se. Ex-addicts and ex-alcoholics have done outstanding work with substance abusers. The down-and-outers in our population need to be able to deal with people they can trust and with whom they can communicate most comfortably. To set up a barrier to employment of such people in hospitals and clinics and other agencies can only serve to alienate the poor further.

An Alternative Approach

I'm not suggesting that we should leave things as they are. Agencies and professional helpers do indeed abuse the oppressed of this society. These institutionalized sources of help are part and parcel of the larger society, thus they are bound to be part of the oppression. We can exhort them to be good, we can force compliance to in-house rules of behavior, we can shift the power balance between professionals and agencies, but none of these steps will really affect the fortunes of the clientele. Not empowerment of social workers but empowerment of the oppressed clients is the way to provide real protection. And not by a few token seats on state licensing boards. The middle class client has other options and the political muscle to make demands. The oppressed client needs to obtain similar options and political muscle. Thus, instead of erecting barriers around social work's turf, we should open the field up to competition. If social work is worth saving, it will survive and prosper.

PRO'S ANSWER

First of all, Con, in view of your apparent concern about social work's level of competence, I'm surprised that you would unleash untrained ex-addicts and ex-alcoholics on unsuspecting clients. You have set up a straw man: Either social work must show impeccable results or its extensive training means nothing. You have cited Fischer's (1973) familiar review of past research purporting to show that casework doesn't work, without citing any of the rather serious criticisms of Fischer's own methods. (See, for example, Gyarfas & Nee, 1973; Alexander & Siman, 1973; Crane, 1976.) You have seized on the tentativeness of Reid and Hanrahan's (1982) language as a sign of weakness of their findings that social work practice *is* effective, instead of recognizing it as the appropriate caution of good social scientists.

You have also pulled the Council on Social Work Education's accrediting standards way out of shape by not distinguishing between the content requirements (which are rigorous) and the way a school meets them (which is flexible, as it should be). You would find the same approach used by other professional accrediting bodies. But in general you seem to hold social work to an unusually high standard; if it cannot meet that, then on with the ex-addicts.

But I don't know anybody who would disagree with your sentiments about elitism. Power to the people! Unfortunately, sentimentality is not going to help anybody. You cite Harry Specht's article on deprofessionalization of social work, Con—at least you have selected one passage that seems to say that professionalism and activism are incompatible. Taking Specht's (1972) comments *in context*, I come up with a different reading. More to the point of what he is saying is the statement that

> Advocacy and activism, if they are to be useful, must not be cast in the image of law or politics; rather, they must be developed as functions or techniques that are articulated with the knowledge, authority, sanction, culture, and professional ethics of social work. Advocacy and activism are still undeveloped as professional social work practice, but the profession nonetheless rushes to claim mastery of these new functions. (pp. 5-6)

To ignore reality and indulge in naive rhetoric can only frustrate our members and discredit us in the eyes of the world. The reality is that social work is not respected, and unless it is it will do blessed little empowering of anybody. There are other realities that you are refusing to face, Con. One is that social workers, being part of the human race, are indeed concerned about their own career interests. You can criticize all you want to, but if you hope to convince social workers of your point of view, you'd better start listening to theirs. If we do respond to the understandable concerns of social workers—yes, the bread and butter concerns, which are just as valid in our field as they are in any other (including, say, the clergy)—then we can indeed get them involved in fighting for the rights of the underdog. Fighting effectively, it might be added, not just with good intentions.

One other reality, which the arithmetic should be telling us: licensure is a thing whose time has come. The movement is spreading, and we can visualize a time in the not too distant future when it will be in effect in every jurisdiction. If minority social workers are interested in avoiding being excluded, they should stop fighting against any kind of legal regulation and instead jump into the debate over the *kind* of legal regulation. Fight over what kind, not whether. That's the way to be inside the room when the decisions are made instead of watching from the sidelines.

There is, finally, the reality of the nature of licensing laws. Con is concerned that the laws in different states vary and we do not have an ideal definition of practice. I'd be interested to find an ideal law of any kind. It is part of the very nature of laws that they are ambiguous and result from compromise. The point is, with a legal framework we can move ahead to develop our practice more fully. Medicine's scientific revolution came after it was licensed, not before. As for whether licensure will increase or decrease the potential for client abuse, I don't think it serves our argument to trot out a few horror stories and say, "That's what social workers are like." Rather, if we look at the nature of social work over the past several years, we have become progressively more sensitive to human need, more oriented to helping the underdog, more involved in the fight against racism and sexism. Find me another profession that is more concerned about human welfare. The guilt trips are something we don't need.

CON'S ANSWER

If recognizing the abusive potential in organized social services and in professional social work is being naive, I'm glad to accept that label. Let's talk about naivete. I think it's naive to assume that social work licensing laws will affect abusive agency practices one iota. Say that a mental hospital staff is beating up on elderly patients. Licensed social worker Jones on staff knows about it but decides not make waves, for fear of losing his job. This comes to the attention of other social workers, who try to get Jones's license revoked. Is it likely that the state licensing board will take any action? No, they won't, which will give Jones a very clear signal.

Or suppose Jones does make waves, and as a result is fired from his post. What will his social work license do to protect him? If Jones's boss is a licensed social worker and somebody tries to revoke the boss's license, it will be easy enough to confuse the issue with questions of Jones's competence.

Or say licensed social worker Smith abuses a patient or has sex with a client or diverts an inmate's funds to his own bank account. We have laws on the books now with which to deal with such criminal acts. If there's too little evidence to get a conviction under those, how likely is it that they will be enough evidence for a license revocation? Smith's criminal record will follow him wherever he goes; action on his social work license will only follow him as far as the state line.

Pro, it looks as if you aren't worried about competence levels after all. You say the raising of technical standards will come after licensure. So the license will be no guarantee of somebody's competence. I wonder which set of circumstances will accelerate technical advancement in social work faster: a monopoly, in which new conceptions of practice can be ruled out of order because their authors lack the proper ticket of admission, or an inclusive system which welcomes new people with new ideas? It's a good thing they didn't have licensure when Dorothea Linde Dix and Jane Addams were around. Otherwise, social work might have a hard time finding heroic figures with which to embellish its folklore.

No, social work licensure will not protect anybody against unethical and incompetent practice. It will just protect those inside the magic circle from competition from outsiders. The profession and its clientele will suffer as a result.

Pro and Con have not exhausted the arguments regarding social work licensure. Debates rarely do. Still, they are an excellent means of smoking out the issues on a subject. With a majority of states having some form of legal regulation of social work and others moving in that direction, the question may be moot in the future. That will not stop the debates about this and other questions of social work's professional status.

Chapter 15

Social Workers as Movers and Shakers

Question: What percentage of all social workers are involved in making social welfare policy?

Answer: 100%. Many social workers would deny that. "I'm a practitioner, I just work with clients." But every social worker affects social policy because there is a political dimension to everything the social worker does. We should define "political" more broadly than the dictionary does, since it includes any use of power to affect policies or social institutions.

When a parent complains to her social worker about the school teacher, the social worker's response is partly political. If the problem is defined as a sign of the parent's hang-ups ("I've noticed you have a lot of negative things to say about people in authority, Mrs. Sims, I wonder why that is") the focus shifts away from the teacher and school policies. The worker's definition may be accurate, but the point is, a political act has taken place.

If the worker and Mrs. Sims focus on her son Johnny's behavior that provoked the teacher's action—again deflecting attention away from the institution—that is a political act. If instead Mrs. Sims and the worker pursue the issue of the teacher's behavior or go on to probe the problems in the school and its treatment of minority children, that, too, is a political decision. Social workers are constantly interpreting clients' problems to them, implicitly encouraging them to use themselves politically or turn their attention elsewhere.

Social workers also affect social welfare policies by making choices in the way they carry them out. The reality of social welfare policy is what actually happens to the consumers of social services. And, as was discussed in Chapter 8, by its nature the service delivery system has to allow a certain amount of discretion to the worker. Social work professionals have additional room for maneuver because they represent a professional community with its own agenda.

This chapter does not deal with policy-making roles requiring specialized training in research and policy analysis, but rather those tasks which any professional social worker could reasonably be expected to undertake as part of basic professional responsibility. We will look at two kinds of politics: one directly concerning policy issues and the other closer to what the general public thinks of as politics, the election of candidates. Social workers have been involved in *issue* politics from the beginning, but they have been getting into *elective* politics as a professional activity only in the last decade. There are several reasons for this. Many social workers have been barred from the latter kind of politics by agency policies and laws governing civil service workers. Many have been concerned lest open support of a candidate, especially a losing candidate, will cut them off from important sources of community support. But partisan political activity has also seemed unprofessional to some social workers. How can you maintain sufficient scientific objectivity if you openly root for a candidate and, by implication at least, side against the opponent? We begin with the other kind of politics in which social workers have been engaged for generations: issue politics.

The young senator, vilified by the press and deserted by most of his friends, gives his maiden speech to a hushed chamber, and then the outburst of applause tells him that his bill will become law. This is the stuff of Hollywood, not the reality of issue politics.

The welfare commissioner's assistant listens impassively to tale after tale of elderly people being dumped in flophouses, glances at her watch and thanks her visitors for sharing their views. "I'll see what I can do," she says, and the group of social workers files out wondering if anything will come of their efforts. That's the reality of issue politics.

Almost casually the lobbyist says, "O.K., why don't we just say *and* instead of *but*," and the legislative aide nods wearily and scribbles something in the margin of the bill.

The social worker presents his testimony, the result of weeks of research, while committee members walk in and out, read the newspaper and hold whispered conferences.

The elaborately staged demonstration in front of city hall gets 20 seconds on the eleven o'clock news on one of the three local TV stations and a three-inch story on page 27 of the next morning's paper.

A major child protection bill is held hostage to an anti-abortion rider and finally dies in committee because the chairman doesn't want to give political mileage to the ranking minority member.

That is the reality of issue politics.

Social workers have had a long acquaintance with issue politics. In Chapter 9 we met Dorothea Lynde Dix, the woman who helped to revolutionize mental health care in the 1840s and 50s. She predated the term "social work," but she is clearly part of the field's rich heritage. She combined intense zeal, boundless energy, and a willingness both to dig out the facts and use her well-placed connections in Massachusetts politics. It is a combination which is still useful today.

Jane Addams shared many of the same attributes, as did other settlement house directors around the turn of the century. There were many dedicated souls who worked with immigrants in America's slums. But leaders like Jane Addams saw the connection between conditions around them and the need to change governmental policies.

During the Depression of 1930s, social workers played a critical role in gathering evidence used in shaping the Social Security Act. It would be an exaggeration to say that political action has been a major focus of professional social work. But this is one of the images the field holds out to itself. Every social work student is expected to be exposed to content in social policy and action in the course of professional training. This sets social work apart from other fields.

In issue politics, victories and defeats are often measured in terms of more or less. One's goal may be to remove the worst features of a bill that seems destined to pass or to trade away part of a good bill without losing the essence in order to assure passage. And always there is the money: dull, boring, complicated, hidden in pages and pages of figures, but the bottom line in issue politics. The wonder is that anything ever gets accomplished, but it does.

Battling Hunger in the Sagebrush State[1]

Wyoming had the lowest poverty rate in the country in 1979, and it ranked fifth in median household income. But Wyoming had hunger: Its rate of nutritionally related neonatal deaths in 1979 was eleventh in the nation, and between 1971 and 1975 almost 9% of all its babies had low birth weights. Despite this, Wyoming was the last hold-out against WIC, the free federal program of nutrition aids for low-income pregnant women, nursing mothers and infants. Because of a campaign started by a few social workers and their allies, Wyoming adopted a WIC program in 1980.

A handful of like-minded individuals cannot get a bill enacted, but because *this* handful of people had the determination to stay with the issue and not be scared off, they were gradually able to build up a sizeable support group. Issue-based campaigns often start that way: a small number of people work very hard to enlist others, and for a while it looks as if no progress is being made. Many campaigns falter at this point because of the lack of apparent success. Knowing this, public officials may start out by ignoring the whole thing, but if the constituency gets big enough, it can't be ignored.

The state human services director in Wyoming finally agreed to set up a task force to study the problem of nutrition among poor women and infants. This can be another stalling tactic but not necessarily. Advocates may figure they've won a victory and rest on their oars after that, or if the study drags on for too many months they may get discouraged and quit. The Wyoming group did neither but instead escalated their campaign. With a few thousand dollars of outside funding they sponsored a series of workshops, launched a petition drive and hired a part-time coordinator for the upcoming legislative session. The news media began to pay attention to them, adding further impetus to the campaign. In the end the state legislature passed the WIC bill by a narrow margin, and the governor, who had originally opposed the idea, signed it into law, twenty-two months after the campaign began.

What can we learn from this experience? One thing is that social workers

---

[1]This account is based on W. H. Whitaker, "Organizing Social Action Coalitions: WIC Comes to Wyoming," in Mahaffey and Hanks (1982), pp. 136-158.

aren't the political marshmallows they are sometimes thought to be. Another is that a few people from outside the formal political system, if they are determined enough, can overcome forces much more powerful than they. There is no magic in this; often there is hard work which doesn't pay off. We will look at the more technical lessons to be learned from the Wyoming case in a moment. In that case, the movers and shakers decided to take the initiative. More often action is forced on social workers by somebody else's initiative.

Social Workers on the Defensive[2]

One of the least known aspects of policy making is the administrative agency that writes regulations with which to carry out the intent of laws passed by Congress or the state legislature. Once those regulations go into effect they have the force of law, so social workers who want to influence policy must understand the rule-making process.

In the winter of 1984, staff members at the National Association of Social Workers (NASW) got a copy of proposed changes in the federal staffing requirements for hospitals receiving Medicare and Medicaid reimbursement. Basically the new rules would have weakened the requirement that hospitals use social workers to provide social services and instead relied on the hospitals to set their own standards. NASW was sure that, once the federal rules were eased, many hospitals would undercut their social services in order to save money.

The Secretary of Health and Human Services (HHS) has the power to write such regulations and the ability of the Reagan administration to get its way was well known, so NASW could have decided it was impossible to stop the action. But experienced activists know that you should never say never in politics. NASW went to work immediately to line up support for its position. Within weeks a coalition of 26 organizations was getting the word out to its members across the country and letters were beginning to pour into HHS and, equally important, to congressional leaders. The role of Congress in policy doesn't stop with the passage of a law. HHS and other agencies have to keep coming back to ask for more money, and congresspersons, knowing that, are able to wield a lot of power with the federal departments.

At the urging of the 26-organization coalition, the heads of several powerful Senate and House committees pressured for a delay in putting the new regulations into effect and called for further study of the plan. The fact that these leaders were from both major parties helped to give the pressure added weight. This was 1984, an election year, a time when the administration would want to avoid controversy. The Secretary of HHS finally sent the proposed regulations back to her staff for further consideration. For the time being, at least, NASW and its allies had been able to stop the undesired action.

---

[2]This account is based on articles appearing in *NASW News* in February, April, May and June, 1984.

There was no guarantee that the proposed regulations would not reappear, maybe in a worse form. Once the election was past, there would be less pressure on HHS to listen to the complaints. In issue politics the action never ends, as we shall see in the next case.

A Win Becomes a Loss[3]

In 1979 the governor of Pennsylvania called for legislation to deny general assistance to employables. The idea had broad support, and many newspapers favored the bill as a way of getting rid of "welfare chiselers." It looked as if the governor's bill would coast to an easy victory in the state legislature. Indeed, it soon passed the House of Representatives by a heavy margin. But then the Senate Public Health and Welfare Committee called for public hearings and studies by outside experts, and action slowed to a crawl. That gave the opposition the time it needed to mount a campaign against the bill.

A major task for the social workers and others fighting the bill was to educate the public about its effects. Without such publicity there would be little to stop the popular governor's plan. Pennsylvania had double-digit unemployment. Not only was there a lack of jobs for general assistance recipients, but welfare payments provided a strong stimulus to the economy. As was pointed out in Chapter 4, every dollar in welfare grants generates about two dollars in economic activity because of what economists call a "multiplier effect" (Stein, 1975). Cut tens of thousands of recipients off welfare and you suddenly introduced a *reverse* multiplier effect. This and other information about the true impact of the bill began to get public notice, and more and more questions were raised in the news media and by public figures about the governor's easy assurances that there were plenty of jobs for those who wanted them. The bill died in the Senate without a floor vote.

The cheering by the opponents had barely died down when the same measure was introduced in the next session of the Legislature. Two things were different from before: the state Senate was now ruled by the governor's party, and some of the opponents had gone on to other issues. The second fight was even fiercer than the first, but the bill was finally enacted.

Was the long fight against the law a waste of time? No. The opposition had been able to modify the bill so as to keep employables on the rolls for three months instead of the one originally proposed. Considering the rapid turn-over in general assistance, that would protect some welfare recipients from being dumped from welfare. Also, the definition of "employables" was modified, allowing more persons to avoid losing their benefits.

NASW was active in the fight against the Pennsylvania bill, but the rank and file of the membership was relatively uninvolved. Unlike the campaign against the hospital staffing regulations in the previous case, general assistance had no

---

[3]Based on Richan (1983).

direct impact on the careers of professional social workers, so they had little personal stake in the issue. Thus, if a leader of NASW urged a legislator to vote against the bill, the latter knew this would not necessarily be translated into large numbers of votes by NASW members in the next election. Contrast that with the battle over social service regulations under the Nixon administration.

Forcing Goliath to Compromise[4]

Fresh from its stunning election victory in November, 1972, the administration of Richard Nixon in early 1973 announced tough new rules for providing social services to welfare recipients and potential recipients. If the regulations went into effect they would have a serious impact on social work services and even affect support of professional education in social work.

As it later would in the case of the hospital regulations, NASW took the lead in putting together a coalition of groups to fight the proposed new rules. Similar coalitions were formed in most large cities around the country. The Department of Health, Education and Welfare (HEW, later the Health and Human Services) was deluged with over 200,000 negative comments on the new regulations, a record. Clearly social workers and others had heard the message that this plan would affect them directly.

Instead of being deterred by the outpouring, however, the Nixon administration signaled that it was going ahead with its plans to implement the new rules. At that point congressional leaders stepped into the picture. Congress cannot rewrite regulations, but it can delay the date of implementation. It did so three times, which allowed the opponents time to act. Congress also began working on new social services legislation. This would nullify the proposed regulations since they were to implement the old policy. Sensing that events were beginning to get beyond its control, the administration approached the opponents and eventually worked out a compromise. The outcome was a new social services amendment to the Social Security Act. What had started out as a rearguard fight against administrative action became a new policy affirming for the first time the federal government's responsibility for social services for other than the welfare poor.

The Importance of Good Information

In all of the above cases, a major weapon for social workers was information. The WIC supporters in Wyoming had to know where to find potential allies. NASW had to have access to the proposed regulations, in the 1973 and 1984 cases, in order to mobilize its forces, and had to know who might help in Congress. Especially in the second round of the Pennsylvania public assistance fight, when the legislative maneuvering became very complicated, it took experienced leaders to know which button to push when. This is *strategic* information: know-

---

[4]Based on Richan (1981), pp. 164-178, and Mott (1976).

ing where the key decisions are made and who has the power to make them and who or what will influence those decisions. Social workers often lack this kind of inside knowledge; that is one of the advantages of teaming up with others in a coalition, along with swelling one's numbers.

But social workers also needed evidence on which to base their arguments—accurate evidence. Give a policy-maker misinformation and you are likely to find that, not only have you lost the current battle, but you may have lost the whole war by discrediting yourself as a trustworthy source. The WIC supporters in Wyoming needed facts and figures on hunger in their state as well as the details about WIC. In Pennsylvania, the opponents of the governor's welfare plan had to offset a general anti-welfare attitude with facts about the true effects of the bill on the economy. At one point the governor claimed that there were plenty of jobs for those who wanted them: just look at the columns of job ads in the papers, he said. The opponents were able to challenge his statement by showing that most such ads were for people with higher educations.

This second kind of information is *tactical*. Here social workers have a special advantage, an ironic result of a disadvantage. The disadvantage is the unpopularity of many of the programs social workers support. Because public assistance and other social welfare programs are not well understood or approved of by the general public, few politicians run on a pro-social service platform. For that reason, there is little political mileage for the public official in getting to be an expert on welfare matters. Instead, they make their reputation on taxes, industrial development and farm policy. So it is possible for social workers to become experts in areas where legislators and congresspersons are relatively ignorant. Especially at the state level, elected representatives have only limited resources for technical experts on their staffs. The result is that social workers can play a key role in shaping welfare policies, just as most lobbyists are primary sources of information for law makers in their particular areas of interest.

Becoming Involved in Issue Politics

The hardest part about getting involved may be deciding what issue to work on—issue, not issues. Social workers are noted for having a large agenda of social concerns, but in order to have an impact it is usually necessary to focus in one place. The bias in this book is on the side of economic issues—inequality of resources and the related problem of powerlessness of oppressed people. From this perspective, the tendency of some turn of the century liberal reformers to pay more attention to civic corruption than exploitation of workers would be seen as a distraction. But regardless of your concerns, concentrating on one problem allows you to build alliances and develop the necessary expertise.

Finding allies may be the easiest part. There are advocacy organizations for just about any cause you can think of, and they are always looking for persons who want to work. People are often surprised at how small the active core of an organization is. By working in coalition with like-minded groups, knowledge-able persons who are commited to working hard can have an impact way beyond their numbers. A person already involved in an issue—for example, the ex-ecutive of a related social agency—knows who is active. Names of leaders and their organizations may appear in news articles and letters to the editor. The peo-ple who are the special targets of these groups—legislators, public administra-tors and news reporters—know them.

Becoming effective calls for a readiness to put in time and effort and keep col-lecting information. Your own value to an organization is directly proportional to your knowledge and your willingness to work at the unglamorous jobs. Most important of all is persistence. Politicians count on short attention spans on the part of their constituents. They figure that many earnest activists will get tired or move on to other issues, so they can afford to wait them out. The case of the Wyoming WIC campaign is an excellent example of what can happen when the zealots refuse to go away and stop pestering. The longer you stay around, the more of an expert you become. Do knowledge and organization and persistence pay off? One of the frustrating things about issue politics is that one never knows. All the hard work may go for naught. The only certainty is that if you do *not* put in the work, you will have no impact.

As one moves from issue politics to elective politics, the tactical information is of a different sort. Issues tend to get sloganized in the heat of a campaign. The rhetoric is partisan and subtleties may be neglected. This causes problems for some social workers.

ELECTIVE POLITICS

In 1972 NASW decided to sit out the presidential election campaign between Richard Nixon and George McGovern and advised its local units that they, too, must not get involved. This was not just an issue of protecting the tax-exempt status of a nonprofit organization but also one of not wanting to be caught on the losing side of a contest whose outcome was foreordained and then having to try to deal with the winners. It was an impasse between issue politics and elective politics. As it turned out failing to back the losers gained NASW no points with the winners, but that could not be known in advance.

In 1984 NASW endorsed Walter Mondale's candidacy for president long before he was even nominated by the Democratic Party. Social workers differed as to the wisdom of this action, but it shows how far NASW had moved in rela-tion to elective politics in twelve years. Not only was Ronald Reagan more clear-ly identified as the enemy of social work than Richard Nixon had been in 1972, but in the interim a major change had come over NASW.

Partly in reaction to criticism of its sidelines role in the Nixon-McGovern campaign and partly in recognition of the inseparability of issue politics and elective politics, the Association in 1976 organized an independent political ac-tion arm: Political Action for Candidate Election for Human Services (PACE). PACE would be able to engage in partisan electioneering and contribute funds to candidates without endangering the tax-exempt status of the parent body. State chapters of NASW set up their own PACE units.

The growth of PACE had been rapid. In 1982 a total of $150,000 in PACE funds went to support congressional candidates. While not on the scale of the National Organization of Women ($1.5 million the same year), organized social work had become a serious participant in elective politics. By husbanding its resources and focusing on key races where limited financial support can make a difference, PACE has been able to claim a role in tipping the balance in some elections.

Social Workers as Politicians

It used to be a rarity to find professional social workers holding elective offices of any kind other than maybe school board positions. Now that has changed. As of the mid-eighties two members of Congress and a least one big city council member were social work professionals.[5] An increasing number of lesser elected officials have come from the ranks of social workers. More typically, social workers are employed as staff aides to elected officials.

Yes, But Is It Professional?

The jury is probably still out on the social work profession's role in elective politics. To an extent NASW and other professional organizations are being forced into this role. When doctors, lawyers and architects have their own political action committees (PACs) raising money and supporting candidates, to say nothing of auto manufacturers and dairy farmers and labor unions, how can social workers stay aloof and hope to have any impact? Simply coming up with good arguments for policies without also being able to deal with the life blood of politics—money and votes—can leave social workers sounding virtuous but impotent. Public officials frequently ask social workers who lobby with them, will you still be around on election day? Are you willing to help *me*?

Some groups want to have PACs abolished. If that applied to all PACs, one might make a case for NASW's abandoning PACE. But as long as PACs are the political reality, it is hard to justify withdrawing from the field. Thus the social work profession, as an organized community, will continue to be involved in elective politics for the foreseeable future.

Different Kinds of Elective Politics

Political action committees like NASW's PACE have the advantage of being an independent voice in election campaigns. By selectively offering support to candidates whose records they approve of, they treat elective politics as an ex-

---

[5]U.S. Representatives Ron Dellums of California and Barbara Mikulski of Maryland, and Detroit City Council member Maryann Mahaffey.

tension of issue politics. They review candidates' records, interview office seekers and circulate questionnaires to see who is likely to advance social workers' professional agenda. It is important to do this publicly so that candidates will understand why they are being supported or not.

A chronic problem for social workers is that they have a very broad set of issues about which they are concerned. If Candidate X favors social work licensure *and* an anti-welfare bill, should she receive PACE's support? Sometimes social work organizations will establish clear priorities among issues or give formal endorsement without also giving financial support to a candidate whose track record is mixed. Because of the divisions within the professional community on many of these issues—for instance, between pro-life and pro-choice factions—it is often hard for social workers to unite the rank and file on a particular slate of candidates.

A way to avoid being trapped into simply choosing between two candidates, both of whose positions are less than satisfactory, is to get involved in the work of developing a party's platform. Social workers have run for positions on platform committees of the national parties where the issues are hammered out or run for delegate to the national or state convention. NASW has also presented testimony to platform committees. By the time all the conflicting interests and cross pressures are resolved, one's special agenda may be lost from view, but it is possible for a constituency with a particular concern to have it reflected in the final platform. Whether it also gets reflected in candidates' positions and their policies if elected is another question.

Unlike British political parties, whose platforms serve as mandates for persons elected under the party banner, American parties are in business primarily for one thing: winning elections. So a Democratic president may be at loggerheads with the dominant congressional leadership from his own party, and there may be sharp factional splits within the party's congressional caucus.

Working for Major Candidates

Working directly in major election campaigns raises a number of professional issues. For one thing, candidates generally demand total loyalty, and no candidate will be simon pure on every issue social workers care about. We are talking about work for candidates who are seriously trying to be elected and who must make concessions along the way. First of all there is the need to sustain a high level of enthusiasm for somebody with whom one disagrees on some issues.

Campaign organizations are not democratic. A few people in the inner circle make most of the critical decisions. There are parts of the campaign that the candidate turns over to others. For a few intensive weeks the candidate does not control his or her own schedule. That falls to somebody called a scheduler. Do you want to know when the candidate will meet a certain group? Don't ask the candidate, ask the scheduler.

Sometimes social workers hold positions of major responsibility, but most of the work of a campaign is repetitive and mind-numbing. Giving the same telephone message in exactly the same words to fifty persons, most of whom don't want to listen to you, requires adoption of a robot mentality, at least for the short run. (''No, don't be creative, say it the way it's written. I know it sounds dumb to you, but that's what you're supposed to say. Don't try to answer questions on abortion. Say you'll have somebody get back to them.'') The same goes for handing out leaflets at a shopping center.

A committee of university professors who were supporting a congressional candidate wanted to issue a public statement, urge people to vote for their candidate and raise money, in that order. The campaign office had a slightly different agenda: raise money, recruit your colleagues to work on the campaign (e.g., in a telephone pool as cited above), and, oh yes, you did say something about a public statement. Why don't you take that up with the issues director? The thoughtfully worded four-page statement was reduced to a few paragraphs and became one of dozens of daily news releases which the news media largely ignored.

Some of the university professors on the committee decided their skills were being under-utilized and dropped out. Some stayed on to do the repetitive and mind-numbing work of getting the candidate elected. What kinds of satisfaction does one get from this sort of experience? The satisfaction of getting the candidate elected. The personal letter from the congressperson thanking you for your important contribution is composed by a campaign staff aide and written by a word processor. It is true that there is now a contact with the congressperson's office, which can be helpful if you want to discuss an issue. But if you urge a vote in support of a particular bill that request will be weighed along with other political considerations by a public official who is constantly running for re-election. It is necessary to understand that and accept it as one of the rules of politics.

Why should we get involved in the grubby, compromising world of elective politics? Because if we do not, we leave the field to others. Elections are what determine the cast of characters who will make the critical decisions—indirectly as well as directly. If we turn our back on elective politics and concentrate on issue politics, we have already given away half the game.

POLITICS AT THE AGENCY LEVEL

So far we have looked at the factors that influence public policy, the official actions by elected and appointed government officials. But, as we said at the outset, everything in social welfare is political. Social workers who decide not to become active in public policy find themselves constantly involved in the politics of agency decisions and practices anyway. The underlying principles are the same as those governing issue and elective politics.

Allies. Just as the social workers in the earlier cases formed coalitions, anyone hoping to influence agency practices must find like-minded colleagues. Groups have more impact than individuals, are less vulnerable to counterpressure or retaliation, can pool information and can be supportive of each other when they are tempted to give up. Particularly important in agency politics are outside supporters who may be able to affect agency resources and are not subject to agency authority.

Self-interest. People will stay with a cause insofar as they see their own interests being affected. Not that people are driven only by self-interest, but as one seeks support it is important to help colleagues see the linkage between the issue and their own concerns. Social workers sometimes have trouble with this, an occupational hazard for "professional altruists," perhaps. But there is evidence that social workers are most effective when they can see the issue affecting both their own interests *and* the welfare of clients or the society as a whole.

Strategic information. Understanding who makes decisions and who and what influences those decisions is probably the most important question for anyone to ask in seeking to affect agency practices. The dynamics of the agency as a social system—discussed in Chapter 8—provide a good framework for doing such an analysis.

Tactical information. Social workers can be very effective in communicating the effects of policies and practices on clients and on staff. Often they are at their best in sharing case anecdotes. They have more trouble with statistics on numbers of persons affected, cost data and other less personal information, but these are also essential if one expects to be listened to seriously by decision-makers. That requires many hours of digging for the critical facts. A useful step in preparing to approach anybody with tactical information is to try out one's presentation in advance with a friend or act as one's own gadfly and raise the prickly questions about the case. It is hard to step back and look critically at your own arguments, but that is the best way to prepare for other people's questions.

INTEGRATORS AND GADFLIES

We started in this final section by looking at social work's role in maintaining the social fabric, integrating disparate elements and supporting social solidarity. We also looked at the other role, of raising difficult questions about the malfunctioning of society. The skills one needs in both of these tasks are essentially the same. The politics of public issues, election campaigns and agency practices lend themselves to the roles of both integrator *and* gadfly. And, at base, the two tasks are inseparable.

The characteristic way in which social workers have acted as gadflies has been not to overthrow the existing order but to improve it. Dissident elements have been supported by social workers the better to bring them into the mainstream. The gadfly's ultimate function has thus been to integrate. Political activism in social work should be understood in that context.

CONCLUSION

This book is guided by two premises: (1) that one must look *beyond altruism* to understand why American society has invested billions in social welfare programs that were at best controversial, and (2) that social welfare and the related profession of social work are part of the liberal tradition in American society. For the person committed to social justice, progress in such a milieu can be maddeningly slow and at times seem to shift into reverse. But, as the saying goes, it is the only game in town. Some readers will disagree with that stark judgment. The writer offers the contents of this book as his evidence.

Does the fact that welfare's ultimate role is to help maintain the evolving social order mean that significant steps toward social justice are impossible? It is an article of the liberal faith that it does not. Opinions differ as to whether there has been any real progress to date. When one looks back on slavery, twelve-hour shifts under unspeakable conditions for young child laborers, the poor farm as the only prospect for millions of elderly Americans, it is hard not to feel that things do improve, if only in limited ways. Judging from the outcry from even the most hardened skeptic when someone proposes rolling back the social legislation of the last fifty years, the belief in progress would seem to be more general than is admitted. Is it enough? Certainly not.

One yearns for a dramatic breakthrough. Thus the lure of radicalism. But it is the writer's conviction that change in the future will come the same way it has in the past: through halting steps, the gains seeming miniscule in comparison with the energy invested. In this way, the political role of social workers is a lot like the clinical role with the individual client. One celebrates the good interview, the small insight, the few days of sobriety, without necessarily looking for the transformed life. Often the goal is to prevent further deterioration rather than hope for improvement. When effective treatment techniques come along which can shortcut this tortoise-like process, they should be adopted. Similarly, radical policy initiatives that work are to be applauded. In the meantime, the reformers must struggle along.

Nothing in what has been said is meant to imply that we should take satisfaction in the status quo or that we should continue to rely on old knowledge and old methods. Greater sophistication in the policy arena is sorely needed. That is also an article of the liberal faith.

Bibliography

Abbott, G. 1938. *The Child and the State*. Vol. II, *The Dependent and the Delinquent Child, the Child of Unmarried Parents*. Chicago: University of Chicago Press.

Abramovitz, M. 1983. Everyone Is on Welfare: "The Role of Redistribution in Social Policy" Revisited. *Social Work* 28:440-445.

Addams, J. 1898. Social Settlements. In *Proceedings, National Conference of Charities and Correction, 24th Annual Session*, 1897. Boston: G. H. Ellis.

Adler, P. T. 1982. Mental Health Promotion and the CMHC: Opportunities and Obstacles. In *Mental Health Promotion and Primary Prevention*, ed. F. D. Perlmutter. San Francisco: Jossey-Bass.

AFSC (American Friends Service Committee). 1971. *Struggle for Justice*. New York: Hill & Wang.

AGI (Alan Guttmacher Institute). 1976. *11 Million Teenagers: What Can Be Done About the Epidemic of Adolescent Pregnancies in the United States*. New York: AGI.

_____. 1981. *Teenage Pregnancy: The Problem That Hasn't Gone Away*. New York: AGI.

_____. Undated. *U.S. and Cross-national Trends in Teenage Sexual and Fertility Behavior*. Photocopy. New York: AGI.

Alexander, L. B., & Siman, A. 1973. Fischer's Study of Studies. *Social Work* 18(4):104-106.

Allison, R. 1983. There Are No Juveniles in Pennsylvania Jails. *Corrections Magazine* 9(3): 12-20.

Altmeyer, A. J. 1966. *The Formative Years of Social Security*. Madison, WI: University of Wisconsin Press.

American Heritage Dictionary of the English Language. 1969. Ed. W. Morris. Boston: Houghton-Mifflin.

Anderson, M. 1978. *Welfare: The Political Economy of Welfare Reform in the United States*. Stanford, CA: Hoover Inst. Press.

Anderson, R. E., & Carter, I. E. 1974. *Human Behavior in the Social Environment: A Social System Approach*. Chicago: Aldine.

Andrews, F. E. 1973. *Foundation Watcher*. Lancaster, PA: Franklin & Marshall University Press.

Arblaster, A. 1984. *The Rise and Decline of Western Liberalism*. London: Basil Blackwell.

Arnaud, J. A., & Mack, C. 1982. The Deinstitutionalization of Status Offenders in Massachusetts: The Role of the Private Sector. In *Neither Angels Nor Thieves: Studies in the Deinstitutionalization of Status Offenders*, ed. J. F. Handler & J. Katz. Washington: National Academy Press.

Arthur D. Little, Inc. 1977. *Responses to Angry Youth: Cost and Social Impact of the Deinstitutionalization of Status Offenders in Ten States*. Washington: Arthur D. Little, Inc.

Atherton, C. R. 1969. The Social Assignment of Social Work. *Social Service Review* 43:421-429.

Atkins, C. M. 1986. 20,000 Choose Paycheck Over Welfare Check. *Public Welfare* 44(1):20-22.

Attinson, Z., & Glassberg, E. 1983. After Graduation What? Employment and Educational Experiences of Graduates of BSW Programs. *Journal of Education for Social Work* 19(1):5-14.

Axinn, J., & Levin, H. 1982. *Social Welfare: A History of the American Response to Need*. Rev. ed. New York: Harper & Row.

Bakal, Y. (ed.) 1973. *Closing Correctional Institutions*. Lexington, MA: Lexington Books.

Barber, B. 1965. Some Problems in the Sociology of the Professions. In *The Professions in America*, ed. K. S. Lynn. Boston: Houghton-Mifflin.

Barnes, H. E. 1930. *The Story of Punishment*. Boston: Stratford.

Bartollas, C., & Sieverdes, C. M. 1982. Juvenile Correctional Institutions: A Policy Statement. *Federal Probation* 46(3):22-26.

Baumol, W. J., & Blinder, A. S. 1979. *Economics: Principles and Policy*. New York: Harcourt Brace Jovanovich.

Beard, C. A., & Beard, M. R. 1960. *The Beards' New Basic History of the United States*. Garden City, NY: Doubleday.

Beck, B. M. 1970. The Voluntary Social Welfare Agency: A Reassessment. *Social Service Review* 4:147-154.

Belknap, I. 1956. *Human Problems of a State Mental Hospital*. New York: McGraw-Hill.

Bell, W. 1965. *Aid to Dependent Children*. New York: Columbia University Press.

————. 1983. *Contemporary Social Welfare*. New York: Macmillan.

Bergland, C., et al. 1980. *Report on House Bill 2044: Consequences for the General Assistance Population*. Report Prepared for Majority Caucus, Pennsylvania Senate Committee on Public Health and Welfare. Philadelphia: Department of City and Regional Planning, University of Pennsylvania. Photocopy.

Bernard, S. E. 1983. Coping With Cutbacks. Unpublished Paper, University of Michigan School of Social Work, Ann Arbor, MI. Photocopy.

————. 1975. Why Service Delivery Programs Fail. *Social Work* 20: 206-212.

Billingsley, A. 1964. Bureaucratic and Professional Orientation Patterns in Social Casework. *Social Service Review* 38:400-407.

———— & Giovannoni, J. M. 1972. *Children of the Storm: Black Children and American Child Welfare*. New York: Harcourt, Brace & Jovanovich.

Black, D. 1976. *The Behavior of Law*. New York: Academic Press.

Bloom, B. L. 1977. *Community Mental Health*. Monterey, CA: Brooks/Cole.

Bluestone, B. 1982. Deindustrialization and the Abandonment of Community. In *Community and Capital in Conflict*, eds. J. C. Raines, L. E. Berson & D. McI. Gracie. Philadelphia: Temple University Press.

Brace, C. L. 1880. *The Dangerous Classes of New York*. New York: Wyncoop.

Bremner, R. H. 1960. *American Philanthropy*. Chicago: University of Chicago Press.

_____. (ed.) 1970. *Children and Youth in America: A Documentary History*. Vol, I, *1600-1865*. Cambridge, MA: Harvard University Press.

Brooks, J. 1982. Annals of Finance (Supply Side Economics). *The New Yorker* (April 19):96-150.

Brown, C. V. 1983. *Taxation and the Incentive to Work*. 2nd ed. Oxford, England: Oxford University Press.

Brown, G. E. (ed.) 1968. *The Multi-Problem Dilemma: A Social Research Demonstration With Multi-Problem Families*, Metuchen, NJ: Scarecrow Press.

Bruno, F. J. 1948. *Trends in Social Work as Reflected in the Proceedings of the National Conference on Social Welfare, 1874-1946*. New York: Columbia University Press.

Bullock, A., & Shock, M. (eds.) 1956. *The Liberal Tradition: From Fox to Keynes*. London: Adam and Charles Black.

Burns, E. M. 1951. *The American Social Security System*. 2nd ed. Boston: Houghton-Mifflin.

Burns J. M. 1956. *Roosevelt: The Lion and the Fox*. New York: Harcourt-Brace.

Butts, R. F. 1947. *A Cultural History of Education*. New York: McGraw-Hill.

California, State Legislature, Joint Legislative Audit Committee. 1974. *California Community Work Experience Program (CWEP)*.

Card, J. J., & Wise, L. L. 1978. Teenage Mothers and Teenage Fathers: The Impact of Early Childbearing on the Parents' Personal and Professional Lives. *Family Planning Perspectives* 10:199-205.

Carlson, E. 1984. Social Security Fix: A Look at What Lies Ahead. *Modern Maturity* 27(4):28-33.

Chein, I., et al. 1964. *Narcotics, Delinquency and Social Policy*. London: Tavistock.

Cherlin, A. 1978. Teenage Pregnancy: Carter Half Sees the Problem. *The Nation* 226(23):727-730.

Chesney-Lind, M. 1977. Judicial Enforcement of the Female Sex Role: The Family Court and the Female Delinquent. *Issues in Criminology* 8(Fall): 51-69.

Chestang, L. 1972. The Dilemmas of Biracial Adoption. *Social Work*, 17(3): 100-105.

Chick, V. 1983. *Macroeconomics After Keynes: A Reconsideration of the General Theory*. Cambridge, MA: MIT Press.

Child Abuse at Taxpayers' Expense. 1974. Citizens' Report on Training Schools in Southeastern Pennsylvania. Media, PA: Friends Suburban Project,

Pennsylvania Program for Women and Girl Offenders & Youth Advocates, Inc.

Children's Defense Fund. 1984. *America's Children and Their Families: Key Facts.* Washington: Children's Defense Fund.

Chimezie, A. 1975. Transracial Adoption of Black Children. *Social Work* 20: 296-301.

Christiansen, K. O. 1968. Recidivism Among Collaborators—A Follow-up Study of 2946 Danish Men Convicted of Collaborating With the Germans During World War II. In *Crime and Culture*, ed. M. E. Wolfgang. New York: Wiley.

Church, R. L., & Sedlak, M. W. 1976. *Education in the United States: An Interpretive History.* New York: Free Press.

Cloward, R. A., & Epstein, I. 1967. Private Social Welfare's Disengagement From the Poor: The Case of Family Adjustment Agencies. In *Community Action Against Poverty*, eds. G. Brager & F. Purcell. New Haven, CT: College & University Press.

Cloward, R. A., & Piven, F. F. 1977. The Acquiescence of Social Work. *Society* 14(2):55-63.

Cogan, J. F. 1978. *Negative Income Taxation and Labor Supply: New Evidence from the New Jersey-Pennsylvania Experiment.* Santa Monica, CA: Rand.

Cohen, R. E. 1979. Chalk Up Another Loss. *National Journal*, 11:2032.

Conte, J. R. 1984. The Justice System and Sexual Abuse of Children. *Social Service Review*, 58:556-568.

Cook, F. J. 1964. *The F.B.I. Nobody Knows.* New York: Macmillan.

Cooper, S. 1977. Social Work: A Dissenting Profession. *Social Work* 22: 360-368.

Corrections Magazine. 1983. Is New York's Tough Juvenile Law a "Charade"? 9(2):40-45.

Crane, J. A. 1976. The Power of Social Intervention Experiments to Discriminate Differences Between Experimental and Control Groups. *Social Service Review* 50:224-242.

Crary, R. W., & Petrone, L. A. 1971. *Foundations of Modern Education*, New York: Knopf.

CSWE (Council on Social Work Education). 1973-1984a. *Statistics on Social Work in the United States.* Annual Series. New York: CSWE.

————, Commission on Accreditation. 1984b. *Handbook of Accreditation Standards and Procedures.* Revised. New York: CSWE.

CQ Almanac. 1979-1984. *Congressional Quarterly Almanac.* Annual. Washington: CQ Almanac.

Demkovitch, L. E. 1979a. No Recess in Hospital Cost Debate. *National Journal* 11:1379-1380.

————. 1979b. Who Can Do a Better Job of Controlling Hospital Costs? *National Journal* 11:219-223.

deSchweinitz, K. 1943. *England's Road to Social Security.* Philadelphia: University of Pennsylvania Press.

Deutsch, A. 1949. *The Mentally Ill in America*. 2nd ed. Garden City, NY: Doubleday.

Dickens, C. 1867. *American Notes and Pictures from Italy*. Boston: Ticknor & Field.

Dinitz, S., Dynes, R. R., & Clarke, A. C. (eds.) 1969. *Deviance: Studies in the Process of Stigmatization and Social Reaction*. New York: Oxford University Press.

Dolgoff, R., & Feldstein, D. 1984. *Understanding Social Welfare*. 2nd ed. New York: Longman.

Dornbusch, R., & Fischer, S. 1984. *Macroeconomics*. 3rd ed. New York: McGraw-Hill.

Durkheim, E. 1972. *Emile Durkheim: Selected Writings*, trans. A. Giddens. Cambridge: Cambridge University Press.

Edelwich, J., & Brodsky, A. 1980. *Burn-out: Stages of Disillusionment in the Helping Professions*. New York: Human Sciences Press.

Ellena, W. J. 1974. 45-15 in a Major School District. *Phi Delta Kappan* 56(1): 65-66.

Elliott, P. 1972. *The Sociology of Professions*. New York: Herder & Herder.

Empey, L. T. (ed.) 1979. *Juvenile Justice: The Progressive Legacy and Current Reforms*. Charlottesville, VA: University of Virginia Press.

Erickson, M. L. 1979. Some Empirical Questions Concerning the Current Revolution in Juvenile Justice. In *The Future of Childhood and Juvenile Justice*, ed. L. T. Empey. Charlottesville, VA: University of Virginia Press.

Etheridge, C. E. 1973. Lawyers v. Indigents: Conflict of Interest in Professional-Client Relations in the Legal Profession. In *The Professions and Their Prospects*, ed. E. Freidson. Beverly Hills, CA: Sage.

Etzioni, A. (ed.) 1969. *The Semi-Professions and Their Organization: Teachers, Nurses and Social Workers*. New York: Free Press.

Evans, J. 1972. Welfare Reform Revisited. *California Journal*. December.

Fanshell, D., & Grundy, J. F. 1975. Child Welfare Information Services, Inc.: *System Level Reports*. New York: Columbia University School of Social Work.

Feldman, S. 1983. Out of the Hospital, Onto the Streets: The Overselling of Benevolence. *The Hastings Center Report* 13(3):5-7.

Fischer, J. (ed.) 1976. *The Effectiveness of Social Casework*. Springfield, IL: Charles C Thomas.

_____. 1973. Is Casework Effective? A Review. *Social Work*, 18:5-21.

Fitzhugh, G. 1960. *Cannibals All! Or, Slaves Without Masters*, ed. C. V. Woodward. Cambridge, MA: Belknap Press.

Flexner, A. 1915. Is Social Work a Profession? In *Proceedings of the National Conference of Charities and Correction*. Chicago: Hildman Printing Co.

_____. 1910. *Medical Education in the United States and Canada*. New York: Arno. Reprinted 1972.

Frazier, E. F. 1950. Problems and Needs of Negro Children and Youth Resulting from Family Disorganization. *Journal of Negro Education* 19: 269-277.

Friedman, M. 1962. *Capitalism and Freedom*. Chicago: University of Chicago Press.

_____ et al. 1975. *Milton Friedman's Monetary Framework: A Debate With His Critics*. Chicago: University of Chicago Press.

Freidson, E. 1970. *Professional Dominance: The Social Structure of Medical Care*. New York: Atherton.

Friedlander, W. A., & Apte, R. Z. 1980. *Introduction to Social Welfare*. 5th ed. Englewood Cliffs, NJ: Prentice-Hall.

Gallup, G. 1978. Growing Number of Americans Favor Discussions of Sex in Classroom. *The Gallup Poll*. News Release, January 23.

Galper, J. H. 1975. *The Politics of Social Services*. Englewood Cliffs, NJ: Prentice-Hall.

Galvin, J. 1983. Prison Policy Reforms Ten Years Later. *Crime & Delinquency* 29:495-503.

_____ & Polk, K. 1983. Juvenile Justice: Time for New Direction? *Crime & Delinquency* 29:325-332.

Garlock, P. D. 1979. Wayward Children and the Law, 1820-1900: The Genesis of Status Offense Jurisdiction of the Juvenile Court. *Georgia Law Review*, 13:341-447.

Garrity, D. L. 1961. The Prison as a Rehabilitative Agency. In *The Prison*, ed. D. R. Cressey. New York: Holt, Rinehart & Winston.

Gibelman, M. 1980. Are Clients Served Better When Services Are Purchased? *Public Welfare* 39(Fall):26-33.

Gilbert, N., & Specht, H. 1974. *Dimensions of Social Welfare Policy*. Englewood Cliffs, NJ: Prentice-Hall.

Gilder, G. 1981. *Wealth and Poverty*. New York: Basic Books.

Gillette, J. M. 1912. Rural Child Labor. *The Child Labor Bulletin* 1:154-160.

Girvetz, H. K. 1950. *From Wealth to Welfare: The Evolution of Liberalism*. Stanford, CA: Stanford University Press.

Glazer, N. 1971. The Limits of Social Policy. *Commentary* 52:51-58.

Glickstein, J. A. 1979. "Poverty Is Not Slavery": American Abolitionists and the Competitive Labor Market. In *Anti-Slavery Reconsidered: New Perspectives on the Abolitionists*, ed. L. Perry & M. Fellman. Baton Rouge, LA: Louisiana State University Press.

Goffman, E. 1961. *Asylums*. Garden City, NY: Anchor Books.

Golding, W. 1962. *Lord of the Flies*. New York: Coward-McCann.

Goldman, S. 1985. Reorganizing the Judiciary: The First Term Appointments. *Judicature* 68:313-328.

Goode, W. J. 1969. The Theoretical Limits of Professionalization. In *The Semi-Professions and Their Organization*, ed. A. Etzioni. New York: Free Press.

Goodwin, L. 1981. Can Workfare Work? *Public Welfare*, 39(4):19-25.

Greenfield, M. 1961. The "Welfare Chiselers" of Newburgh, N.Y. *Reporter* 25 (Aug.):37-40.

Greenwood, E. 1957. Attributes of a Profession. *Social Work* 2(3):45-55.

Grob, G. N. 1983. *Mental Illness and American Society, 1875-1940.* Princeton, NJ: Princeton University Press.

Gueron, J. M. 1986. Work for People on Welfare. *Public Welfare* 44(1):7-12.

Gyarfas, M., & Nee, R. 1973. Was It Really Casework? *Social Work* 18(4):3-4.

Handel, G. 1982. *Social Welfare in Western Society.* New York: Random House.

Handler, J. F., et al. 1982. Deinstitutionalization in Seven States: Principal Findings. In *Neither Angels Nor Thieves: Studies in the Deinstitutionalization of Status Offenders,* eds. J. F. Handler & J. Katz. Washington: National Academy Press.

_____ & Katz, J. (eds.) 1982. *Neither Angels Nor Thieves: Studies in the Deinstitutionalization of Status Offenders.* Washington: National Academy Press.

Haug, M. R., & Sussman, M. B. 1969. Professional Autonomy and Revolt of the Client. *Social Problems* 17 (Fall):153-161.

Hawkins, G. 1976. *The Prison: Policy and Practice.* Chicago: University of Chicago Press.

Helmer, J. 1975. *Drugs and Minority Oppression.* New York: Seabury Press.

Henry, W. E., Sims, J. H., & Spray, S. L. 1971. *The Fifth Profession.* San Francisco: Jossey-Bass.

Hofstadter, R. 1957. *The American Political Tradition and the Men Who Made It.* New York: Vintage.

Holt, L. H., & Chilton, A. W. 1918. *The History of Europe from 1862 to 1914.* New York: Macmillan.

Hudson, R. B. 1978. The "Graying" of the Federal Budget and Its Consequences for Old Age Policy. *The Gerontologist* 18:428-440.

Hughes, E. C. 1965. Professions. In *The Professions in America,* ed. K. S. Lynn. Boston: Houghton-Mifflin.

Huntington, J. O. S. 1893. Philanthropy—Its Success and Failure. In *Philanthropy and Social Progress.* New York: Crowell.

Indianapolis Chapter, American Association of Social Workers. 1952. What Happened in Indiana. *Social Work Journal* 33:35-37.

Institute of Community Studies. 1970. *Citizen Action on Urban Problems.* Report of the Voluntarism in Urban Life Project. New York: United Way of America.

Jamieson, B, Jr. 1982. Surviving the Reagan Onslaught. *Public Welfare* 40(1): 10-15.

Jansson, B. S. 1984. *Theory and Practice of Social Welfare Policy.* Belmont, CA: Wadsworth.

Jobs Watch. 1982. States Cautious in Adopting Workfare; Advocates Report Abuses. (Sept.):1.

Joe, B. 1975. *Welfare Reform California Style—Implications for the Nation.* Washington: National Association of Social Workers. Photocopy.

Joe, T., & Yu, P. 1984. Black Men, Welfare and Jobs. *New York Times* (May 11):A-31.

Kadish, S. 1967. The Crisis of Overcriminalization. *Annals of the American Academy of Political and Social Sciences* 374:158-170.

Kadushin, A. (ed.) 1978. *Child Welfare Strategy in the Coming Years.* Washington: U.S. Department of Health, Education and Welfare.

Kamerman, S. B. 1983a. Child-Care Services: A National Picture. *Monthly Labor Review* 106(12):35-39.

———. 1983b. The New Mixed Economy of Welfare: Public and Private. *Social Work* 28:5-11.

Kansas, Senate. 1974. *An Act Relating to Social Work.* Senate Bill 623.

Kantner, J. F., & Zelnick, M. 1973. Contraception and Pregnancy: Experience of Young Unmarried Women in the United States. *Family Planning Perspectives* 3(Winter):21-35.

———. 1972. Sexual Experience of Young Unmarried Women in the United States. *Family Planning Perspectives*, 4(4):9-26.

Kasun, J. 1978. Teenage Pregnancy: Epidemic or Statistical Hoax? *U.S.A. Today* 107(July):31-33.

Kempton, M. 1962. The Cop as Idealist: The Case of Stephen Kennedy. *Harper's Magazine* 224(March):66-71.

Kentucky, Commonwealth of. 1975. *State Board of Examiners for Social Work.* 335.020(2).

Kobrin, S., & Klein, M. W. 1981. *National Evaluation of the Deinstitutionalization of Status Offender Programs.* Vols. I & II. Washington: U.S. Department of Justice.

Konner, M. J. 1977. Adolescent Pregnancy. *New York Times* (September 24):21.

Kramer, H. J. 1985. Director of Communications, Joseph P. Kennedy, Jr., Foundation. Telephone Interview, March 14.

Kramer, R. 1981. *Voluntary Agencies in the Welfare State.* Berkeley, CA: University of California Press.

Krause, H. D. 1969. The Bastard Finds His Father. *Family Law Quarterly* 3: 100-111.

Kurtz, R. H. (ed.) 1938. *The Public Assistance Worker.* New York: Russell Sage.

——— (ed.) 1960. *Social Work Year Book 1960.* 14th issue. New York: National Association of Social Workers.

Larson, M. S. 1977. *The Rise of Professionalism: A Sociological Analysis.* Berkeley, CA: University of California Press.

Lender, M. E., & Martin, J. K. 1982. *Drinking in America: A History.* New York: Free Press.

Lee, P. R. 1929. Social Work: Cause and Function. In *Proceedings of the National Conference of Social Work.* Chicago: University of Chicago Press.

Levine, J. P. 1983. Jury Toughness: The Impact of Conservatism on Criminal Court Verdicts. *Crime & Delinquency* 29:71-87.

Lewis, H. 1982. *Social Work Education in the 80s: What Is to Be Done?* Address to Opening Plenary Session, Annual Program Meeting, Council on Social Work Education, New York City, March 8. Reprint: Hunter College.

Lewis, O. F. 1922. *The Development of American Prisons and Prison Customs, 1776-1845.* New York: Prison Association of New York.

Lincoln, R. 1978. Is Pregnancy Good for Teenagers? *U.S.A. Today* 107 (July): 34-37.

Lipsky, M. 1980. *Street-Level Bureaucracy: Dilemmas of the Individual in Public Services.* New York: Russell Sage.

Liska, A. E., & Taussig, M. 1979. Theoretical Interpretations of Social Class and Racial Differentials in Legal Decision-Making for Juveniles. *Sociological Quarterly* 20:197-207.

Love, N. 1969. The United Fund Faces Life. *Philadelphia Magazine* 60(12): 90-147.

Lubove, R. 1965. *The Professional Altruist: The Emergence of Social Work as a Career, 1880-1930.* Cambridge, MA: Harvard University Press.

Lueck, M., Orr, A. C., & O'Connell, M. 1982. *Trends in Child Care Arrangements of Working Mothers.* Bureau of Census Special Studies P-23, No. 117. Washington: U.S. Bureau of Census.

Lynd, S. 1967. *Class Conflict, Slavery and the United States Constitution.* New York: Bobbs-Merrill.

Lynn, L. E., Jr., & Whitman, D. de F. 1981. *The President as Policy Maker: Jimmy Carter and Welfare Reform.* Philadelphia: Temple University Press.

Macarov, D. 1978. *The Design of Social Welfare.* New York: Holt, Rinehart & Winston.

Mahaffey, M., & Hanks, J. W. (eds.) 1982. *Practical Politics: Social Work and Political Responsibility.* Silver Spring, MD: National Association of Social Workers.

Martin, J. B. 1954. *Break Down the Walls.* New York: Ballantine.

May, E. 1964. *The Wasted Americans.* New York: Harper & Row.

McCarthy, J., & Menken, J. 1979. Marriage, Remarriage, Marital Disruption and Age at First Birth. *Family Planning Perspectives* 11:21-30.

McKelvey, B. 1936. *American Prisons.* Chicago: University of Chicago Press.

McQuaide, S. 1983. Human Service Cutbacks and the Mental Health of the Poor. *Social Casework* 65:497-499.

Meehan, E. J. 1968. *Explanation in Social Science: A System Paradigm.* Homewood, IL: Dorsey.

Miller, H. L., Mailick, S., & Miller, M. V. 1973. *Cases in Administration of Mental Health and Human Service Agencies.* New York: Institute for Child Mental Health.

Miller, J., & Ohlin, L. E. 1976. The New Corrections: The Case of Massachu-setts. In *Pursuing Justice for the Child*, ed. M. K. Rosenheim. Chicago: University of Chicago Press.

Miller, L. S. 1976. The Structural Determinants of Welfare Effort: A Critique and a Contribution. *Social Service Review* 50:57-79.

Mitford, J. 1973. *Kind and Usual Punishment: The Prison Business*. New York: Knopf.

Moore, K. A. 1978. Teenage Childbirth and Welfare Dependency. *Family Planning Perspectives* 10:233-235.

Morris, N. 1974. *The Future of Imprisonment*. Chicago: University of Chicago Press.

Morris, R. 1977. Caring For vs. Caring About People. *Social Work* 22:353-359.

Moynihan, D. P. 1969. *Maximum Feasible Misunderstanding*. New York: Free Press.

———. 1965. *The Negro Family: The Case for National Action*. Washington: U.S. Department of Labor. (Author not listed.)

———. 1973. *The Politics of a Guaranteed Income*. New York: Vintage.

Murray, C. 1984. *Losing Ground: American Social Policy, 1950-1980*. New York: Basic Books.

Murray, Jane. 1985. Director of Communications, Alan Guttmacher Institute. Telephone interview, March 8.

Myrdal, G. 1960. *Beyond the Welfare State: Economic Planning and Its International Implications*. New Haven, CT: Yale University Press.

Naisbitt, J. 1984. *Megatrends: Ten New Directions Transforming Our Lives*. New York: Warner Books.

NASW (National Association of Social Workers). 1979. Code of Ethics; revised.

———. 1983. *Compilation of Public Social Policy Statements*. Silver Spring, MD.

NASW News. 1974. New Policy Statement on Licensing Issued. (September):12.

———. 1984a. Latest Hospital Rules Undermine Standards. (February): 1, 32.

———. 1984b. Push for Practice Regulation Pays Off; National Tally of State Laws Reaches 34, (May):3.

———. 1984c. Workers Protest "Intolerable Conditions"; Negligency Charged in Child Abuse Cases. (June):5.

Nelson, A. S. 1982. Community Support and Rehabilitation Programs for the Chronically Mentally Ill. In *Handbook on Mental Health Administration*, ed. M. J. Austin & W. E. Hershey. San Francisco; Jossey-Bass.

New York State, Department of Health. 1980. *Quarterly Vital Statistics Review*. Albany: N.Y. State Department of Health.

New York Times. 1937. Supreme Court Backs Security Act on Job Insurance, 5-4, Pensions, 7-2; Roosevelt Asks Wage-Hour Law. (May 25):1, 24.

———. 1973. Homosexuality Is Not a Mental Disorder: APA. (December 16):D-8.

————. 1978a. Funds to Help Pregnant Teen-Agers: An Idea Emerges and Gets a Budget. (January 24):18.

————. 1978b. The Epidemic of Teen-Age Pregnancy. (June 18):E-6.

————. 1981. Senate, 96-0, Bars Two Key Pension Cuts Reagan Had Sought. (May 21):1.

————. 1982. Cutoff of Disability Benefits Challenged. (January 31):XXI-6.

————. 1983a. New York and Other States Defy U.S. Rules for Disability Benefits. (September 12):1.

————. 1983b. Legal Group Asserts Attica Is in "Emergency Situation." (November 23):B-3.

————. 1984a. Labor Board Ruling Further Frees Companies in Moving Operations. (April 11):A-20.

————. 1984b. Blacks See Blacks Saving the Family. (May 7):A-14.

————. 1984c. Treating the Nation's Epidemic of Teen-Age Pregnancy. (June 3):E-5.

————. 1984d. Conservatives on Supreme Court Dominated Rulings of Latest Term. (July 8):1.

————. 1984e. The Right Reform of Disability. (July 24):A-20.

————. 1984f. Almost One in 5 May Have Mental Disorder. (October 3):1.

————. 1984g. Catholic Bishops Ask Vast Changes in Economy of U.S. (November 12):1.

————. 1985a. Angry Citizens in Many Cities Applaud Goetz. (January 7):B-1, B-3.

————.1985b. President's News Conference on Foreign and Domestic Issues. (January 10):B-x.

————. 1985c. U.S. Leads Industrialized Nations in Teen-Age Births and Abortions. (March 13):1.

————. 1985d. Texan Put to Death for a Murder Committed at 17. (September 12):A-19. Official Says He Barred More Prosecutions at Lilly. (September 12):A-23.

————. 1985e. Conferees Agree on a Plan to End Federal Deficit. (December 7):A-1.

————. 1986. Poll Finds Reagan Still Popular; No Ideological Shift. (January 28):A-14.

NIMH (National Institute of Mental Health). 1966. *Consultation and Education: A Service of the Community Mental Health Center*. Washington: NIMH.

Nix, Lulu Mae. 1985. Former Director, Office of Adolescent Pregnancy Programs, U.S. Department of Health & Human Services. Personal Interview, March 8, Philadelphia, PA.

Norton, E. H. 1985. Restoring the Traditional Black Family. *New York Times Magazine* (June 2):43-95.

Nozik, R. 1974. *Anarchy, State and Utopia*. New York: Basic Books.

O'Grady, J. 1930. *Catholic Charities in the United States.* Washington: National Conference of Catholic Charities.

Ohlin, L. E., Coates, R. B., & Miller, A. D. 1974. Radical Correctional Reform: A Case Study of the Massachusetts Youth Correctional System. *Harvard Education Review* 44:74-111.

Ohlin, L. E., Piven, H., & Pappenfort, D. M. 1956. Major Dilemmas of the Social Worker in Probation and Parole., *N.P.P.A. Journal* 2:211-225.

Ostrander, S. A. 1985. Voluntary Social Service Agencies in the United States. *Social Service Review* 59:435-454.

The Oxford English Dictionary. 1959. Oxford: Oxford University Press.

Ozawa, M. N. 1984. The 1983 Amendments to the Social Security Act: The Issue of Intergenerational Equity. *Social Work* 29:131-138.

Parks, Barbara. 1985. Assistant Director of Communications, Alan Guttmacher Institute. Personal Interview, March 4, New York City.

Pechman, J. A., & Timpane, P. M. (eds.) 1975. *Work Disincentives and Income Guarantees: The New Jersey Negative Income Tax Experiments.* Washington: Brookings Institution.

Perlmutter, F. D. 1980. The Executive Bind: Constraints Upon Leadership. In *Leadership in Social Administration*, ed. F. D. Perlmutter & S. Slavin. Philadelphia: Temple University Press.

Personnel Information (NASW). 1962. Agency Exonerated by Commission on Complaint Filed by Member. (November):1.

Perucci, R., & Gerstl, J. E. 1969. *Profession Without Community: Engineers in American Society.* New York: Random House.

Philadelphia Inquirer. 1983. Welfare Projects to Begin. (February 20):B-1.

————. 1985. They're Aiming to Protect Themselves; Some Victims Seek to Make Sure It Won't Happen to Them Again. (January 10):1-C, 4-C.

Piven, F. F., & Cloward, R. A. 1979. *Poor People's Movements: Why They Succeed, How They Fail.* New York: Vintage.

————. 1971. *Regulating the Poor: The Functions of Public Welfare.* New York: Pantheon.

Piven, H. 1961. Professional and Organizational Structure: Training and Agency Variables in Relation to Practitioner Orientation and Practice. Doctoral dissertation, Columbia University.

Polanyi, K. 1944. Speenhamland 1795. In *The Great Transformation.* New York: Holt, Rinehart & Winston. [Reprinted in *The Emergence of Social Welfare and Social Work*, ed. N. Gilbert and H. Specht. Itasca, IL: Peacock (1976).]

Polsky, H. W. 1967. *Cottage Six: The Social System of Delinquent Boys in Residential Treatment.* New York: Wiley.

The PUBLIUS Symposium on the Future of American Federalism. 1972. *Publlius*, 2:95-146.

Rawls, J. 1971. *A Theory of Justice.* Cambridge, MA: Belknap Press of Harvard University.

Reader's Guide and Index to Periodical Literature. Annual. New York: H. W. Wilson.

Rees, A. 1977. The Labor-Supply Results of the Experiments: A Summary. In *The New Jersey Income Maintenance Experiment.* Vol. II, *Labor-Supply Responses*, ed. H. W. Watts & A. Rees. New York: Academic Press.

Reid, W. J. 1971. Sectarian Agencies. In *Encyclopedia of Social Work.* 16th issue. New York: National Association of Social Workers.

―――― & Hanrahan, P. 1982. Recent Evaluations of Social Work: Grounds for Optimism. *Social Work* 27:328-340.

Richan, W. C. 1980. The Administrator as Advocate. In *Leadership in Social Administration: Perspectives for the 1980s*, ed. F. D. Perlmutter & S. Slavin. Philadelphia: Temple University Press.

――――. 1984. The Conflict Between Humanitarian Concern and Agency Demands. Paper presented at Annual Program Meeting, Council on Social Work Education, March 12, Detroit, MI.

――――. 1965. The Influence of Professionalization, Work Environment and Other Factors on Social Workers' Orientation Toward Clients. Doctoral dissertation, Columbia University.

――――. 1983. Obstructive Politics in an Anti-Welfare Era. In *Social Work in a Turbulent World*, ed. M. Dinerman. Silver Spring, MD: National Association of Social Workers.

――――. 1978. Personnel Issues in Child Welfare. In *Child Welfare Strategies in the Coming Years*, ed. A. Kadushin. Washington: U.S. Department of Health, Education & Welfare.

――――. 1973. The Social Work Profession and Organized Social Welfare. In *Shaping the New Social Work*, ed. A. J. Kahn. New York: Columbia University Press.

Rimlinger, G. V. 1971. *Welfare Policy and Industrialization in Europe, America and Russia.* New York: Wiley.

Rosen, G. 1968. *Madness in Society.* Chicago: University of Chicago Press.

Rosenman, S. I. (ed.) 1938. *The Public Papers and Addresses of Franklin D. Roosevelt.* Vol. II. New York: Random House.

Rothman, D. J. 1971. *The Discovery of Asylum.* Boston: Little, Brown.

Rutherford, A. 1974. *The Dissolution of Training Schools in Massachusetts.* Columbus, OH: Academy for Contemporary Problems.

Salamon, L. M., & Abramson, A. J. 1982. *The Federal Budget and the Non-profit Sector.* Washington: Urban Institute.

Santiestevan, H. 1975. *Deinstitutionalization: Out of Their Beds and Into the Streets.* Washington: American Federation of State, County & Municipal Employees.

Schlesinger, A. M. 1951. *The Rise of Modern America.* 4th ed. New York: Macmillan.

Schlesinger, A. M., Jr. 1959. *The Coming of the New Deal.* Boston: Houghton-Mifflin.

————. 1960. *The Politics of Upheaval.* Boston: Houghton-Mifflin.

Schottland, C. I. (ed.) 1967. *The Welfare State.* New York: Harper & Row.

Schultze, C. L. 1977. *The Public Use of Private Interest.* Washington: Brookings Inst.

Schur, E. M. 1965. *Crimes Without Victims: Deviant Behavior and Public Policy.* Englewood Cliffs, NJ: Prentice-Hall.

Scott, W. R. 1969. Professional Employees in a Bureaucratic Structure: Social Work. In *The Semi-Professions and Their Organization: Teachers, Nurses and Social Workers,* ed. A. Etzioni. New York: Free Press.

Scull, A. T. 1977. Madness and Segregative Control: The Rise of the Insane Asylum. *Social Problems* 24:337-351.

Shepherd, R. E., Jr. 1965. The Abused Child and the Law. *Washington and Lee Law Review* 22:182-195.

Sherman, E. A., Neuman, R., & Shyne, A. W. 1973. *Children Adrift in Foster Care: A Study of Alternative Approaches.* New York: Child Welfare League of America.

Sherwood, D. A. 1980. The MSW Curriculum: Advanced Standing or Advanced Work? *Journal of Education for Social Work* 16(1):33-40.

Shriver, E. K. 1977. Teenage Sexuality: There Is a Moral Dimension. *Reader's Digest* 111(November):153-154.

Sieder, V. M., & Hirschbaum, D. C. 1977. Volunteers. In *Encyclopedia of Social Work.* 17th issue. New York: National Association of Social Workers.

Sklar, M. H. 1986. Workfare: Is the Honeymoon Over—or Yet to Come? *Public Welfare* 44(1):30-32.

Sloan, I. 1983. *Child Abuse: Governing Laws and Legislation.* New York: Oceana.

Smith, R. 1981. The Boundary Between Insanity and Criminal Responsibility in 19th Century England. In *Madhouses, Mad-doctors and Madmen,* ed. A. Scull. Philadelphia: University of Pennsylvania Press.

Smith, W. H., & Chiechi, C. P. 1974. *Private Foundations Before and After the Tax Reform Act of 1969.* Washington: American Enterprise Institute.

Social Work Research and Abstracts for Social Workers. Annual. New York: National Association of Social Workers.

Specht, H. 1972. The Deprofessionalization of Social Work. *Social Work* 17(2): 3-15.

SPIGOT (Social Policy Information Group of Temple). 1982. *Closing the Spigot.* Philadelphia: Temple University School of Social Administration.

————. 1983. *The Effects of Cutbacks in Government Funding of Human Services.* Philadelphia: Temple University School of Social Administration.

Stein, I. 1975. *Industry Effects of Government Expenditures: An Input-Output Study.* Washington: U.S. Department of Commerce, Bureau of Economics. COM-75-11157.

Stein, J. L. 1982. *Monetarist, Keynesian and New Classical Economics.* New York: New York University Press.

Stein, T. J. 1984. The Child Abuse Prevention and Treatment Act. *Social Service Review* 58: 302-314.

Steiner, G. Y. 1966. *Social Insecurity: The Politics of Welfare.* Chicago: Rand-McNally.

Stutsman, J. O. 1926. *Curing Criminals.* New York: Macmillan.

Szasz, T. S. 1961. *The Myth of Mental Illness.* New York: Harper & Row.

Tanner, J. M. 1970. Physical Growth. In *Manual of Child Psychology*, Vol. I, ed. M. Carmichael. 3rd ed. New York: Wiley.

This Week in Washington. 1985. Washington: American Public Welfare Association. 4(16):1.

Thomas, C. W. 1976. Are Status Offenders Really So Different? *Crime & Delinquency* 22:438-455.

Thornberry, J. P. 1973. Race, Socioeconomic Status and Sentencing in the Juvenile Justice System. *Journal of Criminology and Political Science* 64: 90-98.

Thurston, H. W. 1930. *The Dependent Child.* New York: Columbia University Press.

Tiffany, F. 1891. *Life of Dorothea Lynde Dix.* Boston: Houghton-Mifflin.

Titmuss, R. M. 1968. *Commitment to Welfare.* New York: Pantheon.

———. 1969. *Essays on the Welfare State.* Boston: Beacon.

———. 1971. *The Gift Relationship: From Human Blood to Social Policy.* New York: Pantheon.

Tobin, J. 1982. *Essays in Economics: Theory and Policy.* Cambridge, MA: MIT Press.

Tocqueville, A. de. 1835. *Democracy in America.* [Quoted in Beard, C. A., & M. R., *The Beards' New Basic History of the United States.* 2nd ed. New York: Doubleday, 1960, p. 219.]

Towle, C. 1945. *Common Human Needs.* Chicago: University of Chicago Press.

Trattner, W. I. 1970. *Crusade for the Children.* Chicago: Quadrangle.

Trolander, J. A. 1973. The Response of Settlements to the Great Depression. *Social Work* 18(5):92-102.

Tropman, J. E., Dluhy, M. J., & Lind, R. M. (eds.) 1981. *New Strategic Perspectives on Social Policy.* New York: Pergamon.

Turem, J. S., & Born, C. E. 1983. Doing More With Less. *Social Work* 28: 206-210.

United Services Agency Evaluation Project. 1977. *Final Report.* Philadelphia: Temple University School of Social Administration.

U.S., Bureau of Census. 1975. *Historical Statistics of the United States, Colonial Times to 1970.* Washington: U.S. Government Printing Office.

———. 1982. *Projections of the Population of the United States: 1982-2050.* Washington: U.S. Government Printing Office.

———. *Statistical Abstract of the United States.* Annual. Washington: U.S. Government Printing Office.

U.S., Commission on Civil Rights. 1966. *Hearing Held in Cleveland, Ohio, April 1-7, 1966.* Washington: U.S. Government Printing Office.

U.S., Comptroller General. 1984. *Report to the Congress.* Washington: General Accounting Office.

U.S., Congress, House of Representatives, Committee on Energy and Commerce, Subcommittee on Health and the Environment. 1981. *Family Planning, Adolescent Pregnancy, and Genetic Disease Programs.* Hearing, April 2, 97th Congress, 1st Session. Washington: U.S. Government Printing Office.

————, Senate, Committee on Agriculture, Nutrition and Forestry, Subcommittee on Nutrition. 1979. *Hunger in America: Ten Years Later.* Hearing, April 30. 96th Congress, 1st Session. Washington: U.S. Government Printing Office.

————, Senate, Committee on Labor and Human Resources. 1981. *Adolescent Family Life.* Report No. 97-161, on S. 1090. 97th Congress, 1st Session. Washington: U.S. Government Printing Office.

U.S., Department of Health, Education & Welfare. 1962. *Work Relief: A Current Look.* Public Assistance Report No. 52. Washington: U.S. Government Printing Office.

U.S., General Accounting Office. 1985. Report to the Chairman, Subcommittee on Intergovernmental Relations and Human Resources, House Committee on Government Operations. Washington: August 27.

U.S., Office of Management and Budget. 1980. *Budget of the United States Government, Fiscal Year 1981.* Washington: U.S. Government Printing Office.

————. 1985. *Budget of the United States Government, Fiscal Year 1986.* Washington: U.S. Government Printing Office.

Whitmer, G. E. 1980. From Hospitals to Jail: The Fate of California's Deinstitutionalized Mentally Ill. *American Journal of Orthopsychiatry* 50: 65-75.

Wicker, T. 1975. *A Time to Die.* New York: Quadrangle/New York Times Book Co.

Wigglesworth, M. 1662. The Day of Doom (Excerpts). In *A College Book of American Literature.* Vol. I. Ed. M. Ellis, L. Pound & G. W. Spohn. New York: American Book Co., 1939.

Wilensky, H. L. 1964. The Professionalization of Everyone? *American Journal of Sociology* 70:137-158.

———— & Lebeaux, C. N. 1958. *Industrial Society and Social Welfare.* New York: Russell Sage.

Wiltse, K. T. 1959. *Public Assistance Personnel: Educational Requirements and Training Facilities.* Berkeley, CA: University of California Press.

———— & Gambrill, E. 1974. Foster Care, 1973: A Reappraisal. *Public Welfare* 32 (Winter):7-15.

Witcover, J. 1977. *Marathon: The Pursuit of the Presidency.* New York: Viking.

Witte, E. E. 1962. *The Development of the Social Security Act.* Madison, WI: University of Wisconsin Press.

Wolfgang, M. E., Kelly, A., & Nolde, H. C. 1962. Comparison of the Executed and the Commuted Among Admissions to Death Row. In *The Sociology of Punishment and Correction*, ed. N. Johnston, L. Savitz & M. E. Wolfgang. New York: Wiley.

Wooden, K. 1976. *Weeping in the Playtime of Others*. New York: McGraw-Hill.

Working Statement on the Purpose of Social Work. 1981. *Social Work*, 26:6.

Young, K. 1942. *Sociology: A Study of Society and Culture*. New York: American Book Co.

Young, L. R. 1954. *Out of Wedlock: A Study of the Problems of the Unmarried Mother and Her Child*. New York: McGraw-Hill.

Zatz, J. 1982. Problems and Issues in Deinstitutionalization: Historical Overview and Current Attitudes. In *Neither Angels nor Thieves: Studies in the Deinstitutionalization of Status Offenders*, ed. J. F. Handler & J. Katz.

Zelnik, M., & Kantner, J. F. 1978. First Pregnancies to Women Aged 15-19: 1976 and 1971. *Family Planning Perspectives* 10:11-20.

————. 1979. Reasons for Nonuse of Contraception by Sexually Active Women Aged 15-19. *Family Planning Perspectives* 11:289-296.

————. 1977. Sexual and Contraceptive Experience of Young Unmarried Women in the United States, 1976 and 1971. *Family Planning Perspectives* 9:55-71.

Zola, I. K., & Miller, S. J. 1973. The Erosion of Medicine From Within. In *The Professions and Their Prospects*, ed. E. Freidson. Beverly Hills, CA: Sage.

Index